A SHORT HISTORY

OF ENGLISH-CANADIAN LITERATURE

# Creative Writing in Canada

## DESMOND PACEY

*Professor of English
and Dean of Graduate Studies
in the University of New Brunswick*

THE RYERSON PRESS    TORONTO

*Third printing, 1964*

## ACKNOWLEDGMENT

In a work of scholarship such as this, the author has
had to make partial quotations from a large number
of works, both prose and verse. Grateful acknowledg-
ment is made to McClelland and Stewart, Limited,
for permission to quote in full "Deeper Into the
Forest" by Roy Daniells, "Over" by Robert Finch and
"Dream River" by Marjorie Pickthall.

*To my students: past and present*
*and especially to the members of my classes*
*in Canadian Literature*

# Preface to the Second Edition

IT IS gratifying to know that this book has been sufficiently well liked by the Canadian and non-Canadian public to make a second edition necessary. It has apparently proved, as was hoped, to be a useful sketch map of the territory of Canadian literature.

In this new edition I have kept to my original purpose of dealing almost exclusively with poetry and fiction; biography, history, and scholarly writings in general have been excluded as beyond its modest scope. The main changes are the addition of Chapter 8 on the literature of the fifties, and the expansion of Chapters 6 and 7 to take into account the work which the writers treated there have done in the last ten years. The Introduction, Conclusion and Bibliography have also been slightly revised and expanded in the light of changes which have recently occurred in the Canadian situation.

I should like to express my gratitude to Mrs. Helen Moore, Miss Nan Gregg and Miss Heather Diplock, of the staff of the University of New Brunswick, for their help in the preparation of this revised manuscript.

DESMOND PACEY

1952

# Preface to the First Edition

THIS BOOK was undertaken at the suggestion of Dr. Lorne
Pierce as a companion volume to *Creative Writing in
Australia*, by John K. Ewers (Georgian House, Melbourne,
1945). In the process of writing and rewriting, it has grown
rather larger than was originally intended. It has remained
a selective survey which does not pretend to be exhaustive,
but aims rather to single out the most interesting work in
each period. As the title suggests, attention has been focussed
on the *belles lettres*, and no effort has been made to include
works of biography, history, or the social and natural sciences.
Writing in French has also been excluded, not because the
author is unaware of the contribution of such writers as
Fréchette and Nelligan, Hémon and Lemelin, but because
their work belongs to a separate if parallel tradition, and
because to have treated it with any adequacy would have
required a book of twice the present length.

My debt to previous critics of Canadian literature is too
extensive to be adequately acknowledged in a brief preface:
the long bibliography will give the reader some conception
of its ramifications. I also owe much to my colleagues and
students at the University of New Brunswick, and to patient
friends in many parts of Canada. Tentative and exploratory
as the book is, it would have been much worse without their
counsel and assistance.

DESMOND PACEY

# Table of Contents

ix

*It is easier to think what poetry should be, than to write it.*

KEATS in a letter to John Taylor, February 27, 1818

CHAPTER ONE

# General Introduction

IN OCTOBER OF 1950 a reviewer in *The Times Literary Supplement* declared that Canada is a country with no indigenous culture. It is difficult to decide what he meant by this declaration. If he used the word "indigenous" in its strict sense, then his view is a defensible one. Certainly Canadian culture has not developed in isolation; at every stage of its progress it has been strongly influenced by English, American and, to a lesser extent, by European models. But it would be almost equally easy to prove that England has no indigenous culture in this sense. Indeed the whole history of Western civilization is a record of the constant interaction of national cultures, and English literature, for example, would be an immensely poorer thing had it been deprived of the stimulation which came, at various times, from Italy, France, Germany and America.

What the reviewer probably meant, however, was that Canada has no distinctive culture. Even this is an ambiguous charge. Of what does distinctiveness consist? Is a distinctive national culture one which reflects that nation's social organization, geography and political history, or is it something more profound than this, the projection of a unique philosophy or the origination of special forms and techniques? If the former, then a good case can be made out for the distinctiveness of Canadian culture. At every stage of its development, Canadian literature has responded to the

1

social, political and physical environment of Canada. Even
if we accept the second sense of distinctiveness, a case can be
made out, though it is less strong. Canadian artists certainly
cannot claim to have invented any very important new
techniques, but they have significantly modified and adapted
existing techniques to suit their own purposes. In painting,
the Group of Seven owed much to the post-Impressionists,
but the Group's canvases have qualities which English and
French critics in the nineteen-twenties immediately per-
ceived to be new and distinctive. E. J. Pratt has certainly
been indebted to the tradition of English narrative poetry,
but his work has its own flavour. Similarly, Frederick Philip
Grove is in a sense merely one of a whole school of naturalistic novelists who flourished in all parts of the western world
in the late nineteenth and early twentieth centuries; and yet
his stark portrayals of the difficulties and dangers of a
pioneer mode of life could not be confused with those of any
other author, not even with those of Hamsun or Rolväag,
whom he most resembles.

Moreover, Canadian art as a whole, and more particularly
Canadian literature, has a distinctive conception of man's lot
on the earth, a conception engendered by the peculiar
features of the Canadian terrain. There is a family resemblance between the paintings of Tom Thomson and Emily
Carr, the poems of Duncan Campbell Scott and E. J. Pratt
and Earle Birney, and the novels of Grove and de la Roche
and Callaghan: in all of them man is dwarfed by an immensely powerful physical environment which is at once
forbidding and fascinating. This assertion I shall attempt to
demonstrate in the course of this survey, and especially in
the conclusion.

But the main purpose of this book is not to prove that
Canada has a distinctive literature, still less to convince our
writers that they should make the achievement of distinctiveness their chief aim. Since we are still dominated by a
romantic conception of the nature and aims of literature, our

tendency is to exaggerate the importance of distinctiveness. The distinctiveness of Canadian literature thus far has been almost wholly an inevitable response to a geographical, climatic and social situation, and this it should and must remain. The main purpose of this book is to consider the *quality* of Canadian writing, to discover where it has succeeded and where it has failed.

Such a task is never easy, and for Canadian literature it is especially hard. Perhaps the chief source of additional difficulty is the fact that so little good criticism of Canadian literature exists. Canadian poetry has been relatively well surveyed and charted, and here one's task is limited to the re-examination and modification of existing judgments; but very little attention has been devoted, at home or abroad, to Canadian prose, and the critic must often proffer opinions which can be checked against those of no one else. Another difficulty is that such a large proportion of good Canadian writing has been done in the last forty years, by people who are still alive and in many cases well known to the critic. Here, obviously, is dangerous scope for the personal fallacy, and temptation to indulge in easy generalities that can offend no sensibilities.

Another special difficulty is the fact that Canadian writers have always had to work under severe handicaps, and the critic must constantly wonder whether he is making enough or too much allowance for these. Two tendencies have always been at war in Canadian literary criticism: the tendency to exalt every poem or novel produced simply because, in the face of appalling obstacles, it has been produced at all; and the tendency to insist that absolutely no account be taken of the extenuating circumstances. Ideally, the latter attitude is the proper one: any literature must submit to judgment by the standards applicable to all literatures. But this impassive ideal is almost impossible to apply in practice, and one's judgment is inevitably affected by one's knowledge of the circumstances in which the writing was done. I shall attempt to approximate this ideal in the following chapters, but that very fact makes me anxious to set down here an account of the main obstacles that have beset the writer in Canada.

A hundred years ago, when Great Britain was at the height of power and even the relatively youthful United States was a potent factor in world affairs, Canada consisted of five weak scattered colonies. These colonies, moreover, had been settled very largely by semi-literate frontiersmen from New York and Pennsylvania and poverty-stricken labourers from England, Ireland and Scotland. Only in Nova Scotia and New Brunswick, where a relatively cultured group of United Empire Loyalists had settled, was there a colonial society capable of creating and sustaining a literary movement of any significance.

Even today, with a population of eighteen million, a very high percentage of literacy and an advanced educational system, Canada is not a particularly favourable environment for the writer. Of the eighteen million, roughly one-third are the French-speaking who concern themselves scarcely at all with Canadian literature in English. The remaining twelve million are spread over half a continent and divided into distinct regional groupings by geographical barriers. Although the last frontier has been closed, the frontier spirit, with its distrust of all but the crudest forms of art, lingers on. No longer a colony in the legal sense, Canada still has many citizens who are colonials at heart, and who look either to Great Britain or to the United States not only for cultural leadership but for all valid cultural performance; for them no Canadian writer can be other than a poor substitute for the real thing.

Most of these factors, however, are temporary, and their influence is already on the wane. More and more, Canadians are coming to concern themselves seriously with their own culture in general and their own literature in particular. If anything, the tendency of late has been to take our literary development too seriously, to attempt to push it forward too far and too fast. Canadian writers are literally festooned with medals, and they must produce in an atmosphere of tense expectancy which looks for each new publication to be The Great Canadian Novel, Poem or Play.

Certainly the geographical barriers are ceasing to obstruct greatly. It is only seventy-six years since the first transcontinental railway was completed, but already the railway has become one of the less significant means by which the country is united. The airplane, and above all the national radio and television systems, have made it possible for the inhabitants of such a sprawling geographical mass as Canada to have a sense of unity. The Canadian Broadcasting Corporation has probably done more than any other single agency to give Canada a sense of cultural identity, and it has provided a market and an audience for Canadian writers such as they have never enjoyed before.

Unfortunately, one of the inhibiting forces mentioned above has not decreased in importance. There is still a wide gulf between the cultures of French and English Canada, and few indeed are the bridges over it. In 1877, William Kirby predicted that in Canada the literary traditions of France and England would in time "be united in one grand flood stream of Canadian literature." That time is not yet; indeed there was more basis for the hope in 1877 than there is today. In the nineteenth century, English-Canadian novels such as Kirby's *The Golden Dog* and Rosanna Leprohon's *The Manor House of de Villerai* were widely read, in translation, in Quebec; but today few if any translations are made. In any case, it is not translations which we should hope for, but a truly bilingual culture which would make translations unnecessary.

This internal division has been matched by an external one. Much of Canadian history can be interpreted as the effort to evade or to reconcile two competing pulls from outside—the pull of the colonial tie with Great Britain, and the pull of the continental tie with the United States. The effects of this struggle have been as apparent in our cultural as in our political history. Enjoying the same language as British and American writers, Canadian writers have found it impossible to resist and difficult to reconcile their influences. Moreover, they have had to compete with them for their audience. When there was a Dickens or a Whitman to be listened to, how should a Kirby or a Carman make his voice heard? When one reflects on this unequal competition, one realizes that the surprising thing is not that the Canadian literary tradition is no stronger but that it has managed to survive at all.

But thus to stress some of the many handicaps which have impeded the development of Canadian literature is to ignore the advantages which our writers have enjoyed. If, for example, American and British competition has made it difficult for our writers to win an audience, it has also stimulated and challenged some of them. Certainly the Canadian writer, if he is at all aware of the outside world, is in little danger of falling into a smug complacency. Moreover, to "speak the tongue that Shakespeare spake," is, in spite of the superficial handicaps which we have mentioned, to be possessed of a literary medium of no mean power. The possibilities of that language, in music and nuance of meaning, are far from exhausted, and the writer who can extract some share of its riches is assured of an audience which extends far beyond the borders of Canada.

If, then, the Canadian writer has cause to be grateful for the British heritage and the American example, he has also cause to be grateful for his Canadian environment. The rugged grandeur of the Canadian landscape has always claimed the attention of her poets, and we may safely predict that it will provide the inspiration for many future poems. Canadian social and political life has not, for various reasons, been explored as thoroughly as might have been expected, but as Canada develops in maturity and influence this aspect of her being will provide endless material for her writers.

The decisive point is that Canada's youth is in reality an advantage rather than a handicap. Her future is almost certain to be greater than her past, and this is the basis for the perpetual hopefulness which pervades her literature and her literary criticism. This sense of the future, however, should not preclude but complement a sense of the past, and it is hoped that the historical survey which follows will do something to quicken both.

CHAPTER TWO

# The Colonial Period

*1750 – 1867*

## 1. Maritime Origins

ENGLISH-CANADIAN literature had its origins in Nova Scotia, the first Canadian colony to be extensively settled by English-speaking people, the first to attain responsible government and the first to develop a sense of cultural identity.

Having been in dispute between England and France for over a century, the colony of Nova Scotia was finally ceded to the former by the Treaty of Utrecht in 1713. It was not, however, until the latter half of the eighteenth century that any serious effort was made to populate the colony with English settlers. For a long time the English residents consisted only of a few soldiers at Annapolis Royal and a few fishermen at Canso, and the bulk of the inhabitants were French Acadians. In 1749 a slightly more positive policy of British settlement was inaugurated with the founding of Halifax and the decision to anglicize the Acadians and compel them to take the oath of allegiance to the British Crown. When the Acadians refused to take the oath, they were expelled from the colony, in 1755, and deported to other English possessions. Three years later the colony was granted a legislative assembly. The result of these two latter moves was to attract, by the prospect of vacant farms and free institutions, a large number of settlers from New England. These New Englanders were joined by a few immigrants from the British Isles and from Germany, and between 1767 and 1775 the population of the province grew from two to

8

seventeen thousand. Constituting two-thirds of the population, the New England Puritans gave the young colony its
dominant cultural tone, but they were neither sufficiently
numerous nor educated well enough to produce a literature.
The one literary figure from this period who is remembered
at all is a religious poet named Henry Alline (1748-1784).
Alline, an itinerant evangelist sometimes known as the Canadian Whitefield, wrote two books, a collection of *Hymns and
Spiritual Songs* (1786) and a prose record of his life and
religious experiences, *The Life and Journal* (1806).

This Puritan interlude was, however, of brief duration.
After maintaining an uneasy neutrality during the War of
the American Revolution, Nova Scotia became, in 1783, the
chief destination for thousands of Loyalists from the dis-
affected southern colonies. These Loyalists, nearly thirty
thousand strong, became in a few short months the dominant
group in the colony. Many of them were of good family and
education, and their coming immediately effected a great
change in the cultural, social and economic life of Nova
Scotia. The colony began to prosper in all phases of its
activity, and for the first time the evolution of a distinctive
culture became possible.

Many of the Loyalist settlers were themselves men of
literary inclinations, but their tastes and interests had been
formed elsewhere and they did not themselves contribute
much of interest to Canadian literature. Poets like Joseph
Stansbury (1740-1809) and Jonathan Odell (1737-1818)
turned out satirical poems directed against the republican
sentiments of the American rebels, nostalgic lyrics in which
they voiced the longings of the exile for home and rousing
patriotic songs in which they celebrated the glories of the
British Flag and Crown, but most of their better work had
been done before they came to Canada and none of it had
any direct relationship with the Canadian scene.

It was the sons and daughters of the original Loyalists who
laid the basis for a genuinely Canadian literature. In the

1820's and 1830's, when this second generation was reaching maturity, the first literary work of lasting significance began to appear.  The whole colony had by this time reached a provisional social and political maturity.  The relative prosperity of the decade following the arrival of the Loyalists had been succeded by an even more prosperous period during the war with France.  With the ports of Europe closed, the trade of the colony with the mother country and the other British possessions increased enormously.  At the close of the Napoleonic War, the last great wave of immigration began: Scottish Highlanders, to the number of forty thousand, poured into the province between 1815 and 1838.  Between 1784 and 1837 the population of the colony increased fivefold.  Along with this material expansion went a corresponding intellectual awakening.  Schools, colleges, libraries, museums, newspapers and magazines were founded; and in the legislative assembly the political debates grew at once more intelligent and more intense.  "By 1828," as Dr. A. G. Bailey expressed it, "the province was responding in full stature to the importunities and possibilities of the age."

The centre of this first Canadian cultural awakening was the city of Halifax.  Halifax had remained since its founding the centre of British influence in Nova Scotia, and its social and cultural tone was distinctly higher than that of the rest of the province with the possible exception of Windsor, seat of King's College.  Professor D. G. Creighton wrote in *Dominion of the North*:

Halifax was the seat of government and bureaucracy, the British naval and military base, the focus of trade with Great Britain, the stronghold of Loyalist political views and conservative social prejudices.  With its wealth, its dignity and gaiety, its aristocratic codes and standards set by government house and garrison, Halifax assumed the right of social leadership in the colony.

It was one such occasion of gaiety which prompted the first native Canadian poet to try his wings.  In his *Autobiography*,

Oliver Goldsmith (1794-1861) tells us that, in 1822, an opening address was solicited for an amateur theatre newly established by some ladies and officers of the Garrison. Goldsmith wrote a verse prologue, and though it was not accepted he "determined on a future effort". This further effort was *The Rising Village* (1825), Canada's first book-length poem in English.

Oliver Goldsmith was the son of a Loyalist who had settled near St. Andrew's, New Brunswick, in 1785. It was at St. Andrew's that the son was born, but shortly afterwards the family moved to Annapolis Royal and thence to Halifax. The father, after various financial misfortunes, had joined the Commissariat Department of the British Army, and the son eventually followed in his footsteps. The one poem by which the latter is remembered, *The Rising Village*, was written at Halifax where its author was employed in the Commissariat Department from 1818 to 1833.

The Canadian Oliver Goldsmith was the grandson of Henry Goldsmith, to whom the English Oliver Goldsmith had dedicated his famous poem, *The Traveller*. In his own poem, the Canadian writer consciously sought to emulate his grand-uncle and to write a sort of sequel to *The Traveller* and *The Deserted Village*. He tells us in the preface that he has "endeavoured to describe the hardships the early settlers experienced, the difficulties which they surmounted, the rise and progress of a young country, and the prospects which promise happiness to its future possessors".

Superficially, *The Rising Village* is very similar to its model, *The Deserted Village*. In structure, each may be broken down into three main divisions: a contrast between past and present conditions; a series of sketches of representative villagers and village institutions; a return to the contrast between past and present, with some thoughts of the future. Both poems are written in heroic couplets, and both attempt to mingle physical description, social history, sentiment and moral teaching.

A close examination reveals many differences. The Canadian poem has little of the wit and none of the passion of *The Deserted Village*, and the elder Goldsmith's diatribes against luxury and the tyranny of wealth have no counterpart in *The Rising Village*. For the Canadian poet, all is for the best in the best of all possible worlds, and his vague benevolence is matched by the vagueness of his descriptions. Only very occasionally, as in his description of the country store, does the younger Goldsmith write as if his eye were really on the object. For the most part he is content with epithets such as "boundless prospects", "heedless passions", "busy mill" and "humble cottage", and he has none of that gift for the memorable phrase which the elder Goldsmith enjoyed in such abundance.

Most critics have agreed that Goldsmith's poem is technically weak, but it has been traditionally hailed for its documentary truth. Even this has been exaggerated. The poem was written during the aftermath of the Napoleonic Wars, when Nova Scotia was restive under the yoke of the political oligarchy in Halifax and the restrictive economic policy of London, but there are no traces of these in the poem. Its accounts of the hardships and triumphs of the settlers are too vague and general to give us much insight into their lives. If it is a document, it is a document not, as one critic has called it, "of the Loyalist migration", but of the cultural awakening of colonial Nova Scotia. The chief significance of *The Rising Village* is that its author had recognized the poetic possibilities of the Canadian social scene.

These possibilities may have been brought to Goldsmith's attention by a man who was himself to do far more to realize them. In 1823, an anonymous pamphlet had appeared in Halifax under the title *General Description of Nova Scotia*, and in Chapter XI there appeared this passage:

The origin and growth of a modern colony affords much matter of curious speculation. To trace the difference between the state of man rising in the progress of years to civilization, and that of an enlightened people operating upon uncultivated nature, is at once an interesting and useful pursuit.

The author then goes on to quote from *The Deserted Village*, and to write what is, in many respects, the prose counterpart of *The Rising Village*. The author of this anonymous pamphlet was Thomas Chandler Haliburton (1796-1865), the first Canadian writer to establish an international reputation.

Loyalist and pre-Loyalist blood mingled in the veins of Thomas Chandler Haliburton. His father, a lawyer and member of the legislative assembly, was of pre-Loyalist stock and had himself been born in Nova Scotia; his mother was the daughter of a Loyalist officer. This ancestry helps to explain the ideas and attitudes which Haliburton was to adopt as a writer: from his father, a staunch and high-principled Tory, he inherited or acquired his political conservatism; from his mother, who had been ship-wrecked in the Bay of Fundy while in flight from the American revolution, he inherited his hatred of America in particular and of republican democracy in general.

Haliburton's Tory and aristocratic bias was intensified by his upbringing and education in the college town of Windsor. This town had become the resort of persons of wealth and official connection, and it boasted that it housed the most aristocratic society outside of England itself. King's College, from which Haliburton graduated in 1815, was a haven of Toryism and Anglicanism.

To such young men as Haliburton, three careers were open: the Church, the Army or the Bar. Haliburton chose the last, and after completing his legal studies in 1820 he began to practise in another strongly Loyalist town, Annapolis Royal. Residence in Annapolis Royal, the second oldest town in North America, encouraged in the young lawyer an interest in the history of his native province, and within three years of settling there he produced the historical pamphlet to which we have already referred. But it was inevitable also that a young man of his parenthood and training should interest himself in politics: before three more years were out he had been elected to the Legislative Assembly.

The great political theme in Nova Scotia at this time—the mid 1820's—was the excessive power of the Legislative Council. Haliburton, as a popular representative, felt it his duty to oppose the Council: but as a Tory Imperialist he found it hard to attack the appointees of His Britannic Majesty. The result was that Haliburton's political record is strangely inconsistent. In some of his speeches he appeared as the champion of popular rights; in others as a constitutionalist of the most conservative character. As V.L.O. Chittick has brilliantly put it: "He occupied, in short, an impossible position in a sort of No-Man's Land, across which he scurried with disconcerting frequency, attacking now this side, now that, each dashing assault being accompanied by a spectacular discharge of oratorical starshells."

There were, however, certain constant elements in Haliburton's speeches in the Assembly, and they are the same elements which underlie all his writings. He was convinced of the necessity of maintaining and strengthening the British connection; he was convinced that the political and social pattern of the United States was crude and false; he was anxious to see Nova Scotia develop her resources in order that she might become a more powerful member of the British imperial system. Above all, he expressed his views, on whatever subject, in a pithy, vigorous and colloquial language.

Haliburton's interests, however, were rapidly shifting from oratory to writing, and he left the Assembly in 1829. At the close of his last session, his colleagues were able to congratulate him upon the first literary work to appear under his own name: *An Historical and Statistical Account of Nova Scotia*. If his medium had changed, however, his purpose had not. As in practically all his writing, Haliburton had in this book a political and social message to communicate: by portraying the history and prospects of his province, he wished to correct the almost universal misconception that Nova Scotia was an ill-favoured brat among the British colonies. Haliburton had spent seven years of research on the book, and although it is not without its errors—as a pioneer historical account it could hardly have avoided them—it remains an indispensable source-book for the study of the early history of the colony.

Although Haliburton had not found his *métier* in this first book, and although it was a financial failure, its publication proved to be a turning point in his life. Largely because of the reputation which the book had earned him, he was appointed to the Bench; as a member of the judiciary he withdrew from the hurly-burly of politics; more and more his real interests came to be identified with writing. The political strife grew more intense as the movement for a more responsible and representative system of government gained momentum, but Haliburton remained above the battle, clinging with one hand to conservative principles which were no longer fashionable even in reactionary circles, and with the other aiming barbs of wit and satire at all those, of whatever party, who aroused his amusement or disgust.

On September 24, 1835, there began to appear in a Halifax newspaper, *The Novascotian*, an anonymous series of articles called "Recollections of Nova Scotia". The Province was in a depressed condition at this time: a series of financial collapses, crop failures and cholera epidemics had strained its limited resources to the breaking point. This series of articles was just the tonic needed, and before it had been completed the demand for publication in book form became so insistent that it could not be denied. In 1836, the articles, with some additions, appeared as *The Clockmaker, or the Sayings and Doings of Sam Slick of Slickville*. Thomas Chandler Haliburton had found his *métier*; Nova Scotia had found its wittiest prophet; and Canada had found its first great humourist.

The appearance of *The Clockmaker* was no freak or accident. It arose in answer to the immediate demands of the province, and it embodied attitudes which had long been maturing in the mind of the author. To a provincial society which seemed about to lose faith in its own destiny, it proclaimed that its salvation lay in its own perseverance and ingenuity; to those members of that society who were tempted to emigrate to the United States (and many emigrated at this period) it held up to ridicule the cheapness and shallowness of American society. The book spoke to them, moreover, in their own language, in an idiomatic prose which combined the witty antitheses of eighteenth century English with the dialectal ingenuity of North America.

*The Clockmaker* is not, perhaps, a great book, but it is an astonishingly good book to have come from a small provincial society in the throes of depression. Like all significant works of art, it blends the particular and the universal; even today, when many of the issues to which it alludes have been forgotten, there is scarcely a page of it which does not hold our interest or arouse our amusement. It exhibits practically every form of humour known to man, and in particular those humorous devices which have come to be labelled, ironically enough in view of Haliburton's prejudices, as "typically American". There is the humour of dialect, in phrases such as "soft sawder" and "a pretty considerable smart horse". There is comic exaggeration, of the type later beloved by Mark Twain: "As for the people on the shore, they know so little of horses that a man from Aylesford once sold a hornless ox there, whose tail he had cut and nicked, for a horse of the Goliath breed". There are puns aplenty: much of the first chapter, for example, consists of various puns on the word "circuit". There is the comedy of situation: Haliburton can turn an anecdote as neatly as he turns a phrase. There is irony in abundance: almost every statement which Haliburton makes can be interpreted in several ways, and many of his sentences are like many-edged weapons which cut us whichever way we turn them. There is, of course, satire: satire at the expense of the shiftless farmers of Nova Scotia, of the lawyers who exploit their credulity and of the Yankee smart alecks who gull them. Above all, there is the humour of character.

*The Clockmaker* swarms with memorable characters. Caricatures they may be, but with a few sure strokes they are drawn and we never forget them. There is, for example, Elder Stephen Gran whose face was "as long as the moral law, and perhaps an inch longer" and who felt that "he had conquered the Evil One and was considerable well satisfied with himself". Greatest of them all, of course, is Sam Slick. He has the ambivalence of so much of the book; Haliburton at once detests and admires him. He is crude, coarse, arrogant, ignorant and downright dishonest, the representative and inevitable product, in Haliburton's eyes, of a republican democracy; but at the same time he is shrewd, practical, self-reliant and inventive, and in this respect the embodiment of an ideal which Haliburton would have his fellow Nova Scotians emulate.

With the publication of the first series of *The Clockmaker*, Haliburton's greatest work came to an end. Even the second series, published two years later, shows a marked decline in his powers. He has become less concrete and more theoretical; the natural flow of his racy idiom is impeded by self-consciousness; the positive aspect of the first series—Haliburton's effort to arouse Nova Scotians from their lethargy—is almost wholly crowded out by his crusade against colonial democracy; there is less wit and more vulgarity; the book is altogether more diffuse and superficial. The faults of the

first series—disorderliness of presentation, repetition and
redundancy, lapses into mere facetiousness—are here magni-
fied and made more apparent.

Much of Haliburton's later life was spent in England
where, until his death on the eve of Confederation, he
devoted his energies to a vain attempt to stem the tide of
responsible government and colonial autonomy. He violently
opposed the Durham Report, one of the charters of Canadian
freedom, and by such acts sacrificed the popularity which his
early books had won him. To the very end of his life he
retained the capacity to turn a witty phrase and to tell an
amusing anecdote, but his later books will not stand comparison with *The Clockmaker*.

*The Clockmaker* is, however, the chief monument of this
first phase of Canadian literature. Before leaving Nova Scotia,
we must glance at the man who was chiefly responsible for
its publication and who himself made a significant if minor
contribution to our early literature. When *The Clockmaker*
began to appear in the pages of *The Novascotian*, its editor
was Joseph Howe (1804-1873); and it was Howe also who
arranged for the publication of the sketches in book form.
Nor was Haliburton the only author who was in Howe's debt.
Howe was the moving spirit in Canada's first literary coterie,
a group of Halifax writers who called themselves "The
Club" and who met to discuss literary questions and to criti-
cize their own work; and in his magazine there frequently
appeared poems by Goldsmith and lesser known writers of
the day, literary essays and travel sketches.

Joseph Howe, like Goldsmith and Haliburton, was of
Loyalist stock. His father had come to Halifax from Boston
at the outbreak of the Revolutionary War, and had brought
with him the press of the old Boston *News-Letter*. In Halifax
he became joint owner of the Halifax *Gazette*, the oldest
newspaper in British North America. The young Howe did
not have much formal education—he would not have been
able to enter King's College, in any event, since his father

was a Sandamanian—but his father gave him a good ground-ing in the Bible and Shakespeare and encouraged the lad to read widely. At the height of his career as a statesman and orator, Joseph Howe displayed a knowledge of world history and literature which would have done justice to the training of any great university. He could recite the poetry of Byron, Scott and Moore, refer eruditely to the literature and history of Greece and Rome, lecture on the Florentine renaissance, and quote from the speeches and writings of Sheridan, Fox, Burke and Macaulay.

All this reading he had to do in the brief leisure moments of an active career as a journalist, politician, legislator and publicist. His working career began at the age of thirteen, when he became a printer's apprentice, and continued to the very end of his life. Seldom can there have been a man of more unbounded energy and enthusiasm. At the age of twenty-four he became the sole owner and editor of *The Novascotian*, and quickly made it the leading newspaper of eastern British North America. He himself did almost all the work of editing the paper; he kept up with the best in contemporary Canadian, American and British journalism and reprinted the pieces which pleased him; he personally reported the activities of the legislature and by his editorial comments upon them raised political consciousness and intelligence to a new level; to learn at first hand the ways and needs of the province he made long journeys on horse-back and wrote the accounts of his travels for his paper. Not content with all this, he was elected to the Legislative Assembly, made a six-hour speech which established the principle of a free press in Canada, and became the recognized leader of the Reform party which sought to break down the autocracy of the Governor's Council in order to establish responsible government. He made several trips to England to further the interests of the province. He long opposed Confederation, fearing that it would endanger the rights and privileges of his native province, but he was eventually won round to the federal idea and became a member of Sir John A. Macdonald's first federal cabinet. His appointment to the lieutenant-governorship of Nova Scotia in 1873 was a fitting reward for his many years of strenuous service.

Busy as he was, Howe could scarcely be expected to have contributed much to our stock of literature. Indeed, his chief literary significance lies in the encouragement which he was able to give, through his editorial post, to other writers, and especially to Haliburton. But somehow, in moments snatched from the frantic round of editing, speaking and travelling, he managed to write a few pieces which Canadians at least are not likely to let die. He wrote poetry, letters and travel sketches, orations on a wide variety of topics, and one short story.

Howe's poetry is markedly inferior to his prose. Where the latter is fresh, idiomatic and flexible, the former tends to be conventional and stiff. He did not take himself seriously as a poet; as one critic has put it, "He wrote poetry as some men will cultivate flowers, purely as an amusement and from a love of the beautiful." His poems are mainly of two sorts: descriptive poems such as "Melville Island" and "Acadia", and patriotic songs such as "The Flag of Old England." In their best passages, these poems have something of Howe's own sincere enthusiasm, but they are all marred by flat lines and pompous phrases. When he is describing action—the Indian massacre in "Acadia" for example—the verse suddenly picks up speed and force; but when he is moralizing he falls into the personifications and periphrases characteristic of eighteenth century verse at its worst.

The prose is much better. His travel sketches—*Western Rambles* (1828), *Eastern Rambles* (1830), *The Nova Scotian Afloat* (1838), *The Nova Scotian in England* (1839)—are lively and humorous. They abound in shrewd comments on the contemporary scene, in quick thumbnail sketches of persons and places, in lively anecdotes and vivid passages of description. His *Letters to Lord John Russell* (1846) are distinguished by their logic, their wealth of illustration, and their passionate sincerity in the cause of Nova Scotia.

Perhaps his best work is contained in his orations. The political speeches are frank and, though often angry, seldom bitter. He had a gift for irony, a corresponding clarity and penetration of mind. The speeches are certainly far above the usual level of political debate, and they reveal the breadth of view with which Howe regarded the problems of his place and time. The orations delivered on general subjects before such bodies as the Mechanics Institute are perhaps of greater interest to the modern reader, however. The language may at times seem somewhat flamboyant, but it is always vigorous and colourful.

Joseph Howe, then, was the centre of a literary movement which, in the four decades prior to Confederation, gave to Nova Scotia a distinctive cultural tone. A small colonial society had produced in him, in Goldsmith, and especially in Haliburton, three writers of whom it could be proud, and through whom it had found distinguished and lasting expression.

## 2. The Beginnings in Upper and Lower Canada

THERE was no such central literary figure as Joseph Howe in the colonies of Upper and Lower Canada, and there was scarcely anything which could be called a literary movement. There were several individual writers of some significance, but they represented much more diverse tendencies than did the relatively close-knit Halifax group.

Upper and Lower Canada, or Ontario and Quebec as they came to be known after Confederation, were several decades behind Nova Scotia in cultural development because they were settled later and by less educated persons. It was not, of course, until after the British conquest of Quebec in 1763 that English settlement of that area began, and it was not until the early nineteenth century that immigration on an extensive scale took place. Quebec for the first few decades after the conquest remained substantially as it had been before. The British settlers were for the most part soldiers and officials, or merchants who speedily took over the French fur trade. A typical member of this small English community, Mrs. Frances Brooke, the wife of an army chaplain, wrote a book which is sometimes called the first Canadian novel; but her *History of Emily Montague* (1769) was certainly no indigenous product. Mrs. Brooke had written extensively before coming to Canada, she remained in Canada at most two years, and she did most of her writing after her return to England. In any case her novel was an isolated phenomenon: the English community was not large or stable enough to develop a sense of cultural identity, still less to produce a literature.

Even the Loyalist migration of 1783 made little difference in this area. Only six thousand Loyalists chose this colony in preference to the Maritimes, and they were of a quite different type. A high proportion of the Maritime Loyalists were officers and professional men; the Quebec Loyalists were almost all farmers, typical frontiersmen from New York and Pennsylvania.

By 1791, the total population of the province was one hundred and thirty thousand, but of this number only twenty-one thousand, or about sixteen per cent, were English-speaking. Most of these English-speaking settlers, however, were situated beyond the Ottawa River, and the Constitutional Act of 1791 made provision for a separate province in that area, to be known as Upper Canada.

Upper Canada grew rapidly. At first the immigrants were mainly American farmers from New York, Pennsylvania and Vermont who followed the natural routes of settlement regardless of political boundaries; they were joined by a few settlers from the British Isles; and by the outbreak of the

War of 1812 it is estimated that there were eighty thousand inhabitants. This war with the United States, which largely overlooked the Maritime Provinces because of the virtual neutrality of the New England states, did much to give these inhabitants a sense of common purpose. Preponderantly American in origin though they were, the bulk of them strenuously resisted the American invasion, and the exploits of such leaders as Brock and his Indian ally, Tecumseh, laid the foundations for a national legend.

After the war, the great tide of immigration began to flow from the British Isles into the two Canadas, and especially into Upper Canada. The new colonists were a mixed lot—Highland Scots, Southern Irish, Ulstermen and Englishmen—but they may be roughly divided into two groups. The great bulk of them were of peasant or labouring stock, but a few of them were relatively well-educated members of the upper middle class—half-pay officers attracted by free grants of land, and the younger sons of good families who sought greater opportunities in a new country.

The former groups made little direct contribution to the development of an indigenous Canadian culture: they lacked the necessary educational background, and they were fully occupied with the job of making a living. Their historic mission was to clear the land and to swell the growing protest against the autocratic and irresponsible form of government in power in both provinces. Their social attitude has been stated in exaggerated form by a member of the genteel group, Susanna Moodie, in her classic documentary study of pioneering life, *Roughing It in the Bush*: "Let them once emigrate, the clog which fettered them is suddenly removed; they are free; and the dearest privilege of this freedom is to wreak upon their superiors the long-locked-up hatred of their hearts." Their agitation was largely responsible for the abortive rebellions of 1837, and for the achievement of responsible government.

A few literary expressions of this attitude have survived.

Perhaps the best known example is the poem "Young Canada, or Jack's as Good as His Master", by Alexander McLachlan (1818-1896).  McLachlan, the son of poor parents in Glasgow, emigrated to Upper Canada in 1840 and ultimately produced three volumes of verse.  His chief model was Burns, and he showed that poet's admiration of the common man and his hatred of cant and hypocrisy.  McLachlan's own poetry, however, is crude and sentimental and seldom rises above the level of doggerel, as this first stanza from "Young Canada" will indicate:

> I love this land of forest grand!
> The land where labour's free;
> Let others roam away from home,
> Be this the land for me!
>
> Where no one moils, and strains and toils,
> That snobs may thrive the faster;
> And all are free, as men should be,
> And Jack's as good's his master.

Although he had little political consciousness, a more important poet from the ranks of this class of immigrants was Charles Heavysege (1816-1876).  Heavysege had little formal education, but had thoroughly digested Shakespeare's plays, the Bible and the poetry of Milton.  Before emigrating to Montreal in 1853 he had published a small volume of poems entitled *The Revolt of Tartarus*.  Although he had almost nothing to say of Canada in his writings, something in the Canadian environment seems to have stimulated him to increased literary activity.  In the next fifteen years he published two long verse dramas—*Saul* (1857) and *Count Filippo* (1860)—three long narrative poems—*The Owl* (1864), *Jephthah's Daughter* (1865) and *Jezebel* (1867)—and a rambling novel called *The Advocate* (1865).  In his own day, Heavysege enjoyed a considerable reputation both at home and abroad.  *Saul* in particular excited attention: Coventry Patmore called it the greatest English poem to be published

outside Great Britain, and Longfellow pronounced Heavysege "the greatest dramatist since Shakespeare". After his
death, however, Heavysege quickly lapsed into obscurity.
Recent attempts have been made by Canadian critics to
revive his reputation, but such attempts are not likely to
have much effect. The best that can be said for Heavysege
and his works is that they are literary curiosities. *Saul*, for
example, is so long and so pompous as to be virtually unread-
able. It has a few good lines, even a few long passages that
attain a kind of noble eloquence, but these are overshadowed
by the awkward imitations of Milton and Shakespeare, the
frequently ridiculous similitudes, and the passages of inflated
rhetoric. What can we say for a play in which a common
Hebrew is made to speak thus:

> But did you not make stipulations, nor
> Propose abatement of the said prerogatives?

How can one take seriously a writer who will compare the
plucking out of the eyes of the dead to "angling unhurt
within those reservoirs of tears"? As for Heavysege's prose,
it has been well said of *The Advocate* that it is the worst of
the many bad novels produced in Canada. Only in his sonnets, and there only very occasionally, does Heavysege achieve
anything that is worthy of the name of art.

The best of the immigrant writers, as we might expect,
were members of the upper class of settlers. Two sisters—
Susanna Moodie (1803–1885) and Catherine Parr Traill
(1802–1899)—made the greatest contribution. Daughters of
a well-to-do Suffolk family, they both married Army officers,
accompanied their husbands to Canada in the early eighteen-
thirties and settled in the bush near Peterborough. Both
had published books before coming to Canada, and both took
advantage of the establishment of *The Literary Garland* in
Montreal in 1838 to augment their incomes by contributing
to it. *The Literary Garland* was the nearest approach in
Upper and Lower Canada to a magazine with the unifying

power exercised in Nova Scotia by Howe's paper. It existed for thirteen years, and printed work by almost all the writers of any stature in Upper and Lower Canada.

Susanna Moodie and Catherine Parr Traill were both prolific writers. Mrs. Moodie wrote poetry, several novels and two autobiographical studies of pioneer life: *Roughing It in the Bush* (1852) and *Life in the Clearings* (1853). Mrs. Traill published seventeen books in all, nine of them, mostly stories for children, before coming to Canada. Of her Canadian books, the best known are *The Backwoods of Canada* (1836), a series of letters from herself to her mother, and *Canadian Crusoes* (1852), a novel which was later republished under the title *Lost in the Backwoods*. The more imaginative work of the two sisters—the poetry, the stories and the novels—is mediocre and conventional: in these they were sentimental, moralistic, imitative and generally uninspired. But in their documentary books, and especially in *Roughing It in the Bush* and *The Backwoods of Canada*, they were much more sincere and vigorous.

Both these books were written for a purpose, for substantially the same purpose. They arose, like Haliburton's *The Clockmaker* and Howe's speeches, from the immediate needs of the hour, for they were written to counteract the illusory propaganda about the advantages of Canada which was being put out by unscrupulous land companies and their agents. Mrs. Traill writes in her foreword:

The writer of the following pages has endeavoured to afford every possible information to the wives and daughters of emigrants of the higher class. . . . Truth has been conscientiously her object in the work, for it were cruel to write in flattering terms calculated to deceive emigrants into the belief that the land . . . is a land flowing with milk and honey, where comforts and affluence may be obtained with little exertion.

The circumstances from which the books arose have disappeared, but the books retain their interest because they bear the imprint of powerful and uncompromising personalities. In their more fanciful works, the sisters spoke conventionally; but here their purpose compelled them to be themselves— and the results are two near-masterpieces. The sisters made no attempt to disguise their sense of social superiority to the impoverished Yankee and British settlers who surrounded them, and though we may deplore their snobbery we must admire their frankness. They honestly record the hardships they encountered, they delight in the odd characters whom they were continually meeting and they describe with a fidelity which has never been equalled the social occasions of pioneer Canadian life. To read Mrs. Moodie's account of a logging bee or Mrs. Traill's account of a house-raising is to feel that one is there, to experience vicariously the life of the pioneers. Their books are written in a homely, unpretentious prose that is most apt for their purpose, and both have a dry, quiet sense of humour. One example must suffice to illustrate both points. Here is Mrs. Traill's account of a day when they were becalmed on the St. Lawrence while on their way to the colony:

So barren of events has that time been that the sight of a party of bottle-nosed whales, two or three seals, and a porpoise, possibly on their way to a dinner or tea party at the North Pole, was considered an occurrence of great importance. Every glass was in requisition as soon as they made their appearance, and the marine monsters were well-nigh stared out of countenance.

So much, then, for the literature produced by the immigrants. The two most important writers in the colonial days of Upper and Lower Canada were not immigrants at all, but native Canadians, and like the Maritime writers both were of Loyalist stock. One was John Richardson, Canada's chief pre-Confederation novelist; the other was Charles Sangster, her chief pre-Confederation poet.

John Richardson (1796-1852), surely one of the most colourful figures in our cultural history, was the grandson of a Detroit merchant, John Askin, and of an Indian squaw. His mother was the daughter of this couple; his father was a surgeon attached to one of the British regiments. When the War of 1812 broke out, Richardson, though only a boy of fifteen, immediately enlisted. After the war was over, he transferred to a British regiment and sailed for Europe to take part in the war against Napoleon. Waterloo was fought while his transport was still at sea, and after a few months of service in the West Indies he was invalided back to England. From 1818 to 1832 he lived in London and Paris, attempting to augment his half pay as a reserve officer by writing. His first effort, a long narrative poem called *Tecumseh* (1828) was a direct reflection of his experiences in the War of 1812, but it appeared at a time when the vogue created by Scott and Byron for that type of poetry had disappeared, and it evoked little attention. In the following year, however, he produced a book which was much more successful: a novel of life in Paris called *Ecarté*. This novel was well reviewed in the British press, and made the subject of a leading article in the *Westminster Review*. Three years later he scored his greatest success with the publication of *Wacousta*, a tale of the Pontiac Conspiracy. *Wacousta* was even more enthusiastically reviewed than *Ecarté*; Richardson was compared with Scott and Cooper; and the book has gone through many editions and is kept in print to this day.

Had Richardson followed up the success of *Wacousta*, he might have become, and remained, an international celebrity; but he was of an unstable, restless temperament, and he was lured away from his desk by the prospect of new adventure. A civil war had broken out in Spain; the British Government, while remaining officially aloof, permitted the raising of a volunteer British Legion; and Richardson joined this Legion as an officer. In 1836 he published an account of his experiences there under the title of *Journal of the Movements of the British Legion*. In this book he paid a tribute to the commanding officer of the force, General De Lacy Evans; but shortly after its publication he was piqued by Evans' failure to promote him, and immediately issued a second edition in which he savagely attacked the general. Since the whole question of the Legion was a lively issue in the British House of Commons, Richardson was quoted there by its opponents and became something of a national celebrity.

At this time, however, there came news of the Rebellion of 1837 in Canada. Richardson, always eager for a fight and strongly loyal to constituted authority, resolved to return to his native land. To supplement his half pay, he accepted an assignment as Canadian correspondent for *The Times* and sailed for Canada early in 1838. There was no fighting to be done, but Richardson found much to excite him. He had returned determined to oppose the proposals for reform, but when he met Lord Durham he recognized a kindred spirit and was attracted by his proposals. To the dismay of "The Thunderer", a bitter opponent of Durham, he began to send back despatches signed "Inquisitor" in which Durham was held up to admiration. After printing a few of these despatches, the editor of *The Times* appended a note to one declaring that its author was an "occasional correspondent" and an obvious partisan of Durham, brought the series to an end, and cut Richardson off his staff.

Richardson found himself stranded in his native land. He hoped that Durham would help him, but the latter's illness and sudden death intervened. He sought the aid of the subsequent governors, he applied for a pension in recognition of his literary services, but all to no avail. For a time he edited a newspaper in Brockville, he wrote a sequel to *Wacousta* called *The Canadian Brothers* (1840), the first part of a projected full-dress *History of the War of 1812* (1842) and several books of reminiscences; but the Canadian public was not even faintly interested in his wares. Indignantly he shook the dust of Canada from his feet and made his way to New York. There he arranged for the reissue in cheap editions of *Wacousta* and *The Canadian Brothers* (under the new title of *Matilda Montgomery*) and produced several potboilers dealing with Indian warfare such as *Hardscrabble* (1850) and *Wau-nan-gee* (1850). He even stooped, in *The Monk Knight of Saint John* (1850), to pornography of the cheapest sort. But try as he would, success was not to be his: he died in 1852 of erysipelas complicated by malnutrition; and he was buried in a pauper's grave.

Richardson's colourful and tragic life is more interesting than his work. Three of his novels—the first three, *Ecarté Wacousta,* and *The Canadian Brothers*—are above the average level of early Canadian fiction, his incomplete *History of the War of 1812* and his volumes of reminiscences are valuable source-books for the historian, but the bulk of his work is shallow and meretricious. His best qualities are clearly evident in the three novels mentioned, and especially in *Wacousta.* He can contrive an intricate plot, full of action and suspense, but not too involved for the reader to follow. He has a gift for singling out dramatic moments, such as the duel scene in *Ecarté* and the shooting of Frank Halloway in *Wacousta.* He can vividly describe social gatherings: the balls, the gambling sessions, and the royal funeral in *Ecarté,* the council of chiefs in *Wacousta,* the gathering of the tribes in *The Canadian Brothers.* He can describe persons and places accurately, and build up an atmosphere of tension or of horror. Where swift action is involved, as in a battle or a chase, he can write with nervous vigour.

But even his best novels are marred by many faults, above all by a kind of artistic irresponsibility which permits deplorable lapses. Even *Wacousta* has passages of the sheerest melodrama: sensation is piled upon sensation, until the modern reader must either laugh or shudder. The book abounds in coincidences, and in episodes which arouse utter incredulity. When we come to such a novel as *The Monk Knight of St. John,* we can only throw up our hands in despair. Here every kind of sexual aberration is displayed, not with the clinical seriousness or the Rabelaisian humour which might make it palatable, but with a kind of sly, lascivious, lip-licking dirtiness which makes one suspect that Richardson's brain was affected when he wrote the book.

Richardson is an isolated figure in the early history of the literature of Ontario. He had no literary acquaintances in this country, very few readers and no disciples. He was the product of a raw provincial society which at his birth was only itself five years old and even at his death was only just emerging from the frontier stage. There was no current of ideas to sustain him, no depth to the cultural soil in which his roots were set.

Charles Sangster (1822-1893) was similarly hampered by isolation and the cultural proverty of his environment. Born in the Loyalist town of Kingston, he was left fatherless while still a boy, and had to begin work filling cartridges at Fort Henry at the age of fifteen. After some years as an Ordnance clerk, he became a journalist and worked on papers in Amherstburg and Kingston from 1849 to 1868. In the latter year he was appointed to a position in the newly created federal Post Office Department at Ottawa, and he remained there almost until his death.

Sangster published only three small volumes of verse—*The St. Lawrence and the Saguenay* (1856), *Hesperus* (1860) and *Our Norland* (1896)—but these were sufficient to win for him general recognition as Canada's leading poet. For some time he fulfilled the functions of an unofficial poet laureate—it was he, for example, who was asked to write the poetical address when a monument was erected at Queenston Heights to the memory of Brock—and his post in the civil service was generally regarded as a reward for his poetic contribution. He was highly praised by his contemporaries, both at home and abroad. Susanna Moodie, for example, exhorted Canada to "be proud of her bard, who has sung in such lofty strains the natural beauties of his native land"; and the *National*

*Magazine* (of London, England) put the same thought much more effusively:

Well may the Canadians be proud of such contribution to their native literature; well may they be forward to recognize his lively imagination, his descriptive powers, his ardent love for the beautiful and good, his never failing charity, his reverence of the god-like, his adoration of the true, his bold, masterly style, and the fullness of his imagery. In some sort, and according to his degree, Mr. Sangster may be regarded as the Wordsworth of Canada.

The Montreal *Transcript* chose rather to compare him with Heavysege: "his genius is not so prolific . . . but his taste is far more refined".

Present-day criticism of Sangster is far less enthusiastic. A provincial Victorian, he has the almost inevitable defects of his place and time: a certain stuffiness and solemnity, a rather narrow moralism, a patriotism that is largely automatic and conventional, a fear of passion, a tendency towards senti- mentality, a refusal to question accepted standards of conduct and belief, a preference for the pretty, the pleasing and the "nice". His philosophy is that of the typical, respectable, middle-class Victorian.

In form he is imitative. The title poem of his first volume is obviously modelled upon Byron's *Childe Harold,* and other poems echo Wordsworth, Moore and above all Tenny- son. The metre of "Locksley Hall" seems especially to have captivated him, and he uses it frequently. There is a good deal of variety in his metres, but it is the variety he found in his models—he made no metrical experiments on his own account.

But his work is not altogether lacking in value, nor in originality. He has some skill in the handling of metaphor and simile; he can describe the Canadian landscape more vividly than any other poet of his period; his lines at times have a lilting, dancing rhythm; he has captured the atmos- phere of pioneer rural life; and he is the first poet to give expression to the national feeling which was to eventuate in Confederation.

We can best illustrate these points by quoting a few representative passages from his poems. These lines, from "The Saint Lawrence and the Saguenay", reveal his gift of imagery and his descriptive power:

> And Darkness, like a Fate, comes stealing down
> In her black mantle, step by step, until
> The trembling stars have dwindled down to one
> Pale, solitary watcher.

This is Sangster at his best. At his worst, he can write a passage of this sort:

> Stand not on the Alps of Error,
> Brother, though the tempting height
> Lure thee to the grassy hilltop,
> Though the view enchant the sight;
> But if sorely tempted thither,
> In some hour of gilded woe
> Stand, and gaze around thee, Brother,
> On the Vale of Truth below.

Unfortunately, good and bad passages are often found side by side in the same poem. "Mariline", a rural idyll in the *Hesperus* volume, contains lines as apt as these:

> Brightly broke the summer morn,
> Like a lark from out the corn,—

and others as bad as these:

> Hunter-up of musty tomes
> Worshipper of deathless poems.

Sangster's patriotism is best expressed indirectly, by his delight in Canadian scenery and customs. His directly nationalistic poems, with the partial exception of "Brock", are rhetorical and uncertain. Even "Brock," after a vigorous opening stanza, declines into conventional clap-trap.

No one today would claim greatness for Sangster, nor indeed for any writer of this colonial period with the possible exception of Haliburton. It is a period spectacular neither in its achievements nor its failures: the literature produced, in both quality and quantity, is just about what might have been expected from a group of pioneer communities. A few lines of *The Rising Village*, Haliburton's *Clockmaker*, some of Howe's speeches, a few passages from *Wacousta*, *The Canadian Brothers*, *Roughing It in the Bush* and *The Backwoods of Canada*, and perhaps a hundred lines scattered through the volumes of Sangster's verse—this is all to which we can point with any assurance. Halifax had, indeed, produced a literary movement of surprising maturity, but it was the product of a soil which, however rich, was limited in area and shallow in depth: Goldsmith, Howe and Haliburton represented the flowering of a small provincial culture rather than the first roots of a national culture. But with the achievement of responsible government in the fifties and of Confederation in the sixties, it seemed that the chief obstacles to the growth of that national culture had been removed.

CHAPTER THREE

# The Confederation Era
## 1867 – 1897

### 1. Introduction

THE RELATIONS between a society and its literature are hypothetical and obscure, and no simple arrangement of cause and effect can be discerned or proven. Perhaps the nearest we can come to a formulation of the relationship is to declare that a state of high excitement within the community, together with some powerful stimulus from outside, is likely to result in the creation of a vivid and vigorous body of writing. These conditions had to some extent been present in Nova Scotia in the 1820's and 1830's; they were present in Canada as a whole during the first few years of her existence as a federated nation.

Confederation was by no means wholly an idealistic experiment in nation-building; among the economic and political factors which precipitated it there were elements of expediency and intrigue. But the desire for a united and strong nation was a powerful motivation, and there was statesmanlike sincerity amid the political rhetoric which welcomed its achievement. The nation was indeed in a state of high excitement. There was so much to do: the newly acquired West to settle, the trans-continental railroad to build, a national economy to create and stabilize. There was also a national spirit to foster, a sense of common purpose to discover.

That this last factor was not ignored is clear from a famous speech of Edward Blake's, a leader of the Reform Party, made in 1874:

We are engaged in a very difficult task, the task of welding together seven Provinces which have been accustomed to regard themselves as isolated from each other. . . . We must find some common ground on which to unite, some common aspiration to be shared, and I think this can be found alone in the cultivation of that national spirit to which I have referred.

Nor was Blake's an isolated voice. In the seventies there arose the "Canada First" movement, whose object it was to unite Canadians on a basis of moral idealism and cultural fervour. Its founder, William Foster, described it as "an intellectual movement", as a "direct product, in some measure of that higher culture which the universities and colleges of our land are steadily promoting", and for a few years it enjoyed wide support.

There was, then, recognition of the fact that a nation does not achieve greatness by a merely material expansion. Never before had Canadians been as ready as in these first three decades after Confederation to welcome a native literary movement, and this public responsiveness undoubtedly had something to do with the marked increase in the quantity and quality of literature during the period. For thirty years, Canada's cultural development almost kept pace with her political and economic expansion. As the West was settled and new provinces added to the Dominion, as the railway pushed gradually across the continent, periodicals and books came from the presses testifying to the new spirit abroad in the land.

As early as 1871, Susanna Moodie, in a preface to a new edition of *Roughing It in the Bush*, captured the new enthusiasm:

Canada is no longer a child, sleeping in the arms of nature, dependent for her very existence on the fostering care of her illustrious mother. She has outstepped infancy, and is in full enjoyment of a strong and vigorous youth. . . . What an advance in the arts and sciences and in the literature of the country has been made during the last few years. . . . Institutes and literary associations for the encouragement of learning are now to be found in all the cities and large towns of the Dominion.

Magazines were founded to serve as media for the new culture. *The Canadian Monthly and National Review* was founded in 1872 and continued for ten years; *The Nation,* official organ of "Canada First", appeared from 1874 to 1876; and in 1883 there began *The Week,* the most brilliant of them all, the counterpart in this period of Howe's *Novascotian* and Gibson's *Literary Garland. The Week,* founded by Goldwin Smith and edited for a time by Charles G. D. Roberts, existed for thirteen years and became the focus of the literary and cultural life of the young Dominion. Almost all the writers to be discussed in this chapter contributed to it at one time or another.

There were other signs of the cultural awakening. The universities expanded their faculties and facilities. To choose three examples from different sections of the country: in the Maritimes, the University of New Brunswick, after undergoing reorganization in 1859, entered its most vigorous period in the seventies and eighties; in Quebec, Laval established, in 1878, a branch in Montreal which subsequently developed into the University of Montreal; and in Ontario, in the eighties, the process began whereby separate denominational colleges were federated into the University of Toronto. A similar symptom was the foundation, in 1881, of the Royal Society of Canada, designed to foster native learning in the arts and sciences. Even the newspapers shared in the movement, the most conspicuous example being that of the Toronto *Globe,* which printed the verse of Canadian poets and opened its pages in the nineties to a literary column edited by Archibald Lampman, Duncan Campbell Scott and William Wilfred Campbell.

## 2. Poetry

The first poet to make his voice heard in this new self-confident Dominion was Charles Mair (1838-1927). As a leading member of the "Canada First" party and one of the pioneers of westward exploration, Mair was in a good position to become the national spokesman; unfortunately his literary gifts were not commensurate with his aspirations.

Born in Lanark, a small Scottish settlement in Ontario, Mair entered Queen's University as a medical student. He published his first book of verse in 1868. This volume, *Dreamland and Other Poems*, is largely a collection of sentimental lyrics in which, however, Mair's characteristic strength and weaknesses are already apparent. The strength resides almost wholly in Mair's capacity to observe and describe the minute details of landscape; the weaknesses are conventional language and uncertain taste. Mair uses a highly artificial poetic diction, and he is given to sudden bewildering descents into bathos. Here are a few lines from a poem called "Innocence" which mark one such descent:

> Oft have I seen her walk
> Through flow'r decked fields unto the oaken pass,
> Where lay the slumbry flock,
> Swoll'n with much eating of the tender grass.

Most of Mair's life was spent in the new West. He accompanied an expedition whose object was to open up an emigration route via Lake of the Woods, engaged in the fur trade in Manitoba and was for many years an Immigration Officer in Alberta and British Columbia. In 1886 he published *Tecumseh, A Drama*, in 1890 *The Last Bison*, in 1901 *Collected Poems*, and in 1908 a prose work called *Through the Mackenzie Basin*.

*Tecumseh* was consciously written as a patriotic exercise. In the preface Mair declares that Canadian history is a mine of character and incident for the poet and novelist, and that the Canadian writer who finds inspiration in his own history is "helping to create for a young people that decisive test of its intellectual faculties, an original and distinctive litera-ture". It cannot be said that Mair's play is a very successful demonstration of his principles. *Tecumseh* is like Heavy-sege's *Saul* not merely in being a closet drama; it is also a literary curiosity. Mair's Indians speak a language even more pompous and rhetorical than that of Heavysege's Hebrews. Only in the descriptive passages, and there only fleetingly, does Mair maintain control over his medium. Here is a sample passage in which he is at or near his rather ponderous best:

> We left
> The silent forest, and, day after day,
> Great prairies swept beyond our aching sight
> Into the measureless West; uncharted realms,
> Voiceless and calm, save when tempestuous wind
> Rolled the rank herbage into billows vast,
> And rushing tides which never found a shore.
> And tender clouds, and veils of morning mist,
> Cast flying shadows, chased by flying light,
> Into interminable wildernesses,
> Flushed with fresh blooms, deep perfumed by the rose,
> And murmurous with flower-fed bird and bee.

*The Last Bison* is even more inept and fantastic. Mair gushes about the oppressed Indians and the disappearing buffaloes, and then describes the arrival of the last mighty bison of the plains. "With stately tread" and "gleaming eyes" it descends to the shore and then proceeds to record the past and foretell the future. It praises the treatment accorded it by the Indians, rehearses the greedy slaughters of the white man, and prophesies the latter's ultimate destruction—all in the language appropriate to an itinerant evangelist!

It is only fair to add that occasionally, in shorter poems

like "August", Mair reaches a slightly higher level. The landscape, the fauna and flora, and the climatic conditions which
he describes in "August" are recognizably those of Canada,
and have been closely observed:

>                    When all the woods
> Grow dim with smoke, and smirch their lively green
> With haze of long continued drought begot;
> When every field grows yellow, and a plague
> Of thirst dries up its herbage to the root,
> So that the cattle grow quite ribby-lean
> On woody stalks whose juices all are spent;
> When every fronded fern in mid-wood hid
> Grows sick and yellow with the jaundice heat,
> While those on hill-sides glare with patchy red;
> When streamlets die upon the lichened rocks,
> And leave the bleaching pebbles shining bare,
> And every mussel shell agape and parched,
> And small snail-craft quite emptied of their crews. . . .

But even at his best, Mair was clearly not the national poet
for whom Canadian critics were impatiently waiting. A much
more likely candidate for that post appeared in 1880, when
Charles G. D. Roberts published *Orion and Other Poems*.
Archibald Lampman, then a student at Trinity College,
Toronto, has told us how the appearance of that book affected
him:

Like most of the young fellows about me, I had been under
the depressing conviction that we were hopelessly situated on
the outskirts of civilization, where no art and no literature
could be, and that it was useless to expect that we could do
it ourselves. I sat up most of the night reading and re-reading *Orion* in a state of the wildest excitement and when I
went to bed I could not sleep. It seemed to me a wonderful
thing that such work could be done by a Canadian, by a young
man, one of ourselves. It was like a voice from some new
paradise of art, calling to us to be up and doing.

Whatever may be the ultimate verdict upon Roberts' own
poetry, his importance as a stimulus to others can never be
questioned. He stimulated Lampman, as the above quota-

tion makes clear, and Lampman in turn stimulated Duncan
Campbell Scott; he stimulated a group of young poets in his
own city of Fredericton, a group which included his cousin
Bliss Carman, his younger brother Theodore Roberts, Francis
Sherman and Barry Straton; and as editor of *The Week* for
a period in the eighties he brought to its columns the work of
practically every new and established writer in the Dominion.

Charles G. D. Roberts (1860-1943) was the product of
three broad cultural influences: the national excitement con-
sequent upon Confederation; the late flowering of the provincial culture of New Brunswick; the external stimulus
provided by the poetry of Swinburne and Rossetti.

About the year 1880, when *Orion* was published, the new
national feeling in Canada was at its height. Sir John A.
Macdonald had returned to power in 1878 and was pushing
forward his three great projects: a national economic policy
which involved the protection of Canada's nascent industries,
the building of the trans-continental railway and the settlement of the West. After the apparently temporary effects of
the economic depression which had begun in 1873, and the
hesitations of Alexander Mackenzie's term of office, it seemed
that the young Dominion was finally launched in pursuit of
its manifest destiny.

That Roberts was responsive to this national excitement is
clear from his poetry. He consciously essayed the role of a
national poet, and in poems such as "An Ode for the Canadian
Confederacy", "Canada", and "Collect for Dominion Day",
he urged Canadians to recognize the greatness of their destiny
and to do their part in fulfilling it. These directly patriotic
poems are far from his best, but they demonstrate beyond all
doubt that he was passionately concerned for his country's
future. His patriotism expressed itself most effectively, however, in less direct and more subtle ways—above all by his
realization of the poetic possibilities in the simple lives of the
New Brunswick farmers.

For Roberts was also a product of New Brunswick, and

knew her life intimately. After a few early years in West-
cock, he had come with his father to the city of Fredericton,
the capital of New Brunswick, attended the Collegiate School
and taken his degree at the University of New Brunswick in
1879.

New Brunswick was originally a part of the colony of
Nova Scotia, but it had been established as a separate province in 1784, soon after the arrival in the St. John River
valley of a group of Loyalists. The cultural development of
the province was delayed, in comparison with that of Nova
Scotia, partly by the later date of its settlement, partly by its
greater geographical diversity and partly by the domination
of its economy during most of the nineteenth century by
what Dr. A. G. Bailey has aptly called "the lawless and specu-
lative spirit of the timber trade". Fredericton, similar in its
loyalism and cultural standard to Halifax, could not dominate its province as Halifax dominated Nova Scotia, because
it did not combine the facilities of a port and commercial
metropolis with its governmental and educational institutions. Fredericton had been, however, ever since its establishment in 1783, a city of strong cultural pretensions and of
modest cultural achievements. The first provincial secretary
was Jonathan Odell, the Loyalist poet; the first novel by a
native Canadian, *St. Ursula's Convent* or *The Nun of Canada*
(1824) by Julia Catherine Beckwith (1796-1867), had been
written there when she was a girl of sixteen.

In the fifties, sixties and seventies, the cultural life of
Fredericton in particular and of New Brunswick in general
began to quicken. The University of New Brunswick was
established on a firmer foundation in 1859, and it soon began
to produce graduates of whom Roberts and Carman were
only the most eminent of a distinguished company. Indeed,
as Dr. A. G. Bailey has said: "The whole society of the province gathered momentum, constructive energies were released, and a vigorous and self-reliant attitude took possession
of its people."

Out of these quickened feelings in the nation and in the province, the poetry of Roberts emerged. But in addition to these factors, there was needed a third—some exciting creative stimulus from the outside world. This was provided by George R. Parkin, Headmaster of the Fredericton Collegiate School, who returned from Oxford in 1875 thrilled by the new poetry of Swinburne and Rossetti. The story can best be told by Roberts himself:

But it was outside school hours that Parkin did most for us two ardent boys [Roberts and Carman]. . . . He would take us favoured two for long hikes over the wooded hills behind Fredericton. . . . England just then was thrilling to the new music, the new colour, the new raptures of Swinburne and Rossetti; Parkin was steeped in them; and in his rich voice he would recite to us ecstatically, over and over until we too were intoxicated with them, the great choruses from "Atalanta in Calydon," passages from "The Triumph of Time," and "Rococo,"—but above all, "The Blessed Damozel," which he loved so passionately that Bliss suspected him of sometimes saying it instead of his prayers.

Roberts published in all ten volumes of verse, but almost all his best work is contained in the first three of them: *Orion and Other Poems* (1880), *In Divers Tones* (1886) and especially *Songs of the Common Day* (1893). Almost to the end of his life, he retained the capacity to write an occasional striking poem—"The Iceberg", for example, which appeared in 1934—but his departure for New York in 1897 was the signal, in part the cause, of a distinct decline in the general level of his achievement. He was essentially a regional poet, a poet of the Tantramar marshes and the St. John River valley, and once he left his region behind him his inspiration began to flag.

His poetry may be divided into six main categories: poems of rural life; poems describing and interpreting Nature; love poems; religious and philosophical verse; patriotic odes; and a miscellaneous group, mainly elegiac in mood. Most of these categories may be briefly dismissed. His patriotic poems we have already mentioned. His love poems are perfervid and artificial; they aim at an exotic sophistication which is quite beyond his power to achieve. Lines like these protest much too loudly that they are passionate:

> The pulses of your throat,
> What madness they denote to me,—
> Passion, and hunger, and despair,
> And ecstacy, and prayer to me!

His religious and philosophical poems are not much better. What he has to offer us is a rather cloudy mysticism, based mainly on Emersonian transcendentalism. His confident faith in the elemental goodness and spirituality of the universe is not even troubled by the timid doubts of Tennyson, nor does his acceptance of the transcendental creed seem to have involved the rejection of orthodox Christianity which it involved for Emerson. In his animal stories he shows himself to have been aware of the difficulties in the way of his optimism—frequently, in his stories, one animal destroys another while innocently fulfilling the law of its own nature —but for some reason no such awareness disturbs his poetry.

A similar vagueness weakens the poems in which he seeks to interpret Nature. Nature heals—but what she heals or how she achieves it is never made clear. But when Roberts is content to describe Nature, his verse takes on a new authority and power. He has the painter's eye, the eye that not merely sees the colour and texture and shape of things but which arranges them into broad patterns, perceives their conformations and their rhythmic interplay of line and plane:

> A high bare field, brown from the plough, and borne
> Aslant from sunset; amber wastes of sky
> Washing the ridge; a clamour of crows that fly
> In from the wide flats where the spent tides mourn . . . .

But these lines are the first part of "The Potato Harvest", a poem which properly belongs to the category of rural life. It is in these poems, found in the volume *Songs of the Common Day*, and to a lesser extent in his elegiac poems, that Roberts is at his best. Simple, unpretentious and accurate, poems such as "The First Ploughing", "The Chopping Bee", "In the Barn-Yard's Southerly Corner", "The Farmer's Winter Morning", "The Sower", "The Pea Fields", "The Mowing", "The Oat-Threshing", and "In an Old Barn" constitute Roberts' most enduring achievement.   Whereas his more ambitious poems are confused and abstract, these are clear and concrete. The self-conscious rhetoric of his patriotic poems, and the exotic images and artificial diction of the love poems, are here replaced by a quiet, casual tone and an unobtrusive plainness of statement.   The poems are so consistent in their level of achievement that it is difficult to select one for quotation, but here are a few passages, selected from various poems, which will give some idea of their quality:

> In billows round the wide red welcoming doors
>     High piles the golden straw; while from within,
>     Where plods the team amid the chaffy din,
> The loud pulsation of the thresher soars . . . .
>                         "The Oat-Threshing"

> Tons upon tons the brown-green fragrant hay
>     O'erbrims the mows beyond the time-warped eaves,
>     Up to the rafters where the spider weaves,
> Though few flies wander his secluded way.
> Through a high chink one lonely golden ray,
> Wherein the dust is dancing, slants unstirred.
>                         "In an Old Barn"

> These are the fields of light and laughing air,
>     And yellow butterflies, and foraging bees,
>     And whitish, wayward blossoms winged as these,
> And pale green tangles like a seamaid's-hair.
> Pale, pale the blue, but pure beyond compare,
>     And pale the sparkle of the far-off seas
>     A-shimmer like these fluttering slopes of peas,
> And pale the open landscape everywhere.
>                         "The Pea-Fields"

The poems in an elegiac mood do not as consistently achieve their intentions, but some of them—"Ave: an Ode for the Centenary of the Birth of Shelley", and "Grey Rocks and the Greyer Sea" for example—are good, and one of them, "Tantramar Revisited", is undoubtedly one of the best poems ever written in Canada. In "Tantramar Revisited" everything is perfectly in keeping. The long lines, the slow melancholy beat of the rhythm, the heavy words made up of long vowels and strong consonants, the accurate pictures of the broad, dull-coloured marshes—all are beautifully adapted to the theme of dissolution and decay. In the descriptive passages we see again Roberts' capacity to arrange a scene as a painter would, to be aware of its planes and lines, its colour and texture:

Skirting the sunbright uplands stretches a riband of meadow,
Shorn of the labouring grass, bulwarked well from the sea,
Fenced on its seaward border with long clay dikes from the turbid
Surge and flow of the tides vexing the Westmoreland shores.

Ah, how well I remember those wide red flats, above tide-mark,
Pale with scurf of the salt, seamed and baked in the sun!
Well I remember the piles of blocks and ropes, and the net-reels
Wound with the beaded nets, dripping and dark from the sea!

Yet, as I sit and watch, this present peace of the landscape,—
Stranded boats, these reels empty and idle, the hush,
One grey hawk slow-wheeling above yon cluster of haystacks,—
More than the old-time stir this stillness welcomes me home.

Roberts was not a great national poet, except in the sense that he initiated the first significant poetic movement in Canada, but he was a good regional poet. His approach to his region was romantic and nostalgic, but it was made fresh by his spontaneous joy in common things, by his interest in and delighted observance of the ordinary processes of rural life and nature.

Bliss Carman (1861-1929) emerged from the same environment and was subject to the same early influences as Charles Roberts, but his poetry is in many respects quite different from that of his cousin. Whereas Roberts is precise and firm in his pictures, Carman tends to be hazy and soft, aiming at suggestiveness rather than clarity. Carman's poetry is, however, much more brightly coloured; the duns and greys and browns of Roberts are replaced by yellows, purples and scarlets. His verse runs or lingers where that of Roberts merely strides; it is more various in its rhythms, and more musical in its skilful arrangements of vowels and consonants.

Carman enjoyed, at the height of his fame, a reputation far greater than that of any other Canadian poet; and even today he remains the Canadian poet whose name and work are most favourably regarded outside our borders. Recent criticism of his work in Canada, however, has been predominantly hostile, and the reaction against his type of romanticism has affected his reputation more adversely than that of any other member of this Confederation groups of poets. The time has come when we must attempt a more judicious estimate of his work.

We must begin by recognizing that Carman wrote far too much and that large masses of his work are unworthy of serious critical attention. In the United States, to which he emigrated in the eighties, he came under the influence of Richard Hovey and began to write a vagabondish type of poetry which was alien to his own temperament. He also wrote love poems of the exotic type then in vogue both in New York and London. It is impossible today to take these poems seriously, but they may afford us amusement if we accept them as light verse. Here is an example:

> My glorious enchantress,
> She went in silken hose,
> With swaying hip and curving lip
> And little tilted nose,
> As full of fragrant fire
> **As any English rose.**

Carman also produced, especially in *Behind the Arras: A Book of the Unseen* (1895), a number of philosophical and mystical poems. They too are of almost negligible value. They contain some effective lines and arresting images, but they are essentially hollow. His philosophy is a shadowy transcendentalism derived from his kinsman Emerson and his teacher Royce, touched with a mildly Keatsian cult of beauty and a shallow paganism taken over from Swinburne and Verlaine. The result of these and other somewhat contradictory influences is a peculiarly jumbled version of the Victorian compromise: the evil in the world is only apparent and temporary ("Evil is a dissonance not a discord. . . . Soon to be resolved in happier phrase"); if Man will put himself in rhythmic harmony with Nature all will be well with him ("let the punctual tides instruct thee, and the planets give thee poise"); we should gratify the senses because that is the true means to spiritual enrichment ("Slake the senses now, that soul hereafter. . . . Go not forth a starved defrauded thing").

Carman's social and political ideas are even less acute and original than his ethical and metaphysical ones. He shares Tennyson's fear of scepticism in religion and of democracy in politics:

> We have scorned the belief of our fathers
> And cast their quiet aside;
> To take the mob for our ruler
> And the voice of the mob for our guide.
>
> "Twilight in Eden"

But such topical verse is rare in Carman. For the most part he seems to move in a social vacuum, unaware of the problems of his time. He has none of the social consciousness which marks Lampman's later poetry.

But if Carman was unaware of his time, he was very vividly aware of his place. Like Roberts he was essentially a regional poet who found in the woods and streams and tides of New

Brunswick the inspiration of all his best work. His best poems are those in which he finds in this native landscape symbols of his mood, and evokes them in a rich and sonorous verbal music. Some critics would include among the best the lyrics contained in *Sappho: One Hundred Lyrics,* published first in 1904 and still kept in print, but I cannot share this view. The Sappho lyrics, delicate and melodious as they are, seem to me artificial; they are, compared with the New Brunswick poems, like mere paper flowers, pretty but inert.

The poems in which Carman creates a mood by exploiting the music of words and the symbolic qualities of the New Brunswick scene may be divided into two main groups. The first and less wholly satisfactory group includes the poems in which he celebrates the coming of spring. Here the mood is ecstatic and rapturous. In the sudden, brief, tumultuous flowering of the Canadian spring, Carman finds symbols all around him:

> Lo, now comes the April pageant
> And the Easter of the year.
> Now the tulip lifts her chalice,
> And the hyacinth his spear . . . .
> > "Resurgam"

> In rocky groves the sugar maples drip,
> Till the sweet sap o'erbrims the shining pails;
> The snow slides from the roofs in the warm sun;
> Along spring-runs the first young green appears;
> The willow saplings in the meadow lot
> Put on their saffron veils with silver sheen
> As if for some approaching festival . . . .
> > "A Bluebird in March"

In these and similar lines we can observe the difference between Carman's approach to landscape and that of Roberts and Lampman. He has little of their regional particularism; he is not concerned with the processes of New Brunswick agriculture, as Roberts was, nor with the precise details of the flora and fauna of his region in the Lampman manner.

He paints with a broader brush, making his effects by bright splashes of colour and by isolating for special attention only those details which are symbolic and suggestive. The result may be somewhat indistinct from the visual standpoint—one never sees a Carman landscape as exactly as one sees the Ontario countryside in Lampman's "Heat"—but there is a greater emotive power and a finer command of verbal melody. Take the stanza:

> And there when lengthening twilights fall
> As softly as a wild bird's wing,
> Across the valley in the dusk
> I hear the silver flute of spring.

The music of these lines is perfect, the imagery is appropriate and suggestive, and the words are evocative and inevitable. How exactly right, for example, is that word "lengthening!" It suggests the sloping rays of the setting sun, the gradual elongation of shadows, the way in which the slow blurring of outlines at twilight makes things seem to stretch out and blend. At the same time it states the simple fact that the days in springtime are gradually growing longer. The same word adds much to the music of the lines; its lingering consonants suggest the drowsiness of twilight and blend with the other sibilants and labials in the stanza, and its vowels fit into the subtle pattern of complementary vowel sounds of which the stanza is composed.

Good as some of these spring poems are—and it must be admitted that they are good in parts rather than as wholes—they are surpassed by Carman's poems in an elegiac mood of hopeless longing and charged regret. On the best of the poems of this second group—"Low Tide on Grand Pré" "A Northern Vigil", "The Eavesdropper", "Marian Drury", and "The White Gull"—his reputation must rest. Here is displayed at its purest his peculiar gift: the capacity to create an effect of haunting melancholy by the use of slow, involved, troubled verbal melodies, and of symbols of decay and desolation drawn from the scenery and climate of his native province.

"Low Tide on Grand Pré", in spite of one weak stanza, is the most nearly perfect poem to come out of Canada in the nineteenth century.   Here Carman found, in the desolate mud flats left by the retreating Fundy tide, the exact symbol for his mood.   As the poem begins, the sun has just gone down, the tide is out, and the reddish brown mud, lit by the sun's afterglow, is temporarily beautiful:

> The sun goes down and over all
>   These barren reaches by the tide
> Such unelusive glories fall,
>   I almost dream they yet may bide
>   Until the coming of the tide.

The reference to "the coming of the tide" leads into the second and third stanzas, in which is evoked the picture of the restless ebb and flow in the rivers and streams along the Fundy coast.   He plays with the fancy that the wandering river is searching for the girl he has lost, and this provides a transition to the central sequence of the poem, in which he recreates the climactic day of their courtship:

> Was it a year or lives ago
>   We took the grasses in our hands,
> And caught the summer flying low
>   Over the waving meadow lands,
>   And held it there between our hands?

Strong indeed must be the prejudice which would resist the appeal of that stanza, with its appropriate waving rhythm, its daring image of the summer as a bird caught on the wing and its disciplined simplicity of statement.

Two almost equally fine stanzas follow, the sixth being remarkable for the way in which its rhythm echoes the rhythm of a drifting canoe.   The seventh stanza, which records a moment of mystical illumination, is relatively loose and abstract, but the eighth regains the level of the first six:

> Then all your face grew light, and seemed
>     To hold the shadow of the sun;
> The evening faltered, and I deemed
>     That time was ripe, and years had done
>     Their wheeling underneath the sun.

The ninth stanza, with its reminiscence of the caught-bird image of the fourth, completes the pattern of the inset memory:

> So all desire and all regret,
>     And fear and memory, were naught;
> One to remember or forget
>     The keen delight our hands had caught;
>     Morrow and yesterday were naught.

But the magnificent tenth and final stanza effectively bursts this bubble of romantic illusion.   Time is inexorable; night must fall. This last stanza completes the pattern of the whole poem; the "unelusive glories" fall no longer; night has replaced twilight; the tide has overwhelmed the land with water and the poet with grief:

> The night has fallen and the tide . . .
>     Now and again comes drifting home,
> Across these aching barrens wide,
>     A sigh like driven wind or foam:
>     In grief the flood is bursting home.

A comparable but not quite equal success is achieved in "A Northern Vigil". Here Carman has found the objective correlative for his mood of hopeless longing in the intense cold of a Canadian winter night:

> The windows of my room
>     Are dark with bitter frost,
> The stillness aches with doom
>     Of something loved and lost.

Again he has used the mutation of the sun to provide the framework; the poem begins at sunset and ends with the coming of dawn:

> Lo, now far on the hills
>   The crimson fumes uncurled,
> Where the caldron mantles and spills
>   Another dawn on the world!

It has some fine stanzas in it, but also some bad ones, and it is too diffuse to match "Low Tide".

We can only glance at the other poems of this group. "The Eavesdropper" contains the perfect stanza:

> Outside, a yellow maple tree,
>   Shifting upon the silvery blue
> With tiny multitudinous sound,
>   Rustled to let the sunlight through.

"Marian Drury", like "Low Tide" though less effectively, employs the symbolism of the marshes and the sea. "The White Gull", Carman's elegy on Shelley, also exhibits his power of finding symbols and suggestion along the Fundy coast:

> The gray sea-horses troop and roam;
> The shadows fly
> Along the wind-floor at their heels;
> And where the golden daylight wheels,
> A white gull searches the blue dome
> With keening cry.

The reputation which Carman enjoyed at the first of this century was undoubtedly an inflated one. It resulted in part from the fact that his best work was done when there was a dearth of great poetry on both sides of the Atlantic: the great Victorians were dead, Yeats was still in his early romantic phase, Eliot, Sandburg and Frost had yet to make their appearance. But Carman is a better poet than much criticism grants him. Faults he has in abundance: he is uncertain in thought and sometimes even in feeling: he can be guilty of astonishing carelessness of technique; his bohemianism is a pose; he is often boisterous to the point of vulgarity; his eroticism is forced and silly; he is ignorant of the social and political forces of his time; he is too facile and too diffuse; his rhythms, themes and moods incline to monotony; the great mass of his work lacks depth and distinction. But he has gifts which we should not overlook, and which go far toward compensating for his deficiencies. He is a master of mood and music. At his best, he achieves a melodic beauty equalled by no other Canadian poet, and he knows better than any other how to employ the distinctive features of his native environment to effect a compelling atmosphere. If there are any masters in Canadian poetry, Carman is of their company.

Another of the masters is Archibald Lampman (1861-1899), whose excitement at encountering Roberts' *Orion* we have already mentioned. Lampman, indeed, who has never attracted much attention outside Canada, has come out of the recent reaction against romantic nature poetry in Canada with less damage than any other poet of his generation. The tendency of recent criticism has been to elevate him above Roberts who inspired him, and above Carman whose reputation once completely overshadowed his. This elevation has been to some extent inspired, I believe, by other than purely aesthetic considerations. Part of it has been a matter of sentiment: he died young, when apparently about to enter the greatest phase of his poetic career. Part of it has been chance: dying young, he was spared the slow decline which marked the later careers of Roberts and Carman and might have marked his. Part of it has been that, in the last years of his short life, he wrote a few poems of the type which were in vogue in the nineteen thirties and early forties—poems of social satire and protest. But Lampman, though he had a more acute social consciousness than Roberts and Carman, was not a great, or even a very good social poet; his best work, like theirs, consists of a few nature lyrics.

The differences between Lampman and Carman and Roberts are differences not of rank but of manner. He was a more even poet than they: he never reached the heights of their finest passages, but he never sank to the depths to which they were capable of sinking. He had not Roberts' manly vigour nor Carman's melodic skill, but he had a greater concern with the detail of craftsmanship and a more patient and faithful watchfulness. He was a less colourful poet than they, but a more restrained and disciplined one. The tone of his poetry is altogether more quiet and its texture finer. His choice of models is significant: whereas the admiration of Roberts and Carman went primarily to Shelley and Swinburne, his was directed toward Keats and Matthew Arnold.

Apart from the fact that Lampman grew up in Ontario and Roberts and Carman in New Brunswick, his background was very similar to theirs. He was descended from a family of Loyalists, and was, like Roberts, the son of an Anglican rector. He attended the Anglican college—Trinity—in the University of Toronto, graduating three years after Roberts' graduation from the University of New Brunswick. Like both Roberts and Carman, he first tried his hand at teaching school. There, however, the similarities end: whereas Roberts and Carman soon began to devote all their time to writing, Lampman went to Ottawa as a civil servant and remained there as a clerk in the Post Office Department until his death.

This residence in Ottawa in some part accounts for the differences between Lampman's poetry and theirs. Living in the federal capital and associated with a government department, he could hardly fail to be aware of the political issues of the day. Frustrated by the routine of his position, he expressed his resentment against a social system which affected him much more directly than it affected the peripatetic New Brunswick poets.

But the first and perhaps the chief effect which the civil service environment had upon Lampman was to turn his eyes to nature as a refuge and an anodyne. In the beautiful wooded hills, rivers, and lakes of the Ottawa Valley he found ample scope for his watchful eye and listening ear. Nature became to him an other-world, a world which, for all its vivid details, was always dream-like, always only half-real:

> And slowly as we heard you, day by day,
> The stillness of enchanted reveries
> Bound brain and spirit and half-closèd eyes
> In some divine sweet wonder-dream astray;
> To us no sorrow or upreared dismay
> Nor any discord came, but evermore
> The voices of mankind, the outer roar,
> Grew strange and murmurous, faint and far away.
>
> "The Frogs"

This is a representative rather than an especially good passage, but in it we can see the qualities which are present even in his best poems. Always the pace is slow, the mood melancholy, the atmosphere dreamy. The famous "Heat" for example, the finest poem he wrote, has the same qualities. The physical details—the "hay-cart, moving dustily/With idly clacking wheels", the water-bugs which "draw close beneath/ The cool gloom of the bridge"—are vivid enough, but it is the vividness of a dream. Everything moves slowly—the hay-cart "slowly steals", the wagoner "is slouching slowly", "even the buttercups are still", the cows "lie waiting", the thrush's song "slides leisurely" and the poet "leans at rest"—so that the whole scene has a trance-like effect.

The same, slow, hesitant music is found in "In November". The poet enters the wood "with loitering step and quiet eye" and soon falls into a kind of trance:

> And all around me the thin light,
> So sere, so melancholy bright,
> Fell like the half-reflected gleam
> Or shadow of some former dream . . . .

The same atmosphere recurs in the sonnet "Solitude," which
begins:

> How still it is here in the woods.  The trees
> Stand motionless, as if they did not dare
> To stir, lest it should break the spell.

And the combination of slow movement, faint sounds and
dream-like reverie is found also in " Sunset at Les Eboule-
ments", a sonnet so fine throughout that it demands full
quotation:

> Broad shadows fall.   On all the mountain side
> The scythe-swept fields are silent.   Slowly home
> By the long beach the high-piled hay-carts come,
> Splashing the pale salt shallows.   Over wide
> Fawn-coloured wastes of mud the slipping tide,
> Round the dun rocks and wattled fisheries,
> Creeps murmuring in.   And now by twos and threes,
> O'er the slow-spreading pools with clamorous chide,
> Belated crows from strip to strip take flight.
> Soon will the first star shine; yet ere the night
> Reach onward to the pale-green distances,
> The sun's last shaft beyond the gray sea-floor
> Still dreams upon the Kamouraska shore,
> And the long line of golden villages.

We may pause here to discuss, with special reference to the
poem just quoted, Lampman's poetic technique.  The sonnet
was easily his favourite form.  In the Memorial Edition of his
*Poems*, published in 1900 by his friend Duncan Campbell
Scott, one hundred and twenty-two, or well over half the
total, are sonnets.  He made no daring experiment with the
sonnet form, but he handled it with a quiet, unassuming
dexterity.  The tone is quiet, the rhythm soft and slow.
There is the precision of detail which we find also in
Roberts' *Songs of the Common Day* but there are none of the
slightly over-ripe expressions of which Roberts is frequently
guilty.  If Roberts' best sonnets remind us of paintings in oil,
Lampman's sonnets are rather like water-colours—softer,

more delicate, almost translucent.  The concreteness of the
poem is remarkable: the mood is communicated almost
entirely by a sequence of sensuous images.  The words have
been chosen with great care. Look, for example, at the second
line.  The alliterated *s*'s give precisely the effect of a scythe
cutting grass. The vowel sounds have been chosen with equal
skill.  The dominant long *i*'s in the first two-thirds of the
line echo the long sweep of the scythe, and the long *o*'s of the
last third suggest the slow roll of the wheels of the haycart.
Fortunately we have external proof of the careful revision by
which such effects were achieved.  The critic, E. K. Brown,
to whom students of Lampman owe so much, once found
several versions of the twelfth line of this sonnet among
Lampman's manuscripts.  At first the line read:

> Where the soft sunshine one long moment more . . . .

Lampman found this too indefinite, and altered it to:

> Where the long light across the lit sea-floor . . . .

This in turn gave way to the line as it stands in the published poem—at once so much more concrete, exact and
musical.

This sort of thing Lampman could do supremely well; but
in his later years he seems to have grown tired of it, to have
felt that it was not enough.  Influenced in part perhaps by
his master Arnold's increasing concern with social and political questions, in part by his own increasing ill health and
mental restlessness, he began to turn his attention from
nature to man.  Sometimes his new attitude took the form of
a more direct expression of his personal melancholy than he
had allowed himself in the nature poems:

> With all dear things that ought to please
>   The hours are blessed,
> And yet my soul is ill at ease
>   And cannot rest.
>
> "Unrest"

Sometimes it took the form of short satirical portraits of those who, in the present social order, were allowed to exploit their fellows:

> He made himself a great name in his day,
> A glittering fellow on the world's hard way,
> He tilled and seeded and reaped plentifully
> From the black soil of human misery . . . .
>
> > "Epitaph on a Rich Man"

On other occasions he saw the ills as being of a deeper origin than in the structure of society, as being the result of the very constitution of the world:

> And the huge presence of this world, at best
> A sightless giant wandering without rest,
> Agèd and mad with many miseries.
>
> > "Despondency"

Sometimes, to counteract such pessimism in himself, Lampman resorted to direct didacticism, to moral admonishment of this sort:

> By deeds not words the souls of men are taught;
> Good lives alone are fruitful . . . .
>
> > "Deeds"

> To those who ever march with faith unbent,
> Preserving in its fervid prime
> A single purpose clear and plain,
> Ready, although the twentieth time
> To strike and fall, and strike again,—
> Fate changes and the Gods relent.
>
> > "Persistence"

Somewhat more successfully, but still in a way which fell far short of his best nature verse, he turned in "The Land of Pallas" to social idealism.  His utopia is obviously modelled on Morris' "Nowhere", and has all the dreamlike features of his model and of his own early verse.  Beauty has replaced wealth as the supreme social value, and as a result all is well. All men and women are equal; the earth is held in common; money, prisons, armaments, judges, marriage contracts and oaths have all disappeared. The prospect may be charming, but the poetry is singularly lacking in the concreteness and precision which mark his nature lyrics.

This final phase did, however, produce two poems worthy to be set beside Lampman's finest: "The City of the End of Things" and "At the Long Sault". In the former the dream has become a nightmare, the influence of Arnold and Morris has been replaced by that of Poe and Thomson. Lampman's soft, slow, hesitant music has been transformed into an angry, maddening roar, the leisurely rhythm into a piston-like beat:

> The beat, the thunder and the hiss
> Cease not, and change not, night nor day.
> And moving at unheard commands,
> The abysses and vast fires between,
> Flit figures that with clanking hands
> Obey a hideous routine;
> They are not flesh, they are not bone,
> They see not with the human eye,
> And from their iron lips is blown
> A dreadful and monotonous cry . . . .

"At the Long Sault" tells the story of an heroic episode in the history of French Canada, when Montreal was saved from the Iroquois by the bravery of Daulac and his few companions. Lampman had tried his hand, unsuccessfully, at a number of narrative poems, but in this story of heroic resistance against overwhelming odds he found at last a congenial theme. Into Daulac's struggle he was able to project himself, for he felt himself to be near death and was increasingly aware of the hostile pressure of his environment. The poem is short and restrained, and its climactic passage, especially the magnificent last line of that passage, is as fine as anything Lampman ever wrote:

Silent, white-faced, again and again
Charged and hemmed round by furious hands,
Each for a moment faces them all and stands
In his little desperate ring; like a tired bull moose
Whom scores of sleepless wolves, a ravening pack,
Have chased all night, all day
Through the snow-laden woods, like famine let loose;
And he turns at last in his track
Against a wall of rock and stands at bay;
Around him with terrible sinews and teeth of steel
They charge and recharge; but with many a furious plunge
          and wheel,
Hither and thither over the trampled snow,
He tosses them bleeding and torn;
Till, driven, and ever to and fro
Harried, wounded and weary grown,
His mighty strength gives way
And all together they fasten upon him and drag him down.

Narrative poetry of this violent sort is unusual in Lampman, but it is the characteristic product of the fourth major
poet of this period, Duncan Campbell Scott (1862-1947).
Scott was a close friend of Lampman's and acted as his literary
executor.   Like Lampman, he was a member of the federal
civil service, but he was connected wtih a department of
government, that of Indian Affairs, which brought him into
contact with the wilder and more inaccessible parts of the
country.  The result is that his nature poetry is usually more
rugged than that of Lampman's, and that much of his poetry
is concerned with violent episodes in the relations between
Indians and white men such as lay quite outside the experience of his friend.

   Scott produced nine volumes of poetry: *The Magic House
and Other Poems* (1893) ; *Labour and the Angel* (1898);
*New World Lyrics and Ballads* (1905) ; *Via Borealis* (1906);
*Lines in Memory of Edmund Morris* (1915) ; *Lundy's Lane
and Other Poems* (1916); *Beauty and Life* (1921); *Collected
Poems* (1926) ; and *The Green Cloister* (1935).   A final

volume, *The Circle of Affection*, containing some additional poems and various prose selections, appeared in 1947. Scott also produced two volumes of short stories—*In the Village of Viger* (1896) and *The Witching of Elspie* (1923)—and a biography of John Graves Simcoe.

The poetry of Duncan Campbell Scott is a poetry of conflict. His pictures of nature are predominantly those of nature in storm, with man withstanding its pressure by virtue either of an inner moral strength or a supreme outer assurance. An example is this stanza from "Rapids at Night":

> Here at the roots of the mountains,
> Between the sombre legions of cedars and tamaracks,
> The rapids charge the ravine:
> A little light, cast by foam under starlight,
> Wavers about the shimmering stems of the birches:
> Here rise up the clangorous sounds of battle,
> Immense and mournful.
> Far above curves the great dome of darkness
> Drawn with the limitless lines of the stars and the planets.
> Deep at the core of the tumult,
> Deeper than all the voices that cry at the surface,
> Dwells one fathomless sound
> Under the hiss and the cry, the stroke and the plangent
>      clamor.

There is a touch of reassurance in this poem: above the battle are the eternal verities symbolized by "the great dome of darkness". But in "The Eagle Speaks" there is no such reassurance, and man appears as a puny earthbound creature which the exultant eagle can destroy at will. Having destroyed him, the eagle speaks thus:

> I swirled low over the earth like flame flattened
> By wind, then with a long loop of swiftness
> Rose sheer up into the bubble of the air
> And left him, carrion with his carrion,
> For the dull coyotes to scent and overhaul
> With snarls and bickerings lower than the dogs.
> Rose to the unattempted heights, spurning

The uséd channels of the air, to the thin reach
Where vapours are unborn and caught the last
Glint of falling light beyond the peak
Of the last mountain, and hung alone serene
Till night, welling up into the void, darkened me,—
Poised with the first cold stars.

The theme of this poem—violent death in a wilderness setting—is the dominant theme of Scott's best and most characteristic poems. In his most famous, and in many ways his most satisfying, single poem, "The Piper of Arll", the climactic episode is the death of the piper and the intruding ship's crew; in "The Forsaken" an old squaw is left alone by the tribe to die in the wilds; in "At the Cedars" there is the double death of a man and his sweetheart in a log-jam. Death is piled upon death in "On the Way to the Mission", where an Indian trapper, hauling the corpse of his wife to the mission for burial, is murdered by two greedy white men. A very similar poem is "Mission of the Trees", in which an Indian father collapses and dies on his way to the mission with the body of his son. A dead son reappears in "A Scene at Lake Manitou"; and "Night Burial in the Forest" and "At Gull Lake: August, 1810" tell the story of fatal love feuds.

The vision of a world in violent conflict also finds expression in Scott's love poems. Almost all of them deal with frustrated love, the frustration resulting from enforced absence, unrequited passion or death. In "Spring on Mattagami" his conception of nature as a violent, frightening but also fascinating power is used to reinforce a similar conception of love:

If she could be here where all the world is eager
    For dear love with the primal Eden sway,
Where the blood is fire and no pulse is thin or meagre,
    All the heart of all the world beats one way!
There is the land of fraud and fame and fashion,
    Joy is but a gaud and withers in an hour,
Here is the land of quintessential passion,
    Where in a wild throb Spring wells up with power.

But this is far from great poetry: the rhythms are too emphatic, the alliteration is too obvious, the lines seem strained and the emotions forced.  Indeed most of his love poems, like those of the other poets of his generation, are weak.

Scott's didactic poems are also relative failures.  The philosophy of life which, in a narrative poem like "The Forsaken", has resonant suggestiveness and restrained intensity, sounds flat and dull when he attempts to express it directly. He is apt to give us uninspired imitations of Victorian poets. "The Height of Land", which is his most ambitious philosophical poem, consists largely of ideas and phrases borrowed from Wordsworth, Browning and Tennyson, as this passage will reveal:

> Here on the uplands where the air is clear
> We think of life as of a stormy sea,—
> Of tempest, of revolt and desperate shock;
> And here, where we can think, on the bright uplands
> Where the air is clear, we deeply brood on life
> Until the tempest parts, and it appears
> As simple as to the shepherd seems his flock:
> A Something to be guided by ideals—
> That in themselves are simple and serene—
> Of noble deed to foster noble thought,
> And noble thought to image noble deed,
> Till deed and thought shall interpenetrate,
> Making life lovelier, till we come to doubt
> Whether the perfect beauty that escapes
> Is beauty of deed or thought or some high thing
> Mingled of both, a greater boon than either . . . .

It is in his narrative poems that Scott is most successful. The finest of them are "The Piper of Arll" and "The Forsaken". The first, in its richness of diction and imagery, its fantasy and eerie atmosphere, represents his early decorative phase; the latter, in its relative starkness and simplicity, is a product of his more restrained maturity.

John Masefield has recorded the effect which "The Piper of Arll" made upon him:

This was the first poem by a living writer to touch me to the quick. It was narrative; it was delicate phantasy; it was about the sea and singing and a romantic end. . . . Its longing, its wistfulness, and the perfection of some of its images made deep impressions on me.  I read it till I knew it by heart: even now, I often repeat it to myself.

It is too long a poem to quote in full, but here are a few stanzas which will give some indication of its quality:

> There were three pines above the comb
> That, when the sun flared and went down,
> Grew like three warriors reaving home
> The plunder of a burning town.
>
> About the coming on of dew,
> The sails burned rosy, and the spars
> Were gold, and all the tackle grew
> Alive with ruby-hearted stars.
>
> Their eyes are ruby in the green
> Long shaft of sun that spreads and rays,
> And upward with a wizard sheen
> A fan of sea-light leaps and plays.

In this poem Scott displays an ability to create the objective equivalents of a mood and to communicate in all its strange, unearthly beauty the substance of a dream.

"The Forsaken" is less musical but more original in substance and form.  Here in two contrasted episodes, related in short lines and plain words, Scott tells the story of an Indian squaw.  In the first episode, she is separated from her tribe by a blizzard; undaunted, she keeps her baby and herself alive by using her own flesh as fish-bait and makes her way to the Fort. In the second episode, she is deliberately deserted by the tribe because she is now old and useless, and with the same bravery she resigns herself to death.

Valiant, unshaken,
She smoothed her dark locks under her kerchief,
Composed her shawl in state,
Then folded her hands ridged with sinews and corded with
     veins,
Folded them across her breasts spent with the nourishing of
     children,
Gazed at the sky past the tops of the cedars . . . .

On the third day, snow falls and covers her.

But in the frost of the dawn,
Up from the life below,
Rose a column of breath
Through a tiny cleft in the snow,
Fragile, delicately drawn,
Wavering with its own weakness,
In the wilderness a sign of the spirit,
Persisting still in sight of the sun
Till day was done.
Then all light was gathered up by the hand of God and
     hid in His breast,
Then there was born a silence deeper than silence,
Then she had rest.

The free verse in which this poem is written suggests
another difference between Scott and his three chief Canadian
contemporaries: he was much more ready to experiment
with metre.  He was fond of strikingly short lines and of
unusually long ones.  Generally, his rhythms are much less
emphatic than those of Roberts and Carman, and his diction
is less ornate.  At its best, his verse is swift, vigorous, direct
and plain.

Scott had, however, no great gift for melody or metaphor.
He never achieved the haunting cadences of Carman at his
finest, and his metaphors and similes are few and far between.
Scott achieved his effects by slower, less spectacular means—
chiefly by the accumulation of accurate bits of physical
description and of emotional insight—rather than by the sud-

den illuminative fusion of thought, feeling and thing which occurs in the finest metaphors and similes.

Scott never enjoyed a reputation comparable to that of his three compeers. He was altogether a quieter, less spectacular artist. In spite of the violent content of so many of his poems, the dominant tone is quiet. There is usually a turbulent climax, but there is always a peaceful close. There is a dialectical pattern to most of his poems: two forces battle one another until their powers are spent or their differences resolved, so that peace may ensue. In "The Piper of Arll", the piper and the crew of the intruding ship exercise their fatal attraction upon each other; a violent climax is reached as the ship suddenly sinks beneath them; but the poem comes to a peaceful close as the ship is pictured on the ocean floor:

> And at the keel a vine is quick
> That spreads its bines and works and weaves
> O'er all the timbers veining thick
> A plenitude of silver leaves.

Throughout most of "Night Burial in the Forest" the birch bark torches roar, symbols of the violence of the events which have preceded the funeral, but quiet peace is the tone of the final stanza:

> Then, as we fare on our way to the shore
> Sudden the torches cease to roar:
> For cleaving the darkness remote and still
> Comes a wind with a rushing, harp-like thrill,
> The sound of wings hurled and furled and unfurled,
> The wings of the Angel who gathers the souls from the
>     wastes of the world.

In "On the Way to the Mission" the white men dog the footsteps of the Indian, kill him, and then, discovering the nature of his load, flee and leave the two corpses in the silent moonlight:

> The moon went on to her setting
> And covered them with shade.

The final peacefulness of these poems is achieved not by the transcendental leap, but by a stoical acceptance of suffering as the inevitable lot of man. The dominant mood is one of heroic endurance, and calm and stability are finally attained through an inner spiritual discipline, not through some magical release. We have the sense of a harsh and lonely world, the vicissitudes of which we can and must endure. Because of his artistic evocation of this mood and attitude, Duncan Campbell Scott will always have, in Canada at least, a small but appreciative audience.

With Scott we reach the last of the four major poets of the Confederation Era. There were, in addition, several minor poets who occasionally wrote verse of some distinction: Frederick George Scott, whose best work has some of the quiet dignity of Matthew Arnold; George Frederick Cameron, a rather too shrill disciple of the Swinburne of *Songs Before Sunrise* and the Tennyson of "Maud"; Pauline Johnson, daughter of an Indian chief, who won great fame by her native dress and dramatic recitals, but the great bulk of whose work is meretricious; Isabella Valancy Crawford; and William Wilfred Campbell. The two latter, by virtue of their more distinctive qualities, deserve separate attention.

Isabella Valancy Crawford (1850-1887) is usually spoken of as the most important Canadian poetess of the nineteenth century. In her own lifetime she was almost unknown, but her work was gathered together by J. W. Garvin and published with an enthusiastic introduction in 1905. The tendency of recent criticism, and especially a most provocative essay by James Reaney, has been to support Garvin's appraisal of her, and to single her out as the most original and authentic poet of her generation. She is praised for her vigour, her metaphorical fecundity and her accurate portrayal of the pioneer life of her time. Much as I admire Miss Crawford's personal courage and tenacity, I cannot share the more enthusiastic estimates of her work.

Miss Crawford was born in Dublin, but came to Canada

with her parents in 1858.   Her father, a country doctor, was
a man of broad culture but of straitened means.   When he
died in 1875, Isabella and her mother were compelled to live
in obscure poverty in Toronto.   Miss Crawford attempted to
augment the family income by contributing poems and
stories to newspapers, and by bringing out a small volume of
poems with the awkward title *Old Spookses' Pass, Malcolm's
Katie, and Other Poems* (1884).   The book, however, sold
only a few copies, and Miss Crawford died in 1887 quite unaware of the recognition that was to come with the publication
of her *Collected Poems* in 1905.

It is easy to see why the recognition came.   Miss Crawford's
poems are vigorous and energetic, and to the description of
a storm or a stampede of cattle she can give compelling speed
and force.   She sees similitudes everywhere, and image is
piled upon image until we are almost breathless from the
pressure:

> The late, last thunders of the summer crash'd,
> Where shriek'd great eagles, lords of naked cliffs.
> The pulseless forest, lock'd and interlock'd
> So closely bough with bough and leaf with leaf,
> So serfed by its own wealth, that while from high
> The moons of summer kissed its green-glossed locks,
> And round its knees the merry West Wind danc'd;
> And round its ring, compacted emerald,
> The South Wind crept on moccasins of flame . . . .

This, surely, gives the sense of the confused intensity of a
Canadian forest.   But even here the confusion is more
apparent than the intensity, and when Miss Crawford turns
from nature to man her essentially melodramatic imagination becomes painfully obvious.   The two title poems of
her collection, for example, are melodramatic extravaganzas
in which the good lines are almost lost in the wild confusion
of the whole.   "Old Spookses' Pass", the account of a cattle
stampede on the prairies, has some fine descriptive passages,
but it also has much trite moralizing, stale sentiment and

strained pathos. "Malcolm's Katie", praised even by the
judicious E. K. Brown as "the best image a poet has given us
of Canadian living in the years following Confederation",
conducts a group of pasteboard characters through a wildly
improbable sequence of events. Violent deaths and fortuitous
rescues occur on almost every page, and the dialogue is stilted
and unnatural.   Even the descriptive passages are frequently
strained, as in this account of an autumn night:

> The land had put his ruddy gauntlet on,
> Of harvest gold, to dash in Famine's face;
> And like a vintage wain deep dyed with juice
> The great moon faltered up the ripe, blue sky,
> Drawn by silver stars—like oxen white
> And horned with rays of light.

Such boldness of fancy is admittedly superior to a timid con-
ventionalism such as Mair or Goldsmith gave us, but it is
surely extreme to call such writing great poetry.   The term
for this type of art, obviously, is rococo: it is tastelessly and
clumsily florid.   No amount of regret for the harsh circumstances among which Miss Crawford's life was lived and her
poetry written should blind us to this fact.

A similar uncertainty of taste is evident in the poetry of
William Wilfred Campbell (1861-1918).   Picking up the
*Collected Poems* (also published in 1905) , we begin with a
misleading introduction. "Simplicity and directness," Campbell wisely declares, "are essential to the highest class of
verse".   Would that he had practised what he preached! His
own poems, with at most two or three exceptions, are anything but simple and direct.

Campbell was a friend of Lampman and Duncan Campbell
Scott, but he had none of their quiet modesty and shy reserve.
He apparently cast himself in the role of unofficial Poet
Laureate, and graced every possible public occasion with a
tribute from his pen: let Macdonald die or Queen Victoria,
Campbell was ready!   Indeed his aspirations seem to have

reached even higher levels: he was to become the Poet Laureate not of Canada alone, but of the Empire, and one section of his poems is impressively headed "The Sagas of Vaster Britain". Unkind as it may be, the temptation to quote a few lines from Campbell's poems of this sort is irresistible. How the Grits must have writhed when Campbell declared of Sir John A. Macdonald:

> God gave this highest honour
> To the nation that upon her
> He was spared to lay the magic of his hand . . . .

But to mourning the death of Queen Victoria, Campbell really brought all his eloquence:

> Roll out earth's muffled drums, let sable streamers flow
> And all Britannia's might assume her panoply of woe!
> Love's holiest star is gone;
>     Wind wide the funeral wreath;
> For she, our mightiest, hath put on
>     The majesty of death.
> Roll forth the notes of woe,
> Let the baleful trumpets blow
> A titan nation's titan, heartfelt throe;
>     'Mid age and storm and night and blinding snow,
>     Death, the pale tyrant, lays our loftiest low.

And that is only the first of twenty-one majestic, woe-filled stanzas.

Apart from such topical poems, Campbell's volume ranges over practically the full gamut of romantic themes. There are poems on nature, love and death; there are poems on classical and mediaeval themes; there are poems in which Campbell sets forth his conception of poetry, religion, philosophy and the state of society. Almost all of them are dull and mediocre. But Campbell had two limited spheres in which he could work with distinction: the creation of an effect of weirdness, at times of morbidity, and the painting of the surface of nature.

The weird and morbid effects are created in poems such as "The Mother", which tells the story of a mother who rises from the grave to suckle her living infant, "The Were-Wolves", who embody the souls of sinners forced perpetually to circle around the Pole, and "The Vengeance of Saki", in which a spurned girl causes horses to trample underfoot her lover and his new mistress. These poems are, in a sense, repulsive; and yet they have a kind of malign fascination. "The Mother" especially, for all its traces of morbid Victorian sentimentality, is a poem which, once read, is difficult to forget.

The number of poems in which Campbell is content simply to paint the surface of nature is very small indeed. Usually he insists on interpreting nature—and always in terms that immediately recall Wordsworth. Very occasionally, however, he gives us a simple, spontaneous, descriptive lyric such as "Indian Summer".

> Along the line of smoky hills
>     The crimson forest stands,
> And all the day the blue-jay calls
>     Throughout the autumn lands.
>
> Now by the brook the maple leans
>     With all his glory spread,
> And all the sumachs on the hills
>     Have turned their green to red.
>
> Now by great marshes wrapt in mist,
>     Or past some river's mouth,
> Throughout the long, still autumn day
>     Wild birds are flying south.

But Campbell's best poems are those in which his capacity to create effects of weirdness and to paint nature are combined. These include "Snowfall", "An October Evening", "How One Winter Came in the Lake Region", and "The Winter Lakes". A stanza from each in turn will give some sense of their quality:

Down drops the snow, the fleecy hooding snow,
  On town and wood and haggard, wind-blown space,
And hushes the storms, and all weird winds that blow
  Upon the world's dead face.

> The bearded swamps are breathing
>   A mist from meres afar,
> And grimly the Great Bear circles
>   Under the pale Pole Star.

For weeks and weeks the autumn world stood still,
  Clothed in the shadow of a smoky haze;
The fields were dead, the wind had lost its will,
And all the lands were hushed by wood and hill,
  In those gray, withered days.

Lonely hidden bays, moon-lit, ice-rimmed, winding,
  Fringed by forests and crags, haunted by shadowy shores;
Hushed from the outward strife, where the mighty surf
    is grinding
  Death and hate on the rocks, as sandward and
    landward it roars.

Here Campbell had found, as Carman found in "Low Tide on Grand Pré", satisfactory objective correlatives for his moods; and the result was poetry immeasurably better than his more pretentious sagas on lofty themes.

## 3. Fiction

Strangely enough, in view of the dominance of prose in the colonial period, the prose output of these first three decades after Confederation fell considerably short of the poetry in both quantity and quality. A great deal of what imaginative prose was written was a by-product of the poetry. Charles G. D. Roberts wrote animal stories and historical romances, of which the best passages are those in which he reveals his gift for describing the surface of nature; Duncan Campbell Scott produced two volumes of short stories which show the same painstaking care for technique, the same preoccupation with violence and the same flashes of descriptive accuracy as his poems; William Wilfred Campbell wrote three historical romances which weave the weird and the beautiful together in his characteristic manner. In all cases, however, with the possible exception of Scott, the prose of these writers is inferior to their best verse. Roberts' stories are good as long as he confines himself to portraying the lives of animals and the environment in which they move, but once he introduces human characters his touch falters and the wildest melodrama results. Campbell's novels, set in the north of Scotland, are late exercises in the Gothic romance, abounding in mysterious trapdoors, torture-chambers, secret passageways and so on. Even Scott's stories are melodramatic in substance, but he treats his themes with a greater subtlety and restraint and achieves in his best stories a haunting suggestiveness quite beyond the reach of his two colleagues.

As the above paragraph would suggest, the favourite form of fiction in Canada in the late nineteenth century was the historical romance. This trend had, indeed, been firmly established during the colonial period. It was in the historical romance that John Richardson was most at home, and almost all the contributors to *The Literary Garland,* including such relatively productive writers as Susanna Moodie, Rosanna Leprohon and Louisa Murray, wrote their novels in this genre.

Confederation gave a renewed impetus to this movement. If Canada was to be given a sense of national pride and destiny, it seemed natural to turn back to dramatic episodes in her past. Certainly it was much easier to do that than to attempt to make fiction out of the fluid society of post-Confederation Canada. Hence it is not remarkable that the two most famous Canadian novels of the late nineteenth century —William Kirby's *The Golden Dog* and Gilbert Parker's *Seats of the Mighty*—are historical romances.

William Kirby (1817-1906) was a Canadian by deliberate choice. Born in England, he emigrated to the United States with his father, lived there for seven years and moved to Canada in 1839 shortly after the Mackenzie–Papineau Rebellion. "War with England was fully expected," he tells us, "and many British born like myself came to a resolution to go to Canada and aid in the defence of the Provinces." From the first he was an ardent Tory Imperialist: catching his first glimpse of the Union Jack flying above Canadian soil he "hailed it as the true flag of Freedom, Justice and Christian civilization". And to the very end of his life he set his face against the democratic, levelling tendencies of the age, and clung to his belief in Britain's divine mission to rule the world. He settled at Niagara and deliberately associated with the old families there, descendants of the officers of Butler's "Greens". He wrote an epic of the Loyalist migration, a history of the Niagara district, editorials expressing his conservative views, and letters to Lord Tennyson, Sir John A. Macdonald, the Duke of Argyll and Gilbert Parker. If he had written only these things, however, he would have been forgotten, or remembered only as a curious anachronism. In the legend of Le Chien d'Or this crusty old Tory discovered a congenial theme and produced a novel which is one of the best of its kind.

In the feudal society of the old French régime Kirby found, as Governors Murray, Carleton and Haldimand had found long before him, values and attitudes which he could admire. It was not to him an alien culture: in its chivalric conventions, its class distinctions, its loyalty to Crown and Empire, its traditionalism and in its religious devotion, it embodied a way of life which Kirby sought vainly to perpetuate. For this reason *The Golden Dog* (1877) is no costume novel: it evokes not merely the surface of life in eighteenth century New France, but its very heart and spirit. The characters are no mere mannequins decked in eighteenth century costume: they are living men and women whom Kirby passionately admires or hates in proportion as they remain true to the chivalric ideals.

But Kirby was not merely an admirer of the old régime; he was also, in his own rather curious fashion, a concerned member of the late nineteenth century Canadian community. He felt, as Roberts and the other poets felt, the stimulation of the new era in Canadian history, and *The Golden Dog* is, in one of its aspects, a novel of the new nationalism. Like the poets, Kirby delights in portraying the beauty of the Canadian landscape. In the very first paragraph of the novel, Peter Kalm the Swedish naturalist is made to exclaim: "Eternity would be too short to weary of this lovely scene— this bright Canadian morning is worthy of Eden, and the glorious landscape worthy of such a sunrising." Similar sentiments are echoed many times in the course of the book: Canada is, as Kalm states on another occasion, "a land worth living for". Kirby also looks forward to the day when the literary heritages of France and England shall be "united in one grand flood stream of Canadian literature".

Kirby's nationalism, however, took a definite form. He was no advocate of Canadian independence: he simply wanted Canada to be a strong branch of the tree of the British Empire. At one point in the novel, he laments that *God Save the King* is no longer heard in France, but rejoices that "it flourishes still with pristine vigour in New France, that olive branch grafted on the stately tree of the British Empire". He never misses an opportunity to inculcate the lesson of devotion to King and Country. He praises La Corne St. Luc and his fellow-colonists because "like brave and loyal men, they did their duty to God and their country, preferring death and ruin in a lost cause to surrendering the flag which was the symbol of their native land".

*The Golden Dog*, then, is no idle literary exercise. It is the fictional expression of Kirby's deep-seated convictions, and this lends to it urgency and authenticity, helps to make it a moving story. It is sustained by a philosophy—not Swedenborgianism, which is something of an excrescence, but the moral philosophy which judges every man and every action in terms of loyalty, integrity and selfless devotion to a cause. Its plot, a skilful blending of three stories drawn from James LeMoine's *Maple Leaves,* moves steadily if somewhat leisurely forward in a procession of vivid scenes. The char-

acters are diverse, individual, consistent and credible.   No
pains have been spared to make the setting, both external and
internal, vivid and exact: the frequent passages of landscape
description are balanced by detailed portrayals of the streets,
houses and rooms in which the action takes place.   Kirby has
a fine sense of atmosphere—look, for example, at the chapter
describing La Corriveau's night visit to Beaumanoir.   He
also has a concern for structure.   The novel is built around
five climactic episodes: Bigot's refusal to give up his life of
debauchery; Angélique's rejection of LeGardeur's love;
Bigot's public denial of Caroline; the murder of Caroline by
La Corriveau; and the killing of the Bourgeois Philibert.   In
each of these scenes a decision is made which inevitably leads
to the events which follow.

Kirby's masters, it is clear, were Scott and Shakespeare.
The five-fold division of the plot, the use of comic relief and
of supernatural warnings (note the parallel between Dame
Rochelle's advice to the Bourgeois and Calpurnia's warning
to Caesar) and the many echoes in phrasing reveal Kirby's
devotion to Shakespeare.   But Scott was his chief model.
Both Scott and Kirby subscribe to feudal and chivalric values;
both divide their characters quite clearly into the sheep and
the goats; both delight in portraying humorous peasant types;
both make extensive use of dialect; both begin their novels
slowly, built them up with deliberate amplitude and end
them in a flurry of activity.

*The Golden Dog* has weaknesses, of course.   There are
touches of melodrama; coincidence sometimes plays a dispro-
portionate part; sometimes Kirby is annoyingly didactic;
sometimes the products of his long years of research are
allowed to impede the plot.   And it is not immune from the
basic flaw of all historical novels: the difficulty of maintaining the uneasy alliance between fact and fiction.   Sometimes
we find ourselves wondering: "Did Bigot *really* have such a
mistress in his Chateau?"—and of course once we get that
sense of another truer reality, the reality of the novel begins

to crumble.   But in spite of these faults, *The Golden Dog* is a great achievement.   Beside it, *Wacousta* seems like the bungling of a clumsy amateur, and even *Seats of the Mighty* the product of a literary hack.

Gilbert Parker (1862-1932) was a much more prolific writer than Kirby.   He wrote a score of novels instead of one, and in addition produced seven volumes of short stories and two volumes of poems.   Much of his work, however, consisted of potboilers, and only two or three of his novels and a handful of short stories are likely to survive.   Even his best novels are marred by melodrama, inadequate character motivation, flamboyant style and moral pomposity.

Parker was born in Camden East, Ontario, the son of a British artillery officer and a Canadian girl of Loyalist descent.   He was educated at the Ottawa Normal School and at Trinity College, Toronto.   He was, then, like Archibald Lampman, the product of a Loyalist, Anglican and Tory environment; unlike Lampman he never reacted against this environment, but retained its outlook to the end of his life. Shortly after graduation he was ordained a deacon in the Church of England and became curate of the parish of Trenton.   Suddenly, for reasons of health, he decided on a sea voyage to England by way of Australia.   In Australia he engaged in journalism and wrote three plays which were produced in Sydney; and in 1889 he moved to England where most of the remainder of his life was spent.   For eighteen years he represented Gravesend in the House of Commons, and was created a knight bachelor in 1902 and a baronet in 1915.

Of Parker's many books, the best are *Pierre and His People*, a book of short stories published in 1892, *When Valmond Came to Pontiac* (1895) and *Seats of the Mighty* (1896).   It is significant that all three of these books were written in the first decade of his literary career: like Carman and Roberts, Parker declined in power with the passing of the years.

In *Pierre and His People* Parker revealed a talent which was to ensure him popularity with his contemporaries: a talent for timing, for selecting the topical subject.   The stories, set in the West, appeared when interest in that area, because of the completion in 1885 of the Canadian Pacific Railway, was at its height.   Few of these stories can hold the attention of the adult reader today: they are too violent in tone, too flamboyant in style, too pompous and pretentious in moral outlook.   In the volume there are a few stories— "The Flood", for example—having an uncanny atmosphere which still exercises a sort of fascination.   But none of them are faithful images of Canadian life comparable with the best poems of Roberts and Lampman: the West to Parker was not so much a region seriously to interpret to the world as a remote area whose romantic connotations he could profitably exploit.   He exploited them so successfully, in the financial sense, that he fathered a whole company of imitators.   Ralph Connor, Robert Service, H. A. Cody, James Oliver Curwood and a host of lesser writers were to follow his example in portraying the Canadian West as a land of snow-covered wastes, picturesque trappers, crafty Indians and heroic and muscular Mounties.

But if Parker's image of the West was a false one, the picture of French Canada which he gives us in *When Valmond Came to Pontiac* and *Seats of the Mighty* is much more authentic.   In his preface to the former novel, Parker writes: "Fantasy as it is, the book has pictures of French-Canadian life which are as true as though the story itself were all true"; and there is some basis for his claim.   Like Kirby, Parker found in French Canada values to which he could subscribe: a simple morality, strong loyalty, a love of tradition and a respect for legend.   Consequently, he was able to portray the life of that area with a sympathy and understanding almost entirely absent from his stories of the West and his novels set in other areas of the world.

The plot of *When Valmond Came to Pontiac,* too intricate

to summarize here, is fantastic enough: it involves a Frenchman who settles in a Quebec village and poses as the son of Napoleon.    In his love of grandeur, tradition and romantic illusion, Valmond is a projection of Parker himself, and it is clear from the preface that Parker felt this identification so strongly that the tragic ending of the book was a positive agony to write.    Writing this book, Parker temporarily forgot his craving for popular success and wrote from the heart.    The result is a story which, for all its improbabilities, is sincerely moving.    The style is still overly emphatic, but there is scarcely any of Parker's usual pompous sententiousness.    The action moves switfly and, once we grant Parker's basic assumptions, with a fine inevitability.    As a contemporary reviewer said in *The Athenaeum*, this novel "set a standard which Parker would find hard to preserve in the future".

He preserved it only once—in *Seats of the Mighty*.    Like *The Golden Dog, Seats of the Mighty* is a story of corruption among colonial officials during the last years of the French régime in Quebec, and it also owes its inspiration to James LeMoine's *Maple Leaves*.    Superior as it is among Parker's novels, however, it falls far short of Kirby's minor masterpiece.    Kirby spent almost eleven years gathering material and writing *The Golden Dog*; Parker spent only two years on *Seats of the Mighty*: the result is that Parker's novel lacks the authenticity of its predecessor.    Moreover, there is less art in his book: the characters are relatively shallow and static, the plot relies more heavily on coincidence, the style is more obtrusive and less natural.    Finally, the morality of the book is at once more obvious and less profound.

The last point can best be proven by reference to the central character of the novel, whose memoir the book supposedly is: Robert Moray, a young Scotsman who has been left an estate in Virginia, settled there, become an officer of the Virginia Regiment, was taken prisoner by the French and is held as a hostage in Quebec.    Parker obviously expects us to admire Moray, and has again projected a good deal of himself into him; but he strikes at least one reader as an arrogant, self-righteous, and morally shoddy young man.  He has sent plans of the fortifications of Quebec to his friends in Virginia, and blithely retorts when accused of this, that his act is justified by the fact that the French have held him as a hostage longer than he thinks proper.  His morality, clearly, is a morality of expediency.

Another great weakness in the novel is the fact that the plot all turns on a situation which is, to say the least, improbable.  Moray has come into possession of some letters desired by La Pompadour to incriminate a rival for the King's favour; and La Pompadour's annoyance at his continued refusal to give them up is alleged to have been the cause of the Seven Years' War!

In spite of this and other almost equally absurd improbabilities, however, *Seats of the Mighty* remains a novel of considerable power.  Its events move rapidly forward and maintain a high level of suspense.  Some of the chapters—those dealing with physical adventures such as escapes, flights, duels and the climactic battle on the Plains of Abraham—are cleverly written.  The characters may be shallow, but they are certainly vivid, and the best of them, such as Doltaire, are quite complex.

*Seats of the Mighty*, to put it briefly, is a novel of intrigue and adventure which can still be read for its value as entertainment.  The trouble is that Parker obviously thought it was more than that.  Its pretentiousness is what most offends us.  We would accept, for the moment, its improbabilities as part of the game—if only Parker would not insist in playing the role of the prophet and the seer!  He seems to suffer from a congenital incapacity to put things plainly: he is always speaking in riddles, attempting to disguise his moral platitudes by dressing them in fancy words and uttering them in an oracular tone.  It was that tendency which completely spoiled his later novels.

Kirby and Parker were not, of course, the only Canadian

novelists of this period to essay the historical romance. In addition to the poets already mentioned, there were W. D. Lighthall, T. G. Marquis, Jean McIlwraith, William Mac-Lennan, and Agnes Laut. None of their novels are especially memorable, but it may be useful to indicate how they illustrate the nationalistic spirit of their period. Lighthall's *The Young Seigneur* (1888), for example, has as its avowed aims "to map out a future for the Canadian nation, which has hitherto been difting without any plan", and "to make some of the atmosphere of French Canada understood by those who speak English". The impulse to develop a sense of Canadian nationality by a portrayal of her dramatic past also lay behind Marquis' *Marguerite de Roberval* (1899), a novel set in the time of Jacques Cartier, and Agnes Laut's *Lords of the North* (1900) and *Heralds of Empire* (1902), which concern the fur traders and explorers of the early West.

A far more important task awaited the Canadian novelist— that of recording and interpreting contemporary social life as sensitively and accurately as the four major poets were portraying the landscape—but there were few ready to attempt it. The growing concern for realism in fiction, which was manifesting itself at this time in France, England and the United States, did have repercussions in Canada, as the columns of *The Week* prove, but the weight of opinion here was almost unanimously against it. Reviews in *The Week* referred with undisguised horror to "the intellectual vivisection methods of the American schools of James and Howells, or, worse still, the loathsome realism and putridity of the school of Zola and France". Among the few defenders of the new realism, however, was Sarah Jeannette Duncan, who herself became a novelist.

Sara Jeannette Duncan (1862-1922) was born at Brantford, Ontario, but abandoned Canada as a permanent place of residence when, at the age of twenty-nine, she married Charles Everard Cotes of the Indian Museum, Calcutta. She became known chiefly as an amusing interpreter of Anglo-Indian customs, but among her many novels is one set wholly in Canada—*The Imperialist* (1904)—and several which reflect, in one way or another, her Canadian background.

Miss Duncan seems to have regarded herself as a light-hearted disciple of Henry James. Her novels, like most of his, are international novels of manners, and have a much more cosmopolitan and sophisticated air than those of any of her Canadian contemporaries. They have not the moral profundity of James' books, however, nor the same painstaking concern for technique. Beside his, her work seems shallow and perfunctory. Only in two of her novels, *The Simple Adventures of a Memsahib* (1893) and *His Honour and a Lady* (1896), did she penetrate beyond transitory manners to universal moral principles. Her other novels—*A Social Departure* (1890), *Those Delightful Americans* (1902), for example—once enjoyed great popularity, but have lost most of their point now that the manners which they satirized have altered.

*The Simple Adventures of a Memsahib* contrasts the triviality of the lives of most members of the Anglo-Indian community with the basic search for the necessities of food and shelter on the part of the native population. In its minor way, and intermittently rather than continuously, this novel is worthy of comparison with E. M. Forster's *Passage to India*. Here is a sample paragraph:

I saw a priest of Kali, wrapped in his yellow chudder, sit hugging his knees under a mahogany tree tonight beside the broad road where the carriages passed reeling into the "cow's dust" of the twilight. A brother cleric of the Raj went by in his victoria with his wife and children, and the yellow robed one watched them out of sight. There was neither hatred nor malice, nor any evil thing in his gaze, only perhaps a subtle appreciation of the advantage of the other cloth.

*His Honour and a Lady* is also set in India, but here we have a study of disintegration of one man rather than of

a social group.   Lewis Ancram has set himself to succeed the
Governor of Bengal in both his office and his wife's affections;
he betrays the governor, succeeds him in his official position,
but is rejected, in a dramatic but restrained scene, by the
ex-governor's wife.   The novel is well built, its style is crisp
and unobtrusive and it impresses one as a sincere and
authentic study of moral degeneration.

Slight as most of Miss Duncan's novels are, she remains
the most interesting of the few Canadian novelists of the
nineteenth century who attempted to maintain a measure of
realism in their work.   Robert Barr and Joanna E. Wood
occasionally struck an authentic note, but both were very
uneven artists whose successes are overshadowed by their
failures.

Robert Barr (1850-1912) was a Canadian in only one sense
of the word.   He was born in Glasgow, came to Canada with
his parents at the age of five, was brought up on a farm near
Toronto and educated at the Toronto Normal School, but he
left Canada for good in 1876 when he joined the staff of the
Detroit *Free Press*.   From 1881 until the end of his life he
lived in England, where from 1881 to 1911 he was co-editor,
with Jerome K. Jerome, of *The Idler*.   However, since his
formative years were spent in Canada and since most of his
serious novels are either set in Canada or have some Canadian connection, there are grounds for considering him in
this study.

Most of Barr's output may be quickly dismissed.   He produced several volumes of short stories (*In a Steamer Chair*,
1892; *The Face and the Mask*, 1893; *A Prince of Good Fellows*, 1902) many detective novels and some historical
romances, all of which were purely ephemeral.   His claim to
serious attention rests on four more realistic novels: *In the
Midst of Alarms* (1894), *The Mutable Many* (1896), *The
Victors* (1901) and *The Measure of The Rule* (1906).   The
first of these is a humorous story of the Fenian Raids; the
best parts of it are those in which Barr reveals his knowledge

of rural Ontario, as in the chapter on the revival meeting; but it is essentially a slight book. *The Mutable Many,* an account of the struggle between labour and capital in a London factory during the eighteen nineties, is a more impressive achievement, and is of some historical interest as the first political novel by a Canadian author. The novel has some strong character portrayal, accurate descriptions of the sordid streets of London which approach those in the novels of George Gissing, and some acute insights in to the nature of capitalism. In *The Victors,* Barr turned his somewhat cynical eye on the meaner aspects of New York. The three men referred to as "the victors" are ambitious climbers who, by various forms of fraud, win their way to positions of influence and affluence in American society. *The Measure of The Rule* applies the same kind of vision to the Ontario educational system and to the Toronto Normal School: the picture which emerges is far from a pleasant one, and is certainly not tinted in rose.

Barr was potentially a good realistic novelist, but his lack of education, his journalistic proclivities and the speed at which he wrote prevented him from realizing this potentiality. He was an acute observer of men and manners, he had a vision unclouded by sentimentality or prudery, and he had broad experience of the world. But he had no sense of literary tradition, little sense of style and none of that single-minded devotion to his art which a great novelist needs. He was at best what he tells us in the introduction to *The Victors* he hoped to be—"an accurate reporter". His best work is only superior journalism.

Joanna E. Wood (died 1919) was also primarily a "popular" novelist. Of her seven novels only one, *The Untempered Wind* (1898), may be called realistic. Inspired by Hawthorne's *Scarlet Letter,* it is a story of the plight of an unmarried mother in an Ontario community of the nineteenth century. The satire at the expense of the smug, self-righteous members of the community who persecute and exploit the girl in the name of Christianity is keen, if rather laboured and obvious. The plot, however, has elements of the incredible, and the style has none of the haunting suggestiveness of Hawthorne's novel.

There is one more writer who must be mentioned in this account of the beginnings of realism in Canadian fiction: Edward William Thomson (1849-1924). Thomson was not a novelist, but he published several volumes of short stories, and in them are a few stories memorable for their humour and their authenticity. Thomson was one of the very few Canadians who enjoyed the realistic novels of Howells and the naturalistic novels of Zola, and though his own work shows disappointingly little trace of their influence, the influence is there: the image of Canadian life he gives us is refreshingly different from that found in the romantic and sentimental novels of his period. Thomson's Scottish farmers get in debt and go to jail; his lumbermen swear and get drunk; his habitants are not idyllic rustics who spend all their time worshipping God in field or church. But Thomson, like Barr, was a busy journalist who had little leisure for serious writing and too keen a sense of his public to be fully consistent or thoroughgoing in his realism. Even his best stories—the title story and "The Privilege of the Limits" in *Old Man Savarin* (1895) for example—suffer from some confusion of purpose and uncertainty of tone, and in many of his other stories, written with an eye to the public of such magazines as the *Youth's Companion,* he descended to sentimental drivel.

## 4. Conclusion

By 1895, when *Old Man Savarin* was published, the momentum of this first national literary movement was almost spent. The brave optimism of the immediate post-Confederation period was giving way to something very close to despair.

By 1897 Roberts, Carman and Thomson had gone to the United States; Gilbert Parker and Robert Barr had gone to England; Sara Duncan had gone to India; Lampman, Crawford, and Cameron were dead. *The Week* ceased publication in 1896. Only Duncan Campbell Scott, a broken-spirited Kirby and an increasingly anachronistic Campbell remained to carry on the tradition. In thirty years, Canadians had produced a considerable body of good writing, though far less than they had hoped; now it looked as if the end had come.

What had happened? Again, in seeking causes, we must be on guard against accepting glib sociological explanations of cultural phenomena. Perhaps the literary movement would have lost its momentum in any case: thirty years is a fairly common life-span for such a movement, as witness the English Renaissance, the Augustan Age and the Romantic Movement. Romantic artists, in particular, seem to be either short-lived or to decline in power as their youth recedes. But what might have been expected was that new writers, with fresh aims and methods, would have begun to appear in Canada in the late nineties: there were none, certainly none of outstanding promise.

At least a partial explanation can be found in the social and political development of Canada during these thirty years. The young Dominion which had so confidently set forth on its national path in 1867 was growing increasingly doubtful of its destiny. A great depression had started in 1873 and continued virtually unabated until almost the end of the century. The enthusiasm which had bound the provinces together into an at least apparent unity of purpose began to give way in the late eighties under the strain of political, economic, religious and racial rivalries. The Maritime provinces awoke to the fact that their economic position was much worse than it had been in the pre-Confederation era; and although Confederation was not the cause it was inevitable that it should bear the brunt of the blame. By

1886, Premier Fielding of Nova Scotia was openly advocating secession in the provincial legislature. The Prairie Provinces were not developing nearly as fast as their settlers had expected, and by the middle eighties were beginning to utter the now familiar outcries against the domination of the central provinces, of the "big interests" and of the Ottawa bureaucracy. Out of this western agitation came Louis Riel's abortive second rising; and the execution of this Catholic half-breed in 1885 stirred up racial and religious animosities throughout the Dominion and especially in the province of Quebec. These resentments culminated in the inter-provincial conference of 1887, at which five provincial premiers met to air their various grievances. It looked as if the brave experiment in nation-building was to fail. Goldwin Smith, indeed, declared in his *Canada and the Canadian Question* (1891) that it had failed, and that the only hope lay in annexation to the United States.

In such an atmosphere, it was not surprising that large numbers of Canadians began to leave the country. By 1890, it is estimated that there were a million Canadians living in the United States, and each year their number greatly increased. Writers like Carman and Roberts were not the only people who sought greener fields south of the border. "There is scarcely a farm house in the older provinces," said the Toronto *Mail* in 1887, "where there is not an empty chair for the boy in the States."

By the mid nineties, then, when the literary movement began to slow down, the pulse of the whole nation was beating feebly. The national excitement which had in part initiated and sustained the first national cultural awakening no longer existed. The period which is often referred to as "the Golden Age" of Canadian life and literature was over. It had not, by world standards, produced much—a few nature lyrics, a handful of narrative poems and short stories, two or three historical romances—but for a young nation of less than five million people there was sound basis for pride.

# CHAPTER FOUR

# The Early Twentieth Century

*1897 – 1920*

## 1. Introduction

IF THE LAST three decades of the nineteenth century to some extent deserved the popular epithet of "the golden age" of Canadian literature, the first two decades of the twentieth were without doubt the age of brass. It was an era of best sellers. Ralph Connor, L. M. Montgomery and Stephen Leacock in prose, and W. H. Drummond, Robert Service and Marjorie Pickthall in poetry, all established popular reputations throughout the English-speaking world. Such survivors of the previous generation as Bliss Carman, Charles Roberts and Gilbert Parker were still attracting wide attention. It appeared that the doubts of the mid-nineties had been groundless, and that Canadian literature was on the high road to world fame.

Indeed Canada's prospects seemed bright in every sphere of activity as the new century dawned. The long depression had finally lifted in 1896, the Canadian prairies became the world's chief granary, gold was discovered in the Yukon and other valuable metals were discovered in Ontario, foreign capital flooded into the country, trade expanded enormously and a new wave of immigration increased the population at an unprecedented rate. Laurier himself declared that the twentieth century was to be "Canada's Century".

In some respects, however, such optimism was unjustified. The sense of national unity inspired by Confederation had been seriously impaired by the depression of the eighties and was still further weakened during this prosperous but rather vulgar era in Canadian life. The rift between French and English which had begun over the execution of Riel and had been widened by the Manitoba Schools Question was

89

broadened still further by the controversy over Canada's role in the Boer War and over her contribution to Imperial Defence. For fifteen years Sir Wilfrid Laurier maintained his government in power by achieving an uneasy balance between the moderates in both camps; but in the election of 1911, the most bitter in Canadian history, he was condemned on the one hand as a tool of the papal hierarchy and on the other as a stooge of the imperialists. It is no wonder that this election provided the subject for two of the most satirical chapters in Stephen Leacock's *Sunshine Sketches of a Little Town.*

And all the time, of course, the country was drifting, along with the whole western world, towards the abyss of war. The war of 1914–1918 had mixed effects on Canada. The controversy over conscription strained Anglo–French relations almost to the breaking point; and yet the exploits of Canadian fighting men, farmers and factory workers did much to build a sense of national pride. The wartime boom brought huge profits to the manufacturers, good prices to the farmers and high wages to the workers; but it also brought the less desirable effects of inflation in the form of increased living costs and scarcities of essential goods. Behind the glamorous front of flags and parades, there was a sharp increase in social unrest. In 1918 there were riots in Quebec, mass demonstrations of farmers in Ontario, angry resolutions at the annual convention of the Trades and Labour Congress. A strong protest movement was also taking shape in the West, and the Winnipeg strike of 1919 was only one symptom of a deep-seated dissatisfaction.

All this was a far cry from the seventies and eighties of the previous century, when it had seemed that Canada could go forward undisturbed by wars and revolutions, evolving a national culture in her own way and at her own speed. The literature which had seemed appropriate enough then—the loitering lyrics of Lampman and Carman, the rustic idylls of Roberts, the leisurely tales of Kirby—was already an anachronism. The Canadian writer was now confronted with a wealthy but divided but restless industrial society.

In the face of such a chaotic period, the writer could do one of four things. He could pretend that the new age did not exist, and go on writing lyrics of nature and love; he could withdraw to the areas of the country which were still untouched by the chaos and write regional idylls; he could accept the vulgar prosperity of the age, flatter its tastes and echo its enthusiasms; or he could challenge it, satirize it and attempt to reduce its chaos to form. Canadian writers chose each of the first three alternatives, but only one of them, and he only partially, chose the last.

Charles Roberts, Bliss Carman and Duncan Campbell Scott virtually ignored the new age of wars and strikes and crises and went on writing much as they had written in the eighties, but with less skill. Marjorie Pickthall, Theodore Goodridge Roberts and a host of lesser songsters followed their example.

The new fashion in escapism, however, was to write idylls of the more secluded areas. Ralph Connor returned to his childhood in Glengarry or showed how its simple virtues could be imposed on the new communities of the West. L. M. Montgomery created idylls of the tiny agricultural province of Prince Edward Island and Marian Keith did the same for rural Ontario. Norman Duncan sought out the fishing villages of Newfoundland, W. H. Drummond the farming communities of old Quebec.

Robert Service and Tom MacInnes, on the other hand, felt perfectly at home in the new coarse but vibrant age. They scorned the pipes and flutes of Lampman and Carman, picked up big guitars and thrummed the tunes that the age demanded. The lust for gold? They shared it. Loose women? They could sing of their charms as well as any. Sentiment? They could pour it out to order.

The one really outstanding writer of the age, Stephen Leacock, was the only one to expose ironically some of its pretensions. It is partly for this reason that his best book, *Sunshine Sketches of a Little Town*, is by far the best book produced in the two decades.

## 2. *Poetry*

The most fashionable type of writing in Canada at this period was the regional idyll. Most of the idyllists chose the form of fiction; its one poetic representative was W. H. Drummond (1854-1907).

In choosing rural Quebec for the locale of his poems, Drummond chose that area which above all remained immune to the new spirit of the twentieth century. Rural Quebec refused to exchange its placid, traditional mode of life for the bustle and greed of the new order. Its values, the values so admired by William Kirby, were those of an agricultural economy, an essentially feudal society and a traditional religion. In books such as *The Habitant* (1897), *Johnny Courteau* (1901) and *The Voyageur* (1905), Drummond sought sincerely to portray this mode of life as seen through the eyes of a successful English-speaking doctor in Montreal. He aimed at a sympathetic understanding of the habitant point of view, regarded his characters with evident affection, and was obviously concerned to help bridge the growing gulf in Canada between the two main races.

To some extent he succeeded. The leading French-Canadian poet, Louis Fréchette, was sufficiently impressed to contribute a foreword to the first volume, and the success of the poems with English-speaking readers was immediate. The reader of today, however, is not likely to find the poems satisfying on either aesthetic or social grounds. They attempt to mingle humour and pathos, a notoriously difficult combination, and the attempt rarely if ever succeeds. It is only in such poems as "The Wreck of the Julie Plante," where the humour completely overshadows the pathos, that a tolerable effect is achieved. Moreover, it may be truly said of Drummond that he "writ no language." The poems are couched in a peculiar dialect of Drummond's own invention, and this forms a barrier to communication which the inherent triviality of the poems scarcely tempts us to surmount. From the social point of view, the poems present us with a patronizing, sentimental view of French-Canadian life. They attracted the early twentieth century generation because they permitted it to chuckle over the quaintness of the habitant and at the same time confirmed it in the belief that the poor habitant was hopelessly backward.

There is no difficulty in accounting for the phenomenal popularity of the verse of Robert Service (1876–1958). The refreshing thing about Service is that he frankly admitted that his aim was merely to entertain his contemporaries and to give them the products for which they were willing to pay. The impression gained from reading Service's autobiography (*Harper of Heaven*, 1948, and *Ploughman of the Moon*, 1951) is of a modest, self-effacing man who was rather surprised by the popularity of his first volume and determined "to hit the jackpot" again as frequently as possible. His frankness is completely disarming. When a lady in Paris exclaimed: "Ah, you are the man who makes poetry pay!" he replied: "No, I merely make rhyming remunerative." He is a *poseur*—and is the first to admit it: "There I was—always playing parts. Would I ever be just myself? Once I played my very self in a cinema drama and the Studio people were dissatisfied. They told me: 'You are not the type'." He was flattered, not insulted, when the Irish writer James Stephens told him that his Yukon ballads were "very good newspaper verse". "I regarded myself," he writes, "as a cross between Kipling and G. R. Sims. I was inclined to agree with the dispraise of the mandarins of letters."

Service was a typical member of his generation. Success to him, as to most of his contemporaries, meant financial success. "I need not have worried about my book [*Rhymes of a Red Cross Man*, 1916]," he wrote. "My publisher wrote predicting its success. And it was—beyond my dreams. The American publishers were enthusiastic. I seemed to have hit the market and for nine months I headed the list of best sellers in *The Bookman*." He had the journalist's eye for "copy": "As I had grabbed my stuff from the Yukon now I would make the War my meat." No pretence about Art, Inspiration and the like for Service: "In orderly sequence I took each of my themes and converted them into a finished set of verses. It was just a job like any other. On an average I wrote three poems a week and in five months I had over sixty."

No one wants to play the mandarin, and in this case it is clearly not necessary. No one, not even Service himself, is in danger of mistaking his verse for poetry or his thrillers for great novels. Nor is it necessary to labour the obvious facts that Service was indebted to the early Kipling for his emphatic rhythms, his slangy diction, his mixture of rapid action and sentimental moralizing, that he never equalled the successes achieved in *Songs of a Sourdough* (1907) and that the great bulk of his work is negligible by any standards. It would be more to the point to rehearse some of the ironies of his strange career: that this quiet, nervous little bank clerk became the spokesman of the rugged gold-miners who hit "the trail of '98"; that he had difficulty finding a publisher for *Songs of a Sourdough* and that it was brought out by the publishing house of the Methodist Church of Canada; and that early Canadian reviewers hailed him for introducing a new era of *realism* to our poetry.

Service harboured no such illusions. "I write," he said in an interview in 1915, "of the things of today for the people of today." He gave them what they wanted: melodrama, coarse brutality, crude sentiment, vigorous excitement, *thrills*. In doing so he produced, in "The Shooting of Dan McGrew" and "The Cremation of Sam McGee", two ballads that are apt to be remembered and enjoyed long after many more pretentious poems have been forgotten. But Service is his own best critic—and his own best apologist. Writing of his novels, but in words which are applicable to all his work, he said:

These books are dead, yet they did what I intended. They kept people awake at night. But they were synthetic—plots, not stories. I was really ashamed of them, and when people praised them I winced. Reviewers were tolerant and frequently used the word "vivid." Yes, they were so vivid they were almost convincing. They were all action, excitement, never to be taken seriously. I think they were competently written, colourful, dramatic. Perhaps for their entertainment power I may be pardoned them. One must be natural, write as one feels. I cannot be dignified. I must try to please people, and my friends are the humble folk of the earth.

Tom MacInnes (1867-1951) was a poet (or rhymester) similar to Service in his emphatic rhythms, his slangy diction and his bohemian pose, but he was a more complex figure. He had an interest in and knowledge of prosody which far exceeded that of Service, and some of his poems call for a serious critical discussion which Service's rough ballads do not warrant. There was also a marked difference in the lives of the two men. Whereas Service always lived on the fringe of the events of his period—he was a bank clerk in the Yukon rather than a miner, an ambulance man in the War rather than a soldier—MacInnes was himself at the centre of the active, acquisitive life of his period. He participated in the Yukon gold rush, served on various government commissions, lived in China and promoted the installation of a modern tramway in the ancient city of Canton.

The difference in experience might lead us to expect a greater authenticity in the poetry of MacInnes, but such expectations are not fulfilled. His Yukon ballads, for example, are less vivid and more unreal than those of Service. His active participation did, however, enable him to act as the spokesman of the new, vulgar generation which rebelled against Victorian standards of respectability in the name of a vague and undisciplined bohemianism.

MacInnes published seven volumes of verse, the first of which, *Lonesome Bar and Other Poems,* appeared in 1909, and the last, *In the Old of My Age,* in 1947.   In spite of this long time-span, however, MacInnes' style and attitude remained fundamentally unchanged.   His poetry is unfailingly romantic—romantic in its lack of discipline, in its strong feeling, in its rebelliousness.   The chief influences upon his work are those of Edgar Allan Poe, Robert Louis Stevenson, Walt Whitman and the Coleridge of "Christabel" and "Kubla Khan."   His general attitude towards life is that of the vagabond: he loves high adventure, exotic women and strange places.   He hates all forms of respectability, smugness, and pedantry.   His language is coarse, slangy, and careless, his rhythms are vigorous and strong, and much of his verse is doggerel.   One aspect of his romanticism is his interest in strange forms and metres—the ballade, the villanelle, the cantel, the mirelle—some of which he borrowed from France, some of which he devised himself, and all of which he delighted to discuss in prose notes and introductions to his poems.

These generalizations are broadly true of all his poetry, but there are subtle differences of tone, style and attitude which deserve notice.   In the first place, the worship of mere strength and the arrogant imperialism of his early collections gave way in the later verse to a somewhat vague humanitarianism which opposed the excesses of the capitalist system while rejecting its most obvious alternative of state socialism. Again, his discovery about 1912 of the French villanelle and ballade forms led him to impose on many of the poems in his subsequent volumes a tighter form and greater precision of language than were found in *Lonesome Bar* and *In Amber Lands* (1910) .   Finally, the rough and tumble optimism of his first two volumes was succeeded in *Rhymes of a Rounder* (1913) and the later collections by an attitude which often approached despair.

The complete personality which emerges from reading MacInnes' seven volumes is in many ways an attractive one. His hatred of sham and hypocrisy, his unashamed sensuous delight in life, his readiness to experiment and to question received authority—these were attitudes which needed expressing in Canadian poetry.   One wishes that from his work several complete poems could be extracted which would satisfactorily embody these attitudes.   Unfortunately, he is a poet of shreds and patches: here and there is a line, a stanza, which commands our admiration, but it is always incorporated in a poem which as a whole is a failure.

"Lonesome Bar", a narrative poem of the Gold Rush, is sheer doggerel. The plot is melodramatic in the extreme, and there are lines as flat as this:

> The typhoid laid me on my back delirious for weeks.

"The Damozel of Doom" is a strange mixture of Coleridge and Poe, full of phantoms and fantasy.   MacInnes' own contribution is in the very un-phantom-like love-making:

> O long—O last supreme caress!
> O ultimate deliciousness!
> O slowly sinking, satiate,
> Erotic swoon!

This is a characteristic theme of the poems in the early volumes—the poet wanders off into a fantastic world where he finds a beautiful girl and proceeds to make violent love to her.   Once, in reiterating this theme, MacInnes hit on a single, inspired stanza which is the finest thing he ever wrote:

> Last night in a land of triangles,
> I lay in a cubicle where
> A girl in pyjamas and bangles
> Slept with her hands in my hair.

Unfortunately, the rest of the poem ("Zalinka") never fulfills the promise of this opening stanza.

It is this humorous note that MacInnes can strike most effectively.   The well-known "Tiger of Desire," which ends

> My teeth are bared, my claws uncurled,
>     Of the red meat I never tire;
> In the black jungle of the World
>     I am the Tiger of Desire!

is only acceptable verse if it is regarded as a slightly grim joke. The best poem in MacInnes' last volume, the title poem "In the Old of My Age" strikes again the same grimly humorous note, and captures something of the ripe disillusionment of Yeats' final phase:

> In the old of my age Life's basement bargain booth
>     Has marked me down from dollar tab to dime . . . .

It is a pity that MacInnes did not strike this note more frequently, instead of attempting to be a serious moralist and apostle of "Beauty". After all, he himself rejected the earnest souls in one of his neatest epigrams:

> These moralists are growing overnice:
> Surely, my friend, some need there is for spice!
> The salt and pepper of impropriety—
> I would not call it vice.

After the doggerel of Service and MacInnes, it is a relief to turn to the poetry of Marjorie Pickthall (1883-1922), the only Canadian poet of this generation with any valid claim to artistic distinction. For Miss Pickthall, in spite of her obvious limitations, was a craftsman sincerely devoted to her calling. Her work is slight in extent and shallow in thought and emotion, but it has a delicate lyricism and an easy grace. She was—like many Canadians—a highly derivative poet, whose work is full of echoes of the pre-Raphaelites and of the poets of the Irish Renaissance, but she at least chose serious models and studied them assiduously. And in her best work she achieves a vision which, if never very penetrating, is clear and individual.

It is not surprising that she should have leaned so heavily upon other writers, for Marjorie Pickthall had little direct experience of life upon which to draw. Always a delicate girl, she was brought up in a sheltered home in Toronto, educated at the fashionable Bishop Strachan School for young ladies, worked in the Victoria College Library, spent the war years in England and died at the age of thirty-nine in Vancouver. Knowing little of the world of men and affairs, she was compelled to draw her inspiration from books, and about all her work there is a bookish, indoor atmosphere.

Her first book, *The Drift of Pinions* (1913), contains almost all her best poetry. In its ninety-four pages are forty-three poems, including such well-known ones as "The Bridegroom of Cana", "The Little Sister of the Prophet", "Père Lalemant", "Duna" and "Saxon Epitaph". As this list of titles suggests, most of her poems are set in remote times and places, in the Palestine of biblical days or the Canada of the early Jesuit missionaries. Only in her nature lyrics does she show any awareness of the immediate world about her, and in them she treats this world in such a romantic fashion that it is almost unrecognizable. Here is one of her nature lyrics which, in its delicate impressionism, its unreal atmosphere, its lush diction and its incantatory rhythms, is typical of her work of this sort.

> Wind-silvered willows hedge the stream,
> And all within is hushed and cool.
> The water, in an endless dream,
> Goes sliding down from pool to pool
> And every pool a sapphire is
> From shadowy deep to sunlit edge,
> Ribboned around with irises
> And cleft with emerald spears of sedge.
>
> O, every morning the winds are stilled,
> The sunlight falls in amber bars.
> O, every night the pools are filled
> With brede of shaken stars.
> O, every morn the sparrow flings
> His elfin thrills athwart the hush,
> And here unseen at eve there sings
> One crystal-throated hermit thrush.
>
> "Dream River"

There are so many poems of this type that they become monotonous. Always the same dreamy, unreal atmosphere is evoked, always the same tremulous note struck, always the same sad-sweet mood established. Her diction in particular is monotonous. She has certain words which she uses over and over again—silver, dream, gold, shadowy, hushed, fairy, sweet —and they are all words of the same rich, lush, romantic quality. One word especially she loves, and in it we can see all her weaknesses brought to a focus—the word "little". Everything in Marjorie Pickthall's vision is "little"—which means that it is made the object of sentimental pathos, reduced to the dimensions of a fairy-tale.

The only variety in the volume is provided by the narrative poems, which are usually cast in the form of dramatic monologues à la Browning. They differ sharply from Browning's monologues, however, in that there is no effort to attain psychological complexity or subtlety. They seek, like her lyrics, rather to evoke a mood of longing, regret or gentle sadness. They have not the strength or substance of great poetry, but they have occasional haunting lines and images:

> Thy lips are bright as the edge of a sword . . .
>
> The shaft of the dawn strikes clear and sharp . . .
>
> Like lotus petals adrift on the swing of the tide . . . .

The best of the poems, undoubtedly, is "The Bridegroom of Cana". The setting of the poem is vague and shadowy; Palestine becomes a dim Garden of Eden:

> Slenderly hang the olive leaves
> Sighing apart;
> The rose and silver doves in the eaves
> With a murmur of music bind our house.

But in spite of the unreality which results from this shadowy setting, the poem rises to a moving climax, in which the bridegroom is torn between the love of his bride and the call of Christ:

Hush, my harp, for the day is begun,
And the lifting, shimmering flight of the swallow
Breaks in a curve on the brink of morn,
Over the sycamores, over the corn,
Cling to me, cleave to me, prison me
As the mote in the flame, as the shell in the sea,
For the winds of the dawn say, "Follow, follow
Jesus Bar-Joseph, the carpenter's son."

Of the other poems of this kind, the best are "Little Sister of the Prophet" and "Père Lalemant". The latter is the only narrative with a Canadian setting. As we might expect, the characteristic ruggedness of the wilderness has been reduced to a gentle softness:

I lift the Lord on high,
Under the murmuring hemlock boughs, and see
The small birds of the forest lingering by
And making melody.

The poem, stressing the priest's loneliness, attains a mild pathos but not tragedy. It is all too soft and muted and un-real—very unlike the great treatment of a similar theme in Pratt's *Brébeuf and His Brethren*.

Marjorie Pickthall's subsequent volumes of verse—*The Lamp of Poor Souls* (1916), *The Wood Carver's Wife* (1922) and *Complete Poems* (1927)—sustained rather than enhanced her reputation. Most of the later poems closely resemble the early ones in both theme and form. There are a few interesting experiments—"On Amaryllis, A Tortoyse", for example, which has a seventeenth century quaintness, and "Wiltshire", which is an amusing dialect poem—and a hand-ful of poems which rival her early best. Of the latter group, "Resurgam", with its soaring anapaestic rhythm and its quietly triumphant close, is probably the finest example. Her patriotic and war poems are, on the other hand, her least successful productions. *The Wood Carver's Wife*, a verse drama of a tragic love-feud in the days of the French régime, is a brave experiment which does not quite come off. Apart from its melodramatic plot, its worst fault is its style. She employs throughout the play her characteristically ornate diction and imagery, and although this style enables her to create some fine descriptive and atmospheric effects, it is fundamentally unsuitable for dialogue.

Marjorie Pickthall's work lacked the imaginative power, the disciplined intensity, of the best romantic verse. But she was a genuine if minor artist, and easily the best poetic craftsman of her Canadian generation.

## 3.  Fiction

The dominant form of Canadian prose fiction during the Confederation period had been the historical romance; in the first two decades of the twentieth century it was the regional idyll.  L. M. Montgomery and Ralph Connor were only the most famous of a large group of writers who between them covered almost every area of the country.  In the Maritimes, in addition to Montgomery, there were Theodore Roberts, Norman Duncan, Alice Jones, F. W. Wallace and Frank Baird; in Quebec there was James Le Rossignol; in Ontario there were Adeline M. Teskey, Isabel E. MacKay, Archibald McKishnie, Marian Keith and R. E. Knowles; in the West there were Mrs. Emily Murphy ("Janey Canuck"), Nellie McClung, Frances E. Herring, Arthur Stringer and, of course, Ralph Connor.  Most of these novelists and their novels have long been forgotten, and few of them are worthy of revival.  They are, however, interesting as a collective phenomenon.  They appeared at a time when the old, predominantly rural Canada was being transformed, and they sought above all to perpetuate the rural virtues.  Avowedly didactic, they aimed to inculcate love of their chosen region, pride in its past and a respect for the Victorian ideals in religion and morality.     It is remarkable that so many of them were closely connected with the Scottish-Canadian settlements and with the Presbyterian Church: Miss Montgomery was the wife of a Presbyterian minister; Baird, Connor and Knowles were Presbyterian ministers themselves.

In a sense, this sudden proliferation of regional fiction was a healthy symptom. Canadians in large numbers were becoming aware of the artistic possibilities of their own place. A good regional literature must precede a good national literature; indeed, it is arguable whether there is any such thing as a national literature apart from its regional components. Moreover, the general attitude of these writers was a commendable one.     The ideals to which they were pledged were far superior to the money values which dominated the new industrialism.

It is when we look deeper that the weaknesses and faults of this regionalist movement become apparent.     Instead of challenging the values of the new industrial society, these writers ignored its existence.     Instead of seeking to show how the old ideals could be adapted to the needs of a new generation, they sought merely to turn the clock back.

If this is to ask too much, at least we might demand that such writers give us an honest account of the life of their region.     This almost all of them failed to do.     Arthur Stringer's prairie trilogy, for example—*The Prairie Wife* (1915) was followed in due order by *The Prairie Mother* (1920) and *The Prairie Child* (1922)—has often been described as a realistic account of prairie life.     But to read these novels with a knowledge of the subsequent work done by Grove, Sinclair Ross and W. O. Mitchell is to be appalled by their triviality, facetiousness and flippancy.     Nellie McClung (1873-1951) came much closer to giving us a true account of prairie life, but even her books stress the virtues of the pioneers and neglect their vices.     Not until the novels of Frederick Philip Grove were published did Canadians of other areas learn how it really felt to live on the prairies.

We might justifiably demand also that these regional novelists pay more than passing attention to the basic principles of the novel as an art-form. Not one of them was an artist of even second rank. Their characters are one-dimensional, their plots are either absurdly melodramatic or absurdly trivial—the plot of Marian Keith's *Duncan Polite* (1908), for example, revolves about a minister's desire to install an organ in his Kirk—their ideas are mere platitudes and their style is plodding and inept.

Even Ralph Connor (1860-1937), the best of these many regional novelists, is vulnerable to almost all the above accusations. His novels, for all their vogue, differ not a whit in kind and only a trifle in degree from those of the rest of the school. What he has to offer us as a system of values is a muscular Christianity which has no theological or ethical subtlety, a hearty masculine back-thumping do-goodism which rests on no philosophical foundations. It is the Christianity of Charles M. Sheldon's *In His Steps* (1896), which makes of Christ at best a superior social service agent and at worst a prying busybody who will not let people alone. There is the same shallowness in his portrayal of character and the same lack of subtlety in his handling of the plot. His characters are all types—the kindly but strict mother who is all altruism, the strong, silent man who has a heart of gold, the ruffian who is really a diamond in the rough—and they are either completely static or, if they change at all, susceptible to incredibly swift conversions. His plots show little regard for probability and are full of melodramatic incidents and coincidence. But there was one thing Connor could do and do well—he could describe physical action economically and vividly. His account of the Varsity-McGill football game in *The Prospector* (1904) is the best work in its very minor kind that has been done in Canada.

Like almost all Canadian writers of this and the preceding generation, Connor did his best imaginative work as a young man. *Black Rock* (1897), *The Sky Pilot* (1898) and *The Man from Glengarry* (1901) are easily the best of his many novels. The finest single book he produced, however, was not a novel at all but his autobiography, *Postscript to Adventure* (1937).

The story of *Black Rock*'s publication has been told too often to warrant repetition. So also has the story of the phenomenal popular vogue which it and its successors enjoyed, a vogue which has resulted in the sale of over five million copies of his books. The most interesting question for discussion is the reason for this popularity.

For one thing, of course, Connor, especially in his novels of the West, was dealing with a region which had recently undergone and was still undergoing a tremendous boom and about which there was great curiosity throughout the English-speaking world. For another, there was in Connor's novels, though in a very mild form, the appeal we find in *Moll Flanders*: readers could comfort themselves with the thought that they were being instructed in virtue while at the same time getting some glimpses of vice. There was another source of comfort in the novels: Connor's unshakeable faith in the essential goodness of human nature. And of course everything always turned out well in the end: the evil-doers were converted rather than destroyed and the good were duly rewarded.

The basic fact was, I believe, that Connor, like Service and MacInnes, was accepting and flattering the spirit of the age. It might appear that in his religiosity and his idealism he was challenging its materialism, but in fact his values were very much the same. His missionaries were red-blooded he-men who tackled the job of winning souls with all the enthusiasm of a commercial traveller bent on setting a new sales record.

A much quieter but no less successful regional writer was Lucy Maud Montgomery (1874-1942). Miss Montgomery was born at Clifton, Prince Edward Island, spent her childhood in Cavendish, the seashore farming community which is called "Avonlea" in her novels, and eventually settled in Ontario as the wife of a country clergyman.

Her first and most famous novel, *Anne of Green Gables* (1908) is a children's classic, and it would be silly to apply adult critical standards to it. Mark Twain called Anne "the dearest and most moving and delightful child since Alice in Wonderland", and the whole book achieves a quaint, naive perfection that is fresh and charming still. The tone throughout is that of pleasant whimsy, the didacticism is, for the most part, implicit and unobtrusive, and the sentimentalism a little less cloying than is usual in books of its type.

There was never any doubt of its popularity. It had all the features of the kind of escape literature which a materialistic and vulgar generation craved: like the poems of Marjorie Pickthall, it was sweetly-sad, innocent and pathetic. Supreme Court justices unashamedly wept over it, and the heads of households were so eager to read it that their children hardly had a chance. It sold in the hundreds of thousands, and is still selling.

Its success prompted its author to turn out more of the same. In *Anne of Avonlea* (1909) she almost maintained the same level, but her subsequent novels showed a marked falling off in both quality and popular success. When she tried her hand at adult fiction—as in *The Blue Castle* (1926)—the product had all the weaknesses of the Anne books and none of their redeeming charm.

Norman Duncan (1871-1916) was also a regional novelist who combined the didactic with the idyllic, and wrote most of his books for children. Since they are set in more rugged parts of the country, however—the coasts of Newfoundland and Labrador, mainly—they have a bleaker atmosphere than Miss Montgomery's novels, and one of them, *The Way of the Sea* (1903), has elements of realism quite alien to the Anne series.

*The Way of the Sea,* a collection of short stories, is one of
those baffling and irritating books which are forever trembling on the verge of greatness and never quite attaining it.
It has some magnificent descriptive passages, it reveals a
close acquaintance with the lives of sailors and fishermen,
it portrays life as a grim and unending struggle, its style
rises at times to true eloquence and it has symbolic overtones
which remind us of *Moby Dick.* It is a book with two characters: Man and his antagonist, Nature, usually in the form
of the sea. Nature always triumphs but Man, in his heroic
resistance, has his moments of glory. *The Way of the Sea*
has, then, elements of greatness—but it is not a great book.
In the first place, it is very uneven: the last story, "The
Fruits of Toil", is a short prose epic, but some of the others
are relatively trivial; and even in "The Fruits of Toil" there
are elements of grandiloquence, sentimentality and melodrama. There is about it all a kind of artistic irresponsibility: Duncan seems to have been unwilling to extort from
himself that final ounce of strength which might have transformed the book into a masterpiece. Too often he is content
to let his effects evaporate in a cloud of rhetoric. A few
precise, disciplined touches would have maintained a perfect
tone, but Duncan "bursts into clamour with the great black
piano appassionato". He will not let the facts carry their
own conviction: he has to drive the message home with the
pile-driver blows of his rhetoric:

Neither in that season, nor in any one of the thirteen years
coming after, did this man catch three hundred quintals
of cod in his trap. In pure might of body—in plenitude and
quality of strength—in the full, eager power of brawn—he was
great as the men of any time, a towering glory to the whole
race, here hidden; but he could not catch three hundred
quintals of cod.

*The Way of the Sea* is a failure: but it is a failure
which comes close to success of a kind quite beyond the reach

of other Canadian novelists of this period. Unfortunately, in his later books, Duncan drifted further way from artistic integrity. The later novels—*Dr. Luke of the Labrador* (1904), *The Cruise of the Shining Light* (1907) and *The Bird-Store Man* (1914), for example—are more imitative and in every respect less compelling. They remind us not of Melville, but of the Kipling of *Captains Courageous* and of the Dickens of the most maudlin scenes in *The Old Curiosity Shop*. The sentimentality grows more oppressive, the rhetoric more bombastic, the melodrama more obtrusive. Norman Duncan had ended by capitulating completely to the vulgarity of his age.

Stephen Leacock (1869-1944) was a much more complex figure than any of the other writers in this chapter. It would be possible to treat him, on the basis of his most famous book (*Sunshine Sketches of a Little Town*), as another regional idyllist, though that would be to ignore the irony which exists in the title and substance of that book. It would be possible also to consider him as a writer of agreeable nonsense, as a professor of economics who discovered a profitable sideline in the production of literary burlesques. The most illuminating attitude, however, is to see in Leacock an ironist and satirist who, alone in his generation, saw through the hypocrisy and pretension of his society. It is true that such an approach leaves out a large proportion of Leacock's phenomenally long list of publications, but it explains and illuminates his best and most enduring productions and relates him significantly to his time and place.

Leacock had an ideal background and preparation for the role of satirist. He had been born in an English village, had come to Canada as a small boy and lived on an Ontario farm, had been head boy at Upper Canada College and, after a thorough training in languages at Toronto and in economics and political science at Chicago, had ultimately become head of the Department of Economics and Political Science at

McGill. His English birth and background gave him at least a glimpse of external standards by which North American civilization might be judged; his years on a farm had accustomed him to a type of life marked by its absence of bustle and its adherence to the traditional processes and decencies. As an ex-head boy of aristocratic Upper Canada and a professor at McGill he had a social prestige which made it difficult to ignore his ironic commentaries. His knowledge of languages helped to give his view perspective, and provided him with models upon which his own satire could be based. As a recognized authority on economics, he could not be brushed aside as an ignorant radical whose distaste for the most ruthless and flamboyant manifestations of unrestricted capitalism arose from a failure to understand it. And the fact that he lived in the commercial metropolis of Montreal and was on intimate terms with many of the leading financiers and industrialists meant that he was ideally situated to survey the rampant materialism of the new century.

Before going on to examine examples of Leacock's satire, it may be well to pause and consider the basis on which his satire rests.

The satirist is one who makes fun of the follies and foibles of mankind, and who does this by relating men's behaviour to some ideal standard or norm from which they depart. Leacock has such a satiric norm: a fundamental unity of outlook underlies all of his best work. He is, to put it briefly, a country squire of the eighteenth century who revolts against the acquisitiveness and arrogant commercialism of the early twentieth century. His values are eighteenth century values: common sense, benevolence, moderation, good taste. His method of presenting these values, however, is the genial Addisonian rather than the savage Swiftian one.

We see the instinct of the country squire in his dress: he wore good tweeds and serges, but he wore them carelessly, chose sizes too large for him and deliberately eschewed the elegant and the up-to-date. We see it also in his maintenance of his country home at Orillia, to which he retreated as soon as the academic session was over. There he played the role of a modern Squire Allworthy. "He liked entertaining in Orillia particularly," his niece tells us in her preface to *Last Leaves*, "to fill the house with weekend guests, friends from everywhere. He liked to look down the broad table and proudly point out that everything was 'off the farm,' except the can of sardines in the *hors d'oeuvres*." We see the same instinct in his deliberate homeliness of speech: Dr. G. G. Sedgwick comments on his use of "ain't" and the racy earthiness of his conversation.

But we see all this even more clearly in his books. In the best of his "serious" books, *The Unsolved Riddle of Social Justice* (1920), we see it directly, without the mask of irony. This book is the attempt of a benevolent man of the eighteenth century to restore some semblance of decency and order to the chaos of an industrial society. When Leacock writes: "The tattered outcast dozes on his bench while the chariot of the wealthy is drawn by. The palace is the neighbour of the slum . . . ." the effect is less like that which we might expect from a contemporary economist than like the reaction of Sir Roger de Coverley suddenly confronted with twentieth century London. It is the sturdy common sense of an eighteenth century squire which dismisses socialism as "a mere beautiful dream, possible only for the angels." It is an eighteenth century instinct which would patch up the present social order rather than destroy it in favour of a new one. And the patching which Leacock suggests is just that which a benevolent squire of that period would have devised. Let us, says Leacock in effect, look after the children, the workless, the aged and the infirm as those people were looked after in the village by the squire and his lady.

But Leacock's satire is seen most clearly in the three books which are, by general consent, his best: *Literary Lapses* (1910), *Sunshine Sketches of a Little Town* (1912) and *Arcadian Adventures with the Idle Rich* (1914). The satire is not confined to these books—it occurs intermittently in even his most trivial efforts—but it finds its most complete and sustained expression in them.

It is no accident that the first and most delightful sketch in *Literary Lapses* describes the plight of a shy youth entering for the first time that temple of modern commerce, a bank.  Beneath all the elaborate clowning of that piece we can detect a serious note: it is inspired by a genuine feeling of being out of place in a commercial civilization.  The next sketch, "Lord Oxhead's Secret", is a satire on the type of commercial fiction which thrives on aristocratic titles, romantic clichés and surprise endings.  "Boarding House Geometry" is perhaps best approached as pure fun, and very good fun it is, but is not the cheap boarding-house with its petty economies and its prying landlady a characteristic product of a commercial society?  The next two sketches are relatively feeble, but we return to the main theme with "How to Make a Million Dollars".  In this piece Leacock, whose satire is usually and deliberately genial, gets rather unkind.

So one evening I asked one of the millionaires how old Bloggs had made all his money.
"How he made it?" he answered with a sneer.  "Why, he made it by taking it out of widows and orphans."
Widows and orphans!  I thought, what an excellent idea. But who would have suspected that they had it?
"And how," I asked pretty cautiously, "did he go at it to get it out of them?"
"Why," the man answered, "he just ground them under his heels, and that was how."

The satire in that, of course, cuts more than one way, and it is a good example of the subtlety with which Leacock's seemingly inconsequential fooling is often conducted.  There is the obvious satire against exploitation; but the man who is making the accusation is himself one of the exploiters and his words are not so much an expression of honest contempt as of disguised envy. Nor does the satire end there: there is satire also at the expense of those who utter the conventional reproaches against great wealth, who over-simplify the complexity of large-scale finance and merely mouth sentimental platitudes about widows and orphans.

It would take too long to itemize each sketch in *Literary Lapses,* and a general summary of the remainder must serve. There is satire on many of the facets of a commercial civilization—on health faddists, for example, on "lonely hearts" columns, on the "progress" which is merely novelty, on our preoccupation with statistics in particular and numbers in general, on so-called advanced education. The sketch entitled "Self-Made Men" strikes the dominant note most clearly: in it, two successful business men, "men with well-fed faces, heavy signet rings on fingers like sausages", try to outbrag each other about the hard uphill struggle they have had—and end characteristically by ordering a very elaborate dinner. One of the very best sketches in the book—"A, B, and C, the Human Element in Mathematics"—may seem at first glance to lie outside the scope of my thesis; but does not part of its appeal arise from our sense of the anonymity of modern man in the huge metropolis? Is it not, like most of the book, an effort to assert the claims of humanity over the claims of mere number?

However that may be, there is little to our purpose in Leacock's second book of humour, *Nonsense Novels* (1911). This series of parodies on popular types of fiction could, of course, be claimed as satire on the commercialization of literature, but it is satire so broad as scarcely to merit the name. It is the prototype of many similar books by Leacock —*Further Foolishness, Moonbeams from the Higher Lunacy, Frenzied Fiction* and a host of others—in which he revels in nonsense for its own sake. Most of these books are already as badly faded as the novels they parodied or the fashions they derided, and it is certainly not on them that Leacock's permanent reputation will rest.

Leacock's next book was his greatest: *Sunshine Sketches of a Little Town*. Here Leacock the gentle ironist and satirist found the ideal subject, and the ideal approach to it. All his best qualities—his benevolence, his common sense, his humanity, his whimsical yet ironic observation—come to a focus in this book. His eighteenth century values and preferences are also quite clearly displayed here. He creates an idyll of a small community based on the farming life of the surrounding area, and for the closest approach to the picture which emerges we must go to the "sweet Auburn" whose passing Oliver Goldsmith so movingly lamented. In Mariposa, life moves at a snail's pace, and there is time for the courtesy and contemplation which have been crowded out in the industrial metropoli. Dean Drone, sitting in his garden over a book of Theocritus, is more like the parson of Auburn than the modern go-getting cleric whom Leacock was later to pillory in *Arcadian Adventures with the Idle Rich*. Josh Smith, with his "chequered waistcoat of dark blue with a flowered pattern", "his shepherd's plaid trousers", "his grey spats and patent leather boots", is an innkeeper whom Fielding would have recognized or Dickens seized upon as a survivor from an earlier and more ample day.

But of course Mariposa is not merely an eighteenth century English or Irish village transferred to twentieth century Canada: it is also recognizably a Canadian small town. There were, and happily there still are, such communities in which the noises of the contemporary industrial era are heard only as a faint and distant murmur, and out of them, as we have seen, dozens of Canadian regional novelists were making their novels. Leacock could write as nostalgically, as sentimentally and more sincerely than any of them about the beauties of his region. He wasn't joking when he wrote, in "The Marine Excursion of the Knights of Pythias", that "You may talk as you will about the intoning choirs of your European cathedrals, but the sound of 'O Canada' borne across the waters of a silent lake at evening is good enough for those of us who know Mariposa."

He wasn't joking—or was he?  It is the ambiguity, the subtle irony of *Sunshine Sketches* which makes it such a fascinating book.  Leacock was aware of the sunshine of Mariposa, but he was also aware of its littleness—for there is irony in the title as everywhere.  In contrast with big cities like Montreal and New York, Mariposa is a utopia, a blessed spot which the tide of industrialism has almost completely passed by.  When "The Whirlwind Campaign in Mariposa" fails to produce the results that a similar financial drive had achieved in the city, Leacock drily comments: "It may be that there are differences between Mariposa and the larger cities that one doesn't appreciate at first sight."  And the flaws in Mariposa life are chiefly things which, like the whirlwind campaign, arise from a misguided desire to ape the cities.  Mariposa isn't content to be a sleepy small town: it wants itself to become a metropolis.  Hence we get genial satire such as this:

In point of population, if one must come down to figures, the Canadian census puts the numbers every time at something round five thousand.  But it is very generally understood in Mariposa that the census is largely the outcome of malicious jealousy.  It is usual that after the census the editor of the Mariposa *Newspacket* makes a careful re-estimate . . . and brings the population up to 6,000.  After that the Mariposa *Times-Herald* makes an estimate that runs the figure up to 6,500.  Then Mr. Gingham, the undertaker, who collects the initial statistics for the provincial government, makes an estimate from the number of what he calls the "demissed" as compared with the less interesting persons who are still alive, and brings the population to 7,000.  After that somebody else works it out that it's 7,500; then the man behind the bar of the Mariposa House offers to bet the whole room that there are 9,000 people in Mariposa.  That settles it, and the population is well on the way to 10,000 when down swoops the federal census taker on his next round and the town has to begin all over again.

The best sustained chapter in *Sunshine Sketches*—"The Speculations of Jefferson Thorpe"—is perhaps the clearest example of this satire upon the corrupting influence of modern industrialism and the worship of material success. This chapter describes the effect upon Mariposa of one of the great financial booms which were characteristic of this generation of Canadian life—the boom occasioned by the discovery of silver deposits in the Cobalt area. The town goes wild, the young bank teller commits suicide and the laconic barber, Jefferson Thorpe himself, loses all his savings. Of course the dominant tone of the piece is farcical, but it is the kind of farce which T. S. Eliot detected in *The Jew of Malta* —farce with a bite to it.

The theme is absent from the tedious chapters of nonsense dealing with the love affairs of young Pupkin, but it reappears in the sketches describing the 1911 election in Mariposa. In election time, Mariposa is inevitably caught up in the stream of the national life. The town exhibits, on a small scale, all the cheap rhetoric which distinguished that most malicious election campaign in Canada history. How neatly, by the slightest of exaggerations, Leacock suggests the falseness of it all:

I only knew that it was a huge election and that on it turned issues of the most tremendous importance, such as whether or not Mariposa should become part of the United States, and whether the flag, that had waved over the school house at Tecumseh Township for ten centuries, should be trampled under the hoof of an alien invader, and whether Britons should be slaves. . . .

It is Josh Smith who wins the election—Josh Smith, the hotel keeper, running as a Tory on a temperance ticket—and he wins by a trick, as the result of a premature election report coming, characteristically, from the city!

The satire in *Sunshine Sketches* is, however, for the most part very mild and gentle. In *Arcadian Adventures with the*

*Idle Rich* it is sharper and more explicit.  The opening pages set the tone:

The Mausoleum Club stands on the quietest corner of the best residential street in the city. . . .

The street in the softer hours of the morning has an almost reverential quiet. . . . The sunlight flickers through the elm-trees, illuminating expensive nursemaids wheeling valuable children in little perambulators. . . . Here you may see a little toddling princess in a rabbit suit who owns fifty distilleries in her own right. . . .

Just below Plutoria Avenue, and parallel with it, the trees die out and the brick and stone of the city begins in earnest. Even from the avenue you see the tops of the sky-scraping buildings in the big commercial streets, and can hear or almost hear the roar of the elevated railway, earning dividends.  And beyond that again the city sinks lower, and is choked and crowded with the tangled streets and the little houses of the slums.

As this passage suggests, the book is an indictment of arrogant plutocracy. The first sketch, "A Little Dinner with Mr. Lucullus Fyshe", is an ironical study of the attempts of a typical plutocrat to lure money from an English peer—who is at the same time eager to *borrow* money to salvage his ancestral estate.  The next two sections concern Mr. Tomlinson who, having made a huge fortune by the chance discovery of gold on his farm, tries vainly to get rid of his wealth only to find that he has acquired a Midas touch. Eventually the mine fails, and Tomlinson is happy to return to his quiet farm.  The satire here is at the expense of the myth of the "hard uphill struggle" of which Leacock's plutocrats are fond of talking, and of the supposed "know-how" which finds itself outmanoeuvred by the simple guilelessness of Mr. Tomlinson.  Leacock came as close in these sections to what he, in *Humour and Humanity*, called "sublime humour" as he was ever to come.  Tomlinson is at once a tragic and a comic figure, and the laughter of the story is always close to tears.

The next two sections of *Arcadian Adventures* are closer

in tone and spirit to the Pupkin sequence in *Sunshine Sketches;* but sections six and seven, dealing with the rivalry between the Anglican Church of St. Asaph and the Presbyterian Church of St. Osoph, resume the main theme. There is excellent satire at the expense of go-getting clergymen, plutocratic elders and the whole paraphernalia of fashionable religion.  It is characteristic that the ultimate merger of the two churches is achieved in the manner of a big business deal—and for the same purpose!

Indeed in this book Leacock holds up to ridicule practically every aspect of the plutocratic society of his time. Entertainment has become a mere adjunct of business: a dinner with Mr. Fyshe is a business conference in disguise. Culture has become a phony outlet for the idle wives of financial barons or a means of display for the barons themselves.  Education, and especially university education, has also been corrupted by the influence of Big Business.  The university is symbolized by the aptly named Dr. Boomer, whose whole aim as an administrator is to pry money out of business men by offering them honorary degrees and similar privileges.  With such a president guiding its destinies, it is no wonder that the university has come to resemble a factory rather than a seat of learning:

The University, as everyone knows, stands with its great gates on Plutoria Avenue, and with its largest buildings, those of the faculty of industrial and mechanical science, fronting full upon the street.

These buildings are exceptionally fine, standing fifteen stories high and comparing favourably with the best departmental stores or factories in the city.

But the man who made these attacks was no social revolutionary who would, in Yeats' phrase, "hurl the little streets upon the great."  Leacock was, in outlook and in actual political affiliation, a Tory; but he was a Tory of the eighteenth century rather than of the twentieth.  His Toryism had nothing of the cynical callousness of Big Business; it was the Toryism of Goldsmith and of Burke, which saw in the traditional decencies and duties of an agricultural society the proper basis for community.  His literary role was similar to that of Chaucer, seeking to preserve amid the growing commercialism and corruption of his century the values of feudal solidarity, chivalric courtesy and the ancestral faith; similar also to that of Addison, attempting to persuade the new middle class to take on something of the culture and humanity of the landed gentry; similar to that of Dickens, calling amid a squalid industrialism for the colour and kindness of a slower age; similar, finally to that of Twain, yearning amid the tinsel of the Gilded Age for the simple virtues of pioneer America.

It was from such men that Leacock learned, and it is with them that he has his closest affiliations.  Like him, they were all genial satirists, laughing philosophers, but in them all, as in him, there was a serious underlying purpose.  Was Leacock their equal?  That is, perhaps, an idle question: time alone can answer it.  The late Dr. G. G. Sedgwick came as close to an answer as anyone is likely to come for decades when he declared: "He is not one of the Great Ones, but he may sit at the same table."

If he was not "one of the Great Ones"—and it is true that the vast bulk of his work is ephemeral and that even his best books leave one with the feeling that the man who wrote these could have written better—it was at least in part because of the nature of Canadian society in his period. The prevailing materialism was too strong even for him, for any one man, to resist.  In most of his books he went along with the crowd and wrote the kind of nonsense for which they were willing to pay.  Canadian culture—as a glance at his literary contemporaries reveals—was still too shallow to support a great artist.  But Leacock came much closer to greatness than any other Canadian writer of his generation, and in *Sunshine Sketches of a Little Town* the period found its chief literary justification.

CHAPTER FIVE

# The Modern Period

## 1920 - 1950

THIS period in Canada in many ways resembled the last three decades of the nineteenth century. There was a similar combination of optimistic nationalism and of progressive political thought; both periods witnessed a severe economic depression which partly restrained their enthusiasm; and both periods, especially in their final ten years, produced an unusual quantity of good literature.

The Canada of 1920 was a nation in ferment, but it was the ferment of new growth rather than of decay. Even the riots and strikes and demonstrations mentioned in the introduction to the fourth chapter of this book were fundamentally healthy manifestations: they were signs that new ideas were stirring, that the industrial workers and the farmers alike were becoming conscious of their power and desirous of exercising a more direct influence on the national life. In the West, and even in relatively conservative Ontario, the farmers joined together to form producers' co-operatives and political parties which won decisive victories in provincial elections and threatened the supremacy of the two traditional parties in the federal sphere. The urban workers were slower to take direct political action, but the trade union movement was expanding rapidly as a means of removing their grievances and advancing their interests.

The twenties also saw a revival of interest in the power and prospects of the nation as a whole. The new nationalism sometimes took extreme and exclusive forms, but on the whole it too was a healthy development. In the political sphere, Canada's status as an equal partner in the British Commonwealth of Nations was officially recognized at the Imperial Conference of 1926, and she soon began to assert this status by appointing first a minister to Washington and subsequently diplomatic representatives in other foreign capitals.

But it was in the cultural sphere, as in the eighteen seventies, the days of "Canada First", that the new nationalism was most apparent and enthusiastic. Again new magazines were founded to serve as media of the cultural revival: *The Canadian Bookman* in 1919, *The Canadian Forum* in 1920, *Dalhousie Review* in 1921, *The McGill Fortnightly Review* in 1925 and *The Canadian Mercury* in 1928. The temper of the period is perhaps most clearly displayed in the introductory essay in the first number of *The Canadian Forum* (October, 1920) in which it is asserted that the magazine "had its origin in a desire to secure a freer and more informed discussion of public questions and, behind the strife of parties, to trace and value those developments of art and letters which are distinctly Canadian".

There was not much Canadian literature about which the early issues of the *Forum* could be enthusiastic, but there was a healthy art movement and what seemed to be the beginning of a great development of Canadian drama. To the work of the Group of Seven in painting and of the Little Theatre Movement in drama the *Forum* devoted a large part of its space. When the paintings of Tom Thomson, A. Y. Jackson, Lawren Harris, J. E. H. MacDonald, Arthur Lismer and the other members of the Group were exhibited in London and Paris in 1924 and received with critical acclaim by English and French reviewers, the editors of the *Forum* glowed with national pride. They were almost equally proud about the Little Theatre Movement, to which for some fifteen years they devoted a special column edited first by Fred Jacob and later by Professor R. K. Hicks. They hailed the work of Carroll Aikins' experimental theatre in Naramata, British Columbia, whose purpose was thus stated on the opening programme (November 3, 1920): "We feel that we have reached that point in our history where we may look for a Canadian literature to record Canadian achievement; and it is in that faith that we have built this theatre for the giving of Canadian plays by Canadian actors." Soon they were able to salute the similar efforts of theatre groups else-where—of the Community Players in Montreal and Winni-peg, of the Drama League in Ottawa, of Hart House Theatre in Toronto, to name only the most outstanding. They searched eagerly for Canadian plays worthy of performance, and found promise in the work of Merrill Denison, Fred Jacob, L. A. MacKay, Duncan Campbell Scott and Mazo de la Roche.

The editors of the *Forum* also searched eagerly for mani-festations of a revival of other literary forms, but it was some years before they found anything about which they could be enthusiastic. Gradually, however, the new names began to appear in their columns. There were, in the twenties, poems by E. J. Pratt, A. J. M. Smith, Robert Finch, Dorothy Livesay and A. M. Klein; short stories by Jean Burton, Mary Quayle Innis, Frederick Philip Grove, Ray-mond Knister and John D. Robins; critical articles by Doug-las Bush, E. K. Brown and A. J. M. Smith; and reviews of novels by Mazo de la Roche, Frederick Philip Grove, Martha Ostenso, Raymond Knister and Morley Callaghan.

There were other signs of a national cultural revival. The Canadian Authors' Association was founded in 1921 "to act for the mutual benefit and protection of the interests of Canadian authors and for the maintenance of high ideals and practice in the literary profession"; the first histories of Canadian literature began to appear, and there were six in the decade; Lorne Pierce, newly appointed and energetic editor of The Ryerson Press, began to issue his series of poetry chapbooks and to publish an ambitious group of books under the general title of "Makers of Canadian Literature"; new editions appeared of the better Canadian books of the nineteenth century, such as Richardson's *Wacousta,* Kirby's *The Golden Dog* and Moodie's *Roughing It in the Bush;* there were book-length studies of Haliburton, Carman and Lampman; and there were several new anthologies of Canadian literature.

All this activity, however, was seriously threatened by the outbreak in 1929 of the most severe economic depression in Canadian history, and by the end of the decade the first wave of post-war enthusiasm was decidedly on the ebb. There had been more talk about Canadian literature than actual production of it. In particular, much energy had been dissipated in a rather futile discussion of the rival merits of nationalism and cosmopolitanism in literature. The Canadian Authors' Association, soon after its foundation, embarked on a programme of "boosting" Canadian literature by means of Book Weeks and the like, and their over-enthusiastic evaluation of mediocre books prompted such young critics as E. K. Brown, Douglas Bush, A. J. M. Smith and Leo Kennedy to attack the whole concept of nationalism in literature. The discussion was largely futile, because neither side yielded ground to the other and both, in the heat of the controversy, lost sight of the fact that the best literature inevitably is rooted in the place of its origin but is not restricted to it. In any case, neither group produced a significant body of work in the decade, and its achievements were not nearly as substantial as had been confidently expected at its beginning. Good work had been done in the novel by Grove, de la Roche, Stead and Callaghan; Pratt had laid the firm foundation of a reputation in poetry and half a dozen younger poets had made promising beginnings; but the movement to create a native drama had almost completely collapsed with the death of Fred Jacob and the departure of Merrill Denison for the United States.

The thirties was, of course, a decade of depression, anxiety and the threat of war in Canada as elsewhere. To the effects of the world-wide economic depression was added the effect of drought on the prairies. The resultant discontent produced, in political terms, the Canadian socialist party, the C.C.F., which attempted to act in the interests of the farmers on the one hand and the industrial workers on the other. In cultural terms, however, the results were almost purely negative. The young poets whose work had been appearing in the magazines should have been publishing their first volumes in the early thirties, but the publishing trade was unable, in the circumstances, to take risks on obscure and experimental writers. The thirties was, consequently, a relatively barren decade in Canadian literature. Of the four leading young Canadian poets—Scott, Klein, Kennedy and Smith—only Kennedy published a volume (*The Shrouding*, 1933) prior to the outbreak of World War II. The others had to be content with publication in the joint anthology *New Provinces* (1936). No new novelists of major significance appeared, and even established novelists such as Frederick Philip Grove and Morley Callaghan found it difficult to get their work published.

The most fruitful development of the decade was in the sphere of criticism—the establishment in 1931 of the *University of Toronto Quarterly* and the initiation in 1935 of its annual symposium "Letters in Canada", which for almost the first time brought mature critical standards to bear on our literary output.

The outbreak of war in 1939 was, strangely enough, the signal for a sudden resurgence of Canadian literature. At first, probably, the cause was not so much the war as the prosperity which was returning just prior to its outbreak; but as the war continued it did stimulate the national morale directly and lead to a renewal of interest in things Canadian. For the first time in years there were, in 1939, three Canadian novels with some claim to be considered as significant interpretations of human experience:    Grove's *Two Generations,* Irene Baird's *Waste Heritage* and Ted Allan's *This Time a Better Earth.* The same year saw the publication of a more vigorous and incisive long poem than had appeared in Canada since Pratt's early "Cachalot"—Anne Marriott's saga of prairie dust storms, *The Wind Our Enemy.* As the war proceeded, the literary movement gained momentum: each year saw the publication of at least one work of major significance. Poets such as A. J. M. Smith, F. R. Scott, A. M. Klein, Robert Finch and Dorothy Livesay at last found publishers and a public eager for their work, and they were joined by other promising new recruits such as Earle Birney, Ralph Gustafson, Irving Layton, Patrick Anderson, Miriam Waddington, P. K. Page, Louis Dudek and Raymond Souster.

The period from 1939 to 1949 was, indeed the most productive and significant period in Canadian literature since that period from 1880 to 1893 when Roberts, Carman, Lampman, Duncan Campbell Scott, Wilfred Campbell and the other members of that generation were producing their best work. All the signs of a literary revival were present: new literary magazines were founded, new anthologies of Canadian writing appeared, and there was a revival of the criticism of Canadian literature. Creatively, the output of poetry was most impressive; but prose fiction was not neglected and even Canadian drama began to develop.

These thirty years, then, saw a strong cultural revival in Canada, but a revival which was broken into two parts by the depression of the thirties. In the twenties, a beginning was made by the establishment of new literary magazines and movements and by the early work of writers like Pratt, Grove, de la Roche, Callaghan and the Montreal Group; this movement was brought almost to a standstill during the thirties; but it revived and made its greatest impact during and immediately after World War II under the stimulation of renewed prosperity and national excitement.

# CHAPTER SIX

# Modern Canadian Poetry

## 1920 - 1950

CANADIAN CRITICS who were stirred by the renewed nationalism eagerly to scan the horizon for new poets had few rewards for their watchfulness in the first five years after World War I. Roberts, Carman and D. C. Scott survived, but they were elderly men whose best work had already been written; Marjorie Pickthall was ill, soon to die; Service and MacInnes had settled into a repetitive routine as popular rhymesters. There were several younger poets who were beginning to establish a reputation about 1920, but only one of them gave promise of major achievement.

Most of these more recent arrivals were content to play minor variations on the romantic themes and manners which had become traditional in Canadian poetry. They might pick up a hint of something new here and there—chiefly from such Georgian poets as Brooke and such Imagists as Amy Lowell—but substantially their poetry belonged to the past rather than to the future. Katherine Hale, in such volumes as *Morning in the West* (1923), Arthur S. Bourinot (*Laurentian Lyrics*, 1915; *Lyrics from the Hills*, 1923), Florence Randal Livesay (*Songs of Ukraina*, 1916; *Shepherd's Purse*, 1923), and even the relatively dexterous and experimental Louise Morey Bowman (*Moonlight and Common Day*, 1922; *Dream Tapestries*, 1924) were merely competent versewriters whose best work was melodically pleasing, pictorially exact, and emotionally suggestive, but had little power or originality of either idea or expression. Arthur Bourinot has been the most consistently productive of this group: he continued to publish deft verses throughout the thirties, forties and fifties, and also did valuable service by publishing the letters of such poets as Archibald Lampman and Duncan Campbell Scott. He did not, however, develop into a major poet.

The one post-war poet of this romantic kind who seemed to his contemporary critics to be destined for greatness was Wilson MacDonald (born 1880), author of *Song of the Prairie Land* (1918), *The Miracle Songs of Jesus* (1921), *Out of the Wilderness* (1926) and of several subsequent volumes. Upon his work, and especially upon *Out of the Wilderness,* the eager critics lavished their superlatives. A critic in *Saturday Night* in October, 1926, for example, was not content to maintain that MacDonald was the first successful challenger of the supremacy of the Group of the Sixties, but also declared him the equal of any poet then writing in Great Britain or the United States. People flocked to Hart House and to other places of assembly to hear him read his poems, and to hear his work praised by the most prominent men of letters of the time.

Such adulation soon provoked its own reaction, and as early as July, 1927, a critic in the *Ottawa Citizen* was able to remark upon the decline of MacDonald's reputation. Today MacDonald's name is scarcely ever mentioned in critical discussions of Canadian poetry, though he has retained some popular reputation as a reader and lecturer and has achieved a vogue in Soviet Russia.

It is not likely that this almost total neglect of MacDonald's poetry will continue. He was undoubtedly overpraised by his contemporaries, but some of his work is considerably better than that of many poets whom critics still take seriously. He was, with the possible exception of Audrey Alexandra Brown, the last important representative in Canada of romantic verse, and by no means a negligible one. His work is too ornate, too

facile, too uneven and too full of obvious echoes of Whitman,
Carman and Rupert Brooke to be truly great, but at its best
it has what Raymond Knister called "a nameless magic", a
capacity to awaken a strange and haunting music. These
qualities are found most abundantly in such descriptive lyrics
as "Muskoka", "Oaks", and "In a Wood Clearing". The
closing lines of this last poem, which appeared in John
Squire's *London Mercury*, will give some idea of his best
work:

> . . . so we stayed,
> Stayed till the bronze moon grew pale from its climbing,
> Stayed till the night was an octoroon lovely to see.
> The air was so silent that even the whip-poor-wills dared not
> sing;
> Nor could we hear aught save the rhythmic advance of our
> hearts
> And the wash of her hair that fell about me like rain.

In such poems MacDonald is at least the equal of Marjorie
Pickthall, and his work has a wider range than hers. He has
written a good deal of satire, for example, and though much
of it is merely petulant, some of it is the powerful expression
of permanent human values. MacDonald holds strong
opinions, frequently unpopular opinions, and is fearless in
expounding them.

In conclusion, I cannot improve upon this summary
judgment of MacDonald's work by the late E. W. Harrold,
which appeared in the issue of the *Ottawa Citizen* already
mentioned: "Wilson MacDonald is neither the supreme poet
of the first group [of critics] nor the mediocrity of the
second. . . . He is the master of deeply moving rhythms, of
a word music that at times attains an exquisite harmony,
and can draw figures and images that have the air of singu-
larity and the freshness of rare beauty. . . . As to the
intellectual content of his poems, little need be said. A
number of the pieces disclose a warm humanity, a lofty pity
and a fine contempt for sham and ugliness and insincerity.

And a number of others merely reveal a schoolboyish nostalgia which every sentient adolescent once railed under but now laughs at."

The decisive fact, however, is that MacDonald represented the end of one tradition rather than the beginning of another. For a fresh start in Canadian post-war poetry we must look not at his work but at that of E. J. Pratt and of the Montreal Group of Scott, Klein, Kennedy and Smith.

The critics may be pardoned for not having seen much that was new or striking in Pratt's first little volume, *A Book of Newfoundland Verse* (1923). Much of it consists of descriptive lyrics in the standard romantic manner and of only moderately successful exercises in imagism. With the wisdom of hindsight, however, we can see that this first book contains many hints of the poet who was to dominate Canadian verse in this thirty-year period. "The Ice-Floes", a narrative of a seal-hunt, reveals that gift for economical and forceful description of heroic action which has marked all of Pratt's longer poems. It also displays for the first time two of the values that Pratt was always to cherish: courage and compassion. Pratt's mingled fascination with and horror of amoral strength is exhibited in "The Shark", and his humour in "Overheard in a Cove" and "The History of John Jones". His mature philosophy of life, which may best be briefly described as Christian humanism, finds expression in "Ode to December, 1917": it is not a successful poem, but it contains the key line "The anthem of a world re-strung to human love and grace."

The effort to re-string the world to human love and divine grace might be described as the central preoccupation of Pratt's verse. He sees man as a creature wavering between the cave and the temple, always in danger of relapsing into primitive barbarity but capable of approximating the divine by the exercise of self-sacrificial love. His three positive values are courage, courtesy and compassion—courage in the sense of a readiness to disregard one's own safety to defend or assist others, courtesy in the true chivalric sense of selfless service and faithful devotion, compassion in the full Christian sense of an ability to identify and feel with all who suffer.

This philosophy can be seen most clearly in certain of Pratt's shorter poems, especially in "The Truant" and "From Stone to Steel". The former poem is an indictment of amoral power and an expression of Christian humanism. Courage, courtesy and compassion mingle in this final climactic speech, in which the truant man sounds his defiance of the mechanical monster who masquerades as God:

> We who have met
> With stubborn calm the dawn's hot fusillades:
> Who have seen the forehead sweat
> Under the tug of pulleys on the joints,
> Under the liquidating tally
> Of the cat-and-truncheon bastinades;
> Who have taught our souls to rally
> To mountain horns and the sea's rockets
> When the needle ran demented through the points;
> We who have learned to clench
> Our fists and raise our lightless sockets
> To morning skies after the midnight raids,
> Yet cocked our ears to bugles on the barricades,
> And in cathedral rubble found a way to quench
> A dying thirst within a Galilean valley—
> No! by the Rood, we will not join your ballet.

This poem, however, expresses Pratt's hopes for man; "From Stone to Steel" is a necessary complement, since it expresses his fears. Man is capable of Christ-like self-sacrifice; but he is capable also of beast-like ferocity and greed. Only two revolutions of the wheel of history separate the violence of Java from the pacificism of Geneva; the savagery of the cave and the self-immolation of the temple are only a hand's breadth apart.

This structure of ideas underlies the three long narrative poems which are Pratt's masterpieces: *The Roosevelt and the Antinoe* (1930), *The Titanic* (1935) and *Brébeuf and His*

*Brethren* (1940). Each of these poems illustrates Pratt's central thesis with growing subtlety and complexity. In *The Roosevelt and the Antinoe,* the narrative of an heroic rescue at sea, the pattern is relatively simple: Captain Freed and his cosmopolitan crew pit themselves with courage, fidelity and compassion against the barbaric forces which lurk in the natural world. When human selflessness has triumphed over the storm's ferocity, the victory is hailed with a divine benediction:

> Through a rift of sky
> A level shaft, the first one for the week,
> Quivered on an edge of cloud, then struck
> A line of foam making for the grey peak
> Of a kingpost, then to waterline from truck,
> Till from the starboard taffrail up the span
> Of the hull, it reached the lettering where it ran
> In crimson coronation of her name,
> As if a god might thus salute the deed,
> And ratify the venture with the screed
> Of an aurora milled in solar flame.

In *The Titanic* the theme is developed more subtly. The struggle here is not a simple one between human courage and natural cruelty: the human beings are themselves torn between the temptation to resort to primitive barbarism and the aspiration towards divine self-forgetfulness; the iceberg, unlike the storm in the earlier poem, is also a mixture of grace and ferocity; and the ship is a mixed symbol of human resourcefulness on the one hand and of human arrogance on the other. In this poem man is, in one sense, defeated, since the ship which he had thought invulnerable is sunk by the gigantic berg; but in the true sense he triumphs, since in the moment of crisis he displays a capacity to rise above self in acts of courage, courtesy and compassion. The berg, on the other hand, seems to win but is really defeated, since at the end it has lost its "temple touch of grace" and has become merely "a grey shape with a palaeolithic face".

The climax of Pratt's poetic career, however, came with the publication of *Brébeuf and His Brethren*. In the sacrificial efforts of the Jesuit missionaries to rescue the Indians from barbarism, the poet found the ideal objective correlative for his major theme. The Jesuit missionaries display to the full the selfless virtues, and the Indians all the barbaric ferocity and cruelty, of which man is capable. Brébeuf faces death with magnificent courage, compassionately thinking more of Lalemant's sufferings than of his own. In his death-agony he sees the vision of the slain but triumphant Christ:

> ... the sound of invisible trumpets blowing
> Around two slabs of board, right-angled, hammered
> By Roman nails and hung on a Jewish hill.

As in *The Titanic*, the forces of barbarism have only apparently triumphed. "The villages fell before a blizzard of axes" but:

The Mission sites have returned to the fold of the Order
Near to the ground where the cross broke under the hatchet.
And went with it into the soil to come back at the turn
Of the spade with the carbon and calcium char of the bodies,
The shrines and altars are built anew, the *Aves*
And prayers ascend, and the Holy Bread is broken.

This bare summary of the poem's theme does not, of course, do justice to the grave dignity of its manner nor to the artistry of its style and structure. To the energy which is always characteristic of Pratt's verse there is here conjoined contemplative grandeur and a wealth of metrical modulation. Thematic images of fire and warfare weave the sections of the poem into a single fabric, and the whole poem moves rhythmically forward to its climax in a series of waves of action and reaction.

The other long poems by Pratt—*The Witches' Brew* (1925), "The Cachalot" and "The Great Feud" (published in 1926 under the joint title *Titans*), *The Iron Door* (1927),

*The Fable of the Goats* (1937), *Dunkirk* (1942), *They Are Returning* (1945), *Behind the Log* (1947) and *Towards the Last Spike* (1952)—are less fully satisfying than those with which we have been dealing, but each in its way contributes it quota to his total vision.

*The Witches' Brew*, an extravaganza celebrating revels at sea, and "The Cachalot", the life story of a great whale, both express most directly Pratt's delight in spontaneity, freedom and heroic energy, and his horror at cunning, captivity and conformity. The former poem hymns the glories of alcohol at a time when prohibition was in fashion; the latter celebrates the spontaneous energy of the whale in contrast with the low cunning of the squid and the commercial greed of the whalers. Each is written in galloping octo-syllabic couplets in a diction which is polysyllabic and allusive, and in images which invoke magnitude and magnanimity. Although these poems were written when Pratt had turned forty, they breathe the spirit of youth: they are the testaments of a mind which has broken with the rigidities of the Protestant ethic and of mechanistic psychology, which glories in a sense of liberation.

"The Great Feud" and "The Iron Door" are more complex poems, and more subdued ones. Although sections of "The Great Feud" retain the exuberance of its predecessors, there is a compensating sense here of the senseless slaughter to which heroic energy may easily deteriorate. Throughout the poem, which narrates a prehistoric battle between elementary creatures of the sea and land, images of maternal solicitude alternate with images of terrible greed and hatred: it is the first prolonged recognition in Pratt's work of the need to complement courage with compassion, freedom with responsibility. Somewhat similarly, in *The Iron Door*, a poem dealing with the question of immortality, the rebellious protests of the early sections give way to the grave reconciliatory lines of the climactic vision: the true conception of liberty is a glad surrender to the Divine Will.

*The Fable of the Goats, Dunkirk, They Are Returning* and *Behind the Log* deal prospectively and retrospectively with World War II. *The Fable,* published before the outbreak of the war, seeks to avert it by revealing that compassion and courtesy are superior to courage, are, in fact, the highest form of courage. Two goats who are traditional antagonists decide to end their feud on the basis of an insight which is described, in unmistakably Christian terms, as "a dagger of apocalypse", "this epiphany", "the redemptive clue". To some extent the poem is a shallow expression of the fashionable pacificism of the thirties, and the whole fable is impaired by the inherent absurdity of its antagonists. That it did not express Pratt's own deepest convictions is clear from the quickness with which, once the War had broken out, he became a spokesman for the Allied cause against Hitlerism. In *The Fable* it was war itself which was seen as the embodiment of the barbaric ferocity of the cave from which man must always seek to free himself; in the other three war poems it is Hitler, and the Nazi regime, who embodies this recidivist savagery. In *Dunkirk* the English are portrayed as a race who have left the cave to worship in the temple, whereas the Germans appear only in the form of tanks and dive bombers which are likened to monstrous beasts and birds of prey. The issue, as perhaps was inevitable in a patriotic poem written in the midst of war, has been grossly oversimplified. Much the same fault is to be found in the other two poems of this group, although in them there is much that commands admiration: Pratt's detailed technical knowledge of ships and seamanship, his talent for precise description and for rapid narration.

*Towards the Last Spike* is also something of a patriotic exercise: it is a narrative of the building of the Canadian Pacific Railway and a glorification of those men of vision who made it possible. It has force, humour, some excellent phrasing, and an unforgettable image of the Laurentian shield as a vast monster lying in the path of the builders, but it is marred by some undigested prose summaries, some passages of forced coyness, and imperfect recognition of the complexity of motives and motions which made the railroad feasible.

More likely to endure than these later, semi-official patriotic exercises are the many fine short poems scattered through Pratt's collections *Many Moods* (1932) and *Still Life and Other Verse* (1943). Worthy to put beside "From Stone to Steel" and "The Truant" are such pellucid descriptions as "Sea-Gulls" and "The Sea-Cathedral", such satires as "The Parable of Puffsky" and "The Prize Cat", and such reflective lyrics as "Silences" and "Come Away, Death". In these poems, as in all his best work, Pratt displays his metrical versatility, his mastery of a clear, colloquial style, his exact response to the concrete sensory world, his deftness in the choice of image and illusion. It is these qualities, plus the vision of man as an errant but ever-seeking pilgrim on the road from the barbaric cave to the divine temple, that make Pratt the finest Canadian poet so far to appear.

As we have seen, Pratt emerged as a solitary poet in Canada, and he has always remained an isolated figure. His ancestry is difficult to trace, and he has had no disciples. He has made no attempt to formulate a poetic creed, and his few published critical articles have been eclectic and tolerant rather than controversial and partisan. But at about the same time that he was beginning to make his presence felt, a group of young poets in Montreal was coming into being, and this group was to be much more vocal and self-conscious. Its members—A. J. M. Smith, F. R. Scott, Leo Kennedy and A. M. Klein—were to lead the first organized movement on behalf of the "new" poetry in Canada.

Though the members of this group did not form a school

in the strict sense of that word, they did possess certain common attitudes. They were anxious poets, in conscious reaction against the easy optimism of Carman and Roberts, Service and MacInnes, and they were determined to face their age rather than to retreat to nature, love, the open road or any of the other romantic refuges. The Group of the Sixties had been conscious above all of their place; these poets were determined to be fully as conscious of their time. They sought to write of contemporary experience in a contemporary vocabulary and in imagery drawn from their immediate environment. In contrast with the sensuous and emotional verse of the Group of the Sixties, their verse was intellectual and passionate. They were deliberately experimental in form, and the chief influences they acknowledged were those of the metaphysical poets of the seventeenth century and of such contemporary poets as Yeats, Eliot and Pound.

The leader and chief spokesman of this group was A. J. M. Smith (born 1902), who has probably exerted a greater influence on the Canadian poetry of his generation than any other single figure. His influence has been out of all proportion to his poetic output, which has consisted so far of only two small volumes, *News of the Phoenix* (1943) and *A Sort of Ecstasy* (1954). More significant than his poetry has been his work as critic and anthologist. As early as 1928, when he was still a graduate student at Edinburgh, Smith published an article, "Wanted—Canadian Criticism" (*The Canadian Forum*, April, 1928) which set the literary dovecots of Canada fluttering. It was Smith who edited *New Provinces* (1936), the first anthology of the new poetry in Canada; and it was his *Book of Canadian Poetry* (1943) which was, more than any other single factor, responsible for the burst of creative and critical activity in the middle and late nineteen forties.

A full-dress analysis and appraisal of Smith's work as a

critic is outside the scope of this essay. He has consistently advocated higher standards of both criticism and creation and he has been the acknowledged leader of the so-called "cosmopolitan school" which refuses to employ parochial standards in the judgment of Canadian literature. His attitude can best be expressed in his own words, addressed to any young Canadian poet: "Set higher standards for yourself than the organized mediocrity of the authors' associations dares to impose. Study the great masters of clarity and intensity. . . . Study the poets of today whose language is living and whose line is sure. . . . Read the French and German poets whose sensibility is most intensely that of the modern world. . . . Read, if you can, the Roman satirists. . . . And remember lastly that poetry does not permit the rejection of every aspect of the personality except intuition and sensibility. It must be written by the whole man. It is an intelligent activity, and it ought to compel the respect of the generality of intelligent men. If it is a good, it is a good in itself."

Certainly Smith has practised what he preached: he has set such high standards for his own verse that he has published little and republished even less. His two volumes contain only some sixty short poems, the distilled product of thirty year of poetic activity. The poems have been so radically revised that many of them are almost unrecognizably unlike their original versions in the magazines. In their final form, they are polished gems which can be handled again and again without dulling their lustre. Of all Canadian poets, Smith most repays re-reading.

At the same time, it must be admitted that Smith is a less original poet than Pratt. At McGill, Smith was especially attracted to the poets of the seventeenth century, to the early Eliot and the later Yeats; at Edinburgh he wrote a thesis under Grierson on the religious poetry of the seventeenth century; and the influence of these admirations is apparent in his own verse. Of all the influences, that of Yeats is dominant. Smith, like Yeats, makes use of intellectual symbols and of taut, tense rhythms; and he shares Yeats' ideal of the hard, aloof, aristocratic poise amidst the contemporary chaos and commercialism. Like Yeats also, he attempts, though less successfully, to combine the bitter and the gay, to be at once really responsible and apparently irresponsible.

It is bitterness which predominates in Smith's poetry. His chief themes are loneliness and death, fear and renunciation. The dominant tone of his poetry is created by his choice of diction—his favourite words, in order of frequency, are "cold", "sharp", "lonely", "bitter" and "hard". Everything combines to enhance this effect of stark deprivation. His favourite images are those of pain — everything "cuts", "wounds", "sears" or "tears". Shadows to Smith are "as sharp as glass"; kisses leave bruises; cedar and fir trees "uplift sharp barbs"; the currents in a stream are "arrows of direction, spears of speed"; a sky is "icicle-sharp"; "torches make a slow wound on the gray mist". Sores, lances, darts, sickles, swords, scars, shears and knives are everywhere.

His vision, in other words, is a highly distinctive one: nowhere else in modern poetry can we find such concentrated agony. The frequent echoes of other poets in his work are misleading, for they suggest a derivativeness which exists only on the surface. It is true that he is sometimes tempted to write poems which do not express his personal vision—"Son-and-Heir" and "The Face", for example, which are both clever but superficial imitations of Auden—but in his best poems he is unmistakably himself. Only Smith could have written "The Lonely Land", the finest poetic counterpart of Tom Thomson's paintings:*

---

*It is interesting to note that in the original version of this poem, there were several explicit "Canadian" references. The early Smith was himself strongly influenced by the nationalism of the twenties.

Cedar and jagged fir
uplift sharp barbs
against the gray
and cloud-piled sky;
and in the bay
blown spume and windrift
and thin, bitter spray
snap
at the whirling sky;
and the pine trees
lean one way.

A wild duck calls
to her mate,
and the ragged
and passionate tones
stagger and fall,
and recover,
and stagger and fall
on these stones—
are lost
in the lapping of water
on smooth, flat stones.

This is a beauty
of dissonance
this resonance
of stony strand,
this smoky cry
curled over a black pine
like a broken
and wind-battered branch
when the wind
bends the tops of the pines
and curdles the sky
from the north.

This is the beauty
of strength
broken by strength
and still strong.

Smith is, admittedly, a minor poet, though he has been a major influence on Canadian poetry. But he is a minor *poet,* and no mere versifier; and he is the finest and most conscious craftsman of his generation.

When A. J. M. Smith published his article "Wanted—Canadian Criticism" he elicited a mild rebuke from one of his chief lieutenants in the Montreal Group, F. R. Scott (born 1899). Scott agreed with Smith in deprecating the booster-like activities of the Canadian Authors Association, but he disagreed with Smith's argument that a mature criticism could create a mature literature. He demolished the argument with one of those sallies of wit that have been Scott's chief contribution to our literature: "As well hope to hasten the harvest by assembling the harvesters in May."

Wit is the dominant characteristic of Scott's best poetry. He has a keen mind, a gift for clear and forceful expression, and a quick eye for absurdity and pretension. He sees a gaping tourist—and straightway impales her on the barb of his satire:

> This fat woman in canvas knickers
> Gapes seriously at everything.
> We might be a city of the dead
> Or cave men
> Instead of simple town folk.
> We have nothing to show
> That can't be seen better somewhere else,
> Yet for this woman the wonder ceases not.
> Madam, the most extraordinary thing in this town
> Is the shape of your legs.
> O communication!
> O rapid transit!

Poems of this sort—"Saturday Sundae", "The Canadian Authors Meet", "Financier", "Professor" are other examples—are the most immediately attractive of Scott's productions.

But he writes at least two other types of poetry with distinction. There are poems in which Scott, an ardent socialist, sets forth his idealistic vision of a planned society;

and there are poems in which he writes passionately of nature or of love. The former group are the least successful. Like Spender's "programme poems", which they often closely resemble, many of them already seem dated. But his lyrics, though less superficially exciting than his satires, have a clear precision and easy grace which make them memorable. Here, for example, is "North Stream":

> Ice mothers me
> My bed is rock
> Over sand I move silently
>
> I am crystal clear
> To a sunbeam.
>
> No grasses grow in me
> My banks are clean.
>
> Foam runs from the rapid
> To rest on my dark pools.

Scott, like Smith, is also a minor poet. He has published only three volumes—*Overture* (1945), *Events and Signals* (1954) and *The Eye of a Needle* (1957)—and the bulk of his energies has been devoted to his professorial duties at McGill and his political activities for the C.C.F. His verse has not the concentrated richness of Smith's, nor the ample vigour of Pratt's, but it is valuable for its quick wit, its clear intelligence and its cool precision.

F. R. Scott was one of the four editors of *The Canadian Mercury*, founded in 1928 to act as a medium for new writing in Canada. Another editor was Leo Kennedy (born 1907), whose early work, appearing chiefly in *Mercury* and *The Canadian Forum*, gave promise of a brilliant career as poet, critic and short story writer. A provocative article entitled "The Future of Canadian Literature" (*The Canadian Mercury*, April, 1929) indicated his cosmopolitan outlook. Declaring that Canada had as yet produced no literature of value, Kennedy wrote: "Having as yet no worthwhile tradition of their own, the young men are inclined, and wisely, to look abroad. After three or four years apprenticeship to the English classics, they are concerned usually with the work of moderns . . . of men . . . whose writing reveals their own wounds, and echoes the cry which they have not yet managed to utter."

Whether or not this statement was an accurate account of the tastes of young Canadians in general, it certainly was a true indication of Kennedy's own leanings. His poetry bears the imprint of Eliot and Pound, his stories have the sardonic wit of the early Huxley and of Sherwood Anderson, and wounds are almost as frequent in his work as in that of A. J. M. Smith.

Death, however, as the title of his single volume, *The Shrouding* (1933), would indicate, is the dominant theme of Kennedy's early poetry, and around this theme and that of resurrection he weaves motifs borrowed from his reading of Eliot and Sir James Frazer. A Catholic who gave up the faith, he sought substitutes for the Christian doctrine of immortality in the fertility and vegetation myths of primitive man. The results are often rich and suggestive, as in his "Words for a Resurrection":

> Each pale Christ stirring underground
> Splits the brown casket of its root,
> Wherefrom the rousing soil up thrusts
> A narrow, pointed shoot,
>
> And bones long quiet under frost
> Rejoice as bells precipitate
> The loud, ecstatic sundering,
> The hour inviolate.
>
> This Man of April walks again—
> Such marvel does the time allow—
> With laughter in His blessèd bones,
> And lilies on His brow.

But for all their suggestiveness, delicacy of phrasing and verbal melody, these early poems of Kennedy become monotonous. Their intensity is contained within too narrow limits, and the images of split and bleeding hearts, of bones and cerements, are reiterated until they lose their power to move us. Kennedy must have sensed this himself, for he announced in his poem "Calling Eagles" that he was going to devote himself henceforth to the poetry of social struggle:

> Come down into life, Eagles, where iron grinds bone,
>     hands falter
> And brave men perish for a tyrant's peace;
> Come where Spain strangles in blood, Ethiopia
> Groans at the iron-cased heel, Vienna
> Numbers the dead, remembers Weissel and Wallisch;
> Scream for Brazilian dungeons where Prestes rots
> And fascist madmen rattle gaoler's keys . . . .

Shortly after issuing this proclamation, however, Kennedy left for the United States, and he has published little since his exile.

The actual creative performance of the whole group of Montreal poets has been less than might have been expected. Of the four, Smith has increasingly devoted himself to criticism, Scott to politics and Kennedy to advertising and book reviewing. The poet of this group whom we have yet to consider, A. M. Klein (born 1909), has not published any poetry since 1948.

If the source of Smith's anxiety was chiefly personal, of Scott's chiefly political and of Kennedy's chiefly religious, Klein's has been chiefly racial. He is a Jew who has always been conscious of his Jewishness, and who has felt deeply the persecutions to which his race has been subjected in this and in other periods. His early poetry is saturated in the history, philosophy, social conditions and religious rites of Jewry. The poems in *Hath Not a Jew* . . . (1940) and *Poems* (1944) are thoroughly Jewish in content, and *The Hitleriad* (1944) is an angry satire upon the Jews' chief contemporary oppressors. His single novel, *The Second Scroll* (1952), is a parable-like travelogue symbolizing the quest of the Jew for his ancestral home in Israel. His latest and finest volume of verse, *The Rocking Chair* (1948), is French-Canadian rather than Jewish in emphasis. This shift is not surprising, for French Canada has much in its life which would appeal to Klein's temperament. He has always loved Montreal (though he has been quite aware of its meaner aspects); he has always delighted in ancient cultures and traditions; he has always been interested in religious rites, ceremonies and hierarchies; he has always loved domesticity, the ties of family and the pleasures of home; and he has always been interested in the fate of minorities. All of these things he could find as readily in French Canada as in Jewry.

In all his verse, from the earliest days to the present, certain common characteristics may be observed. Here, for example, are the opening lines of a very early poem, "Business":

> And for the sake of you I am become
>   A trafficker in stars, and barter my
>   Knapsack of constellations for some high
> Rare compliment for you; I am become
>   A hawker of the moon, who, never dumb,
>   Runs through the streets and shouts his wonders. . . .

And here is a passage from a later poem, "Lone Bather":

> Upon the ecstatic diving board the diver,
> poised for parabolas, lets go
> lets go his manshape to become a bird.
> Is bird, and topsy-turvy
> the pool floats overhead, and the white tiles snow
> their crazy hexagons. . . .

Both poems exhibit Klein's audacity, energy, and richness. The technique of the later passage is at once looser, in the sense of being released from the restraints of regular metre, and more intense, since no words are used to make a rhyme or fill a line. But both passages exhibit Klein's mastery of brilliant technical effects. The choice and arrangement of words is perfectly adapted to give the sense, in the first poem of leaping, and in the second of diving. As always in Klein's poetry, the dominant effect is of vigour and power. His lines are filled with strong open vowels, hard decisive consonants, active verbs and daring scintillating images. His rhythms are emphatic, and his lines have a buoyancy which reminds one of E. J. Pratt.

But Klein is no mere technician. His feelings and thoughts are as strong and vigorous as the words in which he expresses them. Whether in praise or blame, he is direct and unequivocal. Indeed it is Klein's frankness, his readiness to reveal his undisguised self, which makes him outstanding amidst a poetic generation which has so often sought to cloak its confusion in obscurity and its vacillation in irony. Klein is a man of deep sympathies and warm passions, and he is not afraid to admit it. His poetry glows with sympathy for the oppressed, or burns with hatred for the oppressor.

Sometimes, however, his poetry borders on sentimentality or invective. Poems such as "The Sugaring" and "For the Sisters of the Hotel Dieu", in *The Rocking Chair,* are over-sweet, sticky with sentiment; and most of *The Hitleriad* is invective rather than poetry. But at his best he avoids these extremes by his wit, by his intellectual range and quickness. There is a tough reasonableness in his best poems, and his humour ranges all the way from the boisterous and broad, through the tender and subtle, to the dry and ironic. He has a gift for portraits—such as that of Mayor Houde in *The Rocking Chair*—in which sympathy and satire are piquantly compounded. He also has a gift for symbols: as a recent writer in *Poetry Commonwealth* put it, "give him a rocking chair or a spinning wheel and he will describe you a time, a place, and a people".

The members of the Montreal Group were not the only Canadian poets who were beginning to appear in the magazines in the late twenties and early thirties. There were traditionalists who continued to write the kind of romantic nature and narrative verse which had dominated Canadian poetry during the previous periods; and there were modernists who were variously influenced by such movements abroad as imagism and symbolism. Of the more traditional poets, the most competent was Audrey Alexandra Brown; of the modernists, the best were probably Robert Finch and Dorothy Livesay, although Raymond Knister and W. W. E. Ross also produced some finely observant imagist lyrics.

Audrey Alexandra Brown (born 1904) has her closest affiliation, among Canadian poets, with Marjorie Pickthall: like her, she is most attracted to the legendary and heroic past, and she writes in a musical diction which tends to be too ornate and lush. She also resembles Marjorie Pickthall in her tendency to fall too completely under the sway of previous poets, whether it be that of Keats, de la Mare or Christina Rossetti. She has published four volumes of verse— *A Dryad in Nanaimo* (1931), *The Tree of Resurrection* (1937), *Challenge to Time and Death* (1943) and *All Fools' Day* (1948)—but there has been little significant development in her work and, indeed, she has never equalled the best and longest poem in her first collection, "Laodamia". "Laodamia" is, like many of her poems, rather too diffuse, but it reveals her finest qualities: a gift for vivid, colourful description, for haunting musical cadence and for the sympathetic portrayal of human frustration and longing. Even these qualities cloy, however, when they are presented in such abundance, and one longs even in this poem for a more disciplined mode of utterance, for a greater severity of form and austerity of tone.

Such a capacity for conciseness and restraint is found in the work of Robert Finch (born 1900), who has always been distinguished for his verbal ingenuity and wit. The best of his early poems are examples of *vers de société* such as Eliot published, also under French influence, in the early

Prufrock volume. Here, for example, is a little poem by Finch which appeared in 1925:

> I know a man who's too discreet!
> He has apologetic feet,
> His nose and mouth and chin retreat—
> He seems just leaving when you meet.

There is the same wit, and an Eliotian use of ironic contrast, in another early poem, "Furniture":

> How many a tree whose lofty dome
> Gave magic birds a magic home
> Now shelters in its varnished shade
> Books, handkerchiefs, and marmalade!

This gift for epigrams has remained with Finch. *The Strength of the Hills* (1948) contains such neat little verses as "Race":

> While the professor flies ahead
> Time flies too, on wings of lead.

Finch's verbal ingenuity sometimes leads him into mere idle word-spinning, as in "Measure":

> The lady little less
> Than beautiful? Confess
> That little less gives her the sort of
> Beauty beauty falls short of.

At other times, however, it enables him to create poems as fine as "Over":

> It is over, the ceaseless search is over,
> Souls may collide but not like bodies mate,
> After collision they must separate,
> Minds are not twins as Calais is to Dover.

> Searching was half the world while searching lasted,
> Finding was all the world created new,
> Losing was hardest to believe come true,
> But search, find, loss, not one of them is wasted

That shed this timeless moonlit week on week
In an uncumulative series.  Frost
Could not quietlier gild and geld the fall.

There is no search when nothing is left to seek,
Nothing to find when what was found is lost,
Nothing to lose when what is lost was all.

Finch is a musician and a painter as well as a poet, and
some of his best poems reflect his other interests.  He is very
conscious of the music of words, and achieves many striking
effects by the subtle interweaving of vowel sounds, as in the
line: "Could not quietlier gild and geld the fall".  He also
uses his poetry on occasion as a substitute for painting and
etches clear word-pictures in the manner of the Imagists.

Delicacy, restraint, and precision are the chief qualities of
Finch's agreeable minor verse.  These, too, were the qualities
of the poems which Dorothy Livesay (born 1909) published
in her first two small volumes, *The Green Pitcher* (1928) and
*Signpost* (1932).  At this stage she was under the influence
of Imagist poets such as H. D. and Elinor Wylie, and of Emily
Dickinson.  Her early poems are brief, epigrammatic and
intense; they are stylized emotional cries in which she utters
her sense of loneliness and her yearning for love.  Here are
two examples of this early verse, "Time" and "If It Were
Easy":

> The thought of you is like a glove
> That I had hidden in a drawer.
> But when I take it out again
> It fits, as close as years before.

> Fire creeps into my bones, and drowsily
> I lean against the flame and drink
> Succour from burning wood.

> If it were as easy as this
> To creep close up to love
> And gather strength

> There would be none of these
> Cold heavy evenings
> Storm-bound, outside the door.

But whereas Finch has continued to write in this manner, Miss Livesay turned, in the thirties, to social verse. In Paris, doing graduate work at the Sorbonne in 1931–1932, she came into close contact with Henri Barbusse's League of Revolutionary Writers, and she returned to Canada to take up a career as a social worker and to devote her poetry to the cause of social revolution. In 1935 she published her first revolutionary poem, "The Outrider". In it, following the influence of the English left-wing poets of the thirties, she used a modern vocabulary, contemporary images of industrial power and social stagnation, and emphatic jazz rhythms:

> Early morning
> stirs the street
> men go by
> on urgent feet
> Early morning
> litter still
> in the gutters
> on the sill. . . .

A similar poem is "Day and Night", which provided the title for her third volume, published in 1944. It portrays the deadening effects of the mechanical routine of a modern factory:

> One step forward
> Two steps back
> Shove the lever,
> Push it back

> We bear the burden home to bed
> The furnace glows within our hearts:
> Our bodies hammered through the night
> Are welded into bitter bread.

Bold and passionate as are the poems in this volume, they seem to me to generate more heat than light. When she is expressing indignation or anger, she can speak forcibly and intelligently; but like that of most of her contemporaries, her voice falters when she attempts to set forth a remedy for

the abuses she so clearly sees. There is an anonymity about
these poems—they often sound more like a loudspeaker than
a personal instrument.

In *Poems for People* (1947), and in the later poems
included in her *Selected Poems* (1957), there is an attempt
at a fusion of the personal and the social, and in the best
poems of the collections, such as "Preludium", the fusion is
almost perfect. In "Preludium", the account of a child's
development into self-hood, the dogmatic collectivism of the
*Day and Night* volume has been replaced by a simple but
strong humanism:

> And if the tower builded then
> Be bold and venturesome
> Not all negations, whipping, snares
> Not all the frantic obstacles to face
> Can down the darer. . . .

Poems such as "The Mother" and "Small Fry" are less
pretentious than her earlier efforts, but they are more sincere,
more simple and natural. The jazz rhythms of "Day and
Night" are here employed, more pleasingly, to create a child's
sense of a carnival:

> Save me a little
> Silver wheel
> A chariot moving
> On the world's reel. . . .

Anger has been largely replaced by pity—see, for example,
"Sonnets for a Soldier" and "Railway Station"—and indignation by admiration for those, such as Franklin Roosevelt,
who have faced life courageously.

Dorothy Livesay has been one of the leading representatives
of the so-called "native tradition" in Canadian poetry. She
has usually selected her themes from Canadian life, but she
has never been narrowly parochial in her outlook. She has
in her own verse exhibited the qualities which she has asked
for in the work of others: objectivity, lyricism and passion.

Disillusioned with dogmatic solutions to the problems of our time, she has turned, for a basis of hope, to the promise of children, the courage of strong men, the delights of love and the beauty of nature.

A poet in many respects similar to Dorothy Livesay is Earle Birney (born 1904). He belongs to the same generation as far as age goes, but he made his reputation as a poet much later: with the publication of *David and Other Poems* in 1942, when he was thirty-eight. Since that time he has published three other volumes of verse—*Now Is Time* (1945), *The Strait of Anian* (1948) and *Trial of a City* (1952)—and two novels—*Turvey* (1949) and *Down the Long Table* (1955).

Like Dorothy Livesay, Birney is a Westerner, and his poetry exhibits the vigour and heartiness which we associate with that relatively youthful area. Like Dorothy Livesay, also, he came to intellectual maturity during the great depression of the thirties and was for some years an avowed Marxist; like her again he has turned in late years from dogmatic Marxism to an idealistic humanitarianism. Both poets have been unafraid of the "nationalist" label, and have been aware of the Canadian scene, alert to Canadian problems and concerned with interpreting world events in Canadian terms.

These and other similarities between the two poets should not, however, blind us to their differences. Whereas Miss Livesay served her apprenticeship to Emily Dickinson, the Imagists and the French symbolists, Birney was attracted as an undergraduate to Anglo-Saxon verse and to the poetry of Chaucer. His doctoral dissertation—Birney is a professor of English—was concerned with Chaucer's irony, and he has published scholarly articles on pre-Chaucerian verse. These interests have had their influence on his own poetry. In some poems—notably "Anglo-Saxon Street"—he deliberately imitates Anglo-Saxon poetic techniques, using the alliterative line, the mid-line hiatus and archaic words such as "carl" and "leman". More often the Anglo-Saxon influences are less obvious but equally real, and take the form of direct energy of expression, the sparing use of adjectives and a sinewy litheness of verse movement. There are also marked Chaucerian influences: like his master, Birney is primarily a narrative poet, interested in the people and events of his own time rather than in the subtleties of his own mind, and concerned to present a realistic but richly ironic and occasionally satirical picture of the life about him.

These influences, however, are general rather than specific. There are few echoes in Birney and, next to Pratt, he is the most original poet of Canada. The temporal distance which separates him from his chief influences precludes imitation. Unlike most contemporary Canadian poets, Birney is not given to echoing Eliot, Auden or Dylan Thomas. He is not always successful, as a poet, but he is always himself.

His greatest success, undoubtedly, was the poem which first brought him fame, "David". In a rather over-enthusiastic article, Roy Daniells has compared this poem, as the turning-point in the development of a literary tradition, to Spenser's *Shephearde's Calendar*. The judgment is too kind, but we can see why it was made. "David" is a poem to which almost anyone can respond, and yet one which will repay almost any amount of literary analysis. This story of mountain-climbing and of a final tragic fall is ideally suited to Birney's various talents. Birney can describe nature accurately and suggestively; he can build a story to a climax by a series of small, telling moves; he can reveal human strength and human weakness; he can supply realistic detail and at the same time suggest symbolic overtones. All these things he does to perfection here. As Daniells has shown, Birney has employed every means at his disposal—a flexible verse-form, enjambment, echoes and partial correspondences of sound, alliteration, images of motion, a mounting series of sub-climaxes—to give to the poem a sense of uninterrupted movement. The tragic climax, when it comes, seems at once inevitable and unexpected.

But Birney has never since risen to the heights he achieved in this, his first important poem. The *David* volume contains other good poems—notably "Anglo-Saxon Street", "Slug in Woods", "Hands" and "Dusk on English Bay"—but none which approach the title poem. The average level of *Now Is Time* is, if anything, higher, but there is no single poem to set beside "David". Here Birney's tendency to root his poems in the present—the tendency suggested by his choice of title— frequently betrays him, as it also has betrayed Pratt in recent years, into writing not only of but merely for the moment. This is not true, however, of the best poems in this second volume, such as "Man on a Tractor", "Joe Harris" and "World Conference". This last poem, the best in the book, will give some idea of his quality:

> The quiet diesel in the breast
> 　propels a trusting keel
> Whether we swing toward a port
> 　or crocodiles of steel.
>
> The compassed mind must quiver north
> 　though every chart defective
> there is no fog but in the will
> 　the iceberg is elective.

Birney's third volume, *The Strait of Anian*, proved, disappointingly, to be mainly a reprinting of poems selected from his two first volumes. The best of the new poems, however—"Man is a Snow", "Prairie Counterpoint" and "This Page my Pigeon"—show him in full possession of his own distinctive gifts. In 1952 he published *Trial of a City,* containing a verse play and thirteen new poems. The play is a minor triumph, but the poems are disappointing. The play is ostensibly the trial of the City of Vancouver, but it broadens out into a trial of humanity, and into a final vindication of the value of human life. It provides an opportunity for the display of many of Birney's best qualities: his humour, his strong sense of topicality, his irony and his sturdy common sense. Only occasionally does the humour become too "literary", too self-conscious and coy. The short poems in the book, however, with the possible exceptions of "North Star West" and "Takkakaw Falls", are much too obviously contrived.

In recent years, Birney's output of verse has been very sparse, and he has devoted the major portion of his attention to prose fiction and criticism. It will be a pity if he gives up the craft of verse, for although he is not a brilliant poet he has distinctive gifts: a sensuous precision which has no need of rhetoric to be effective, a loose, loping energy which seems designed for the long run rather than the short sprint, a knowledge of the work and ways and manner of thought of the ordinary man which makes his verse more genuinely a people's poetry than much self-conscious proletarian verse.

Earle Birney was only one of the many Canadian poets who made their reputations during World War II. Charles Bruce, Ralph Gustafson, Anne Marriott, Irving Layton, Patrick Anderson, Miriam Waddington, P. K. Page, Louis Dudek and Raymond Souster—all these poets produced at least one volume of verse between 1939 and 1946. In addition to these, there were many poets who contributed good verse to magazines and anthologies: Margaret Avison, Ronald Hambleton, Kay Smith, A. G. Bailey, Bertram Warr, Floris Clark McLaren, James Wreford and Elizabeth Brewster. There is obviously not space to give detailed treatment to all of these; instead we must be content to indicate the main tendencies of the period.

Canadian poets of the forties were decidedly leftist in politics and experimental in verse form. They derived their attitudes from the English left-wing poets of the thirties, especially from Auden and Spender, and their forms from these poets and from Dylan Thomas and George Barker. Most of them were poets of the city rather than of the farm or the sea, and their manner was more frequently satirical than lyrical. They found media for publication in the little magazines which were founded during the war years (*Contemporary Verse*, 1941; *First Statement*, 1942; *Preview*, 1942; *The Fiddlehead*, 1945) and in various anthologies (Ralph Gustafson's *Canadian Poetry (English)*, 1942; Smith's *Book of Canadian Poetry*, 1943; *Unit of Five*, 1945; and John Sutherland's *Other Canadians*, 1947).

Seven individuals deserve special thanks for this unprecedented outburst of poetic activity: Alan Crawley, Patrick Anderson, A. J. M. Smith, Ralph Gustafson, Lorne Pierce, John Sutherland and E. K. Brown. Alan Crawley founded *Contemporary Verse* in 1941 with the specific object of encouraging the new poetry in Canada, and showed almost impeccable taste in the choice of good poetry and in providing sympathetic and perceptive reviews of the current output of verse. Patrick Anderson arrived from England in 1940 full of the rhythms of Dylan Thomas and fired with the conviction that poetry must play its part in the social struggle. He proceeded to establish *Preview* and to gather an eager band of disciples around him. Smith and Gustafson, through their anthologies, brought the new poetry to the attention of a far wider audience than read the little magazines. Lorne Pierce, as editor of The Ryerson Press, kept a watchful eye on the magazines and brought out volumes by the young poets as soon as he felt they were ready for book publication. John Sutherland founded and edited *First Statement*, arranged its merger in 1945 with *Preview* to form *Northern Review*, initiated in 1945 a series of little books known as "The New Writers Series", and edited a lively anthology called *Other Canadians* for which he provided a provocative introduction. E. K. Brown's role was the publication of *On Canadian Poetry* (1943), which championed the cause of the new poetry and stirred Canadian interest in it, and the annual reviews of Canadian poetry which he contributed to the *University of Toronto Quarterly* series, "Letters in Canada".

Much of the poetry of the war period, undoubtedly, was

ephemeral, and much of it already seems dated. To re-read *Preview* now, with its naive talk of making poetry a weapon, is a disillusioning process. There was so much solemn cant about it: one would have thought the whole Canadian war effort, the very defeat of Fascism, depended on the continued existence of this little mimeographed monthly. "Two events of great importance to the Writer have occurred in recent weeks", wrote Anderson solemnly in February, 1943. "One is the Russian offensive, the other the conference at Casablanca". In the same issue he wrote: "Our task is clear: not only to help in the winning of the war by our literary work . . . but also to supply something of the personal, the graceful and the heroic to the atmosphere of this half-empty Dominion". Mr. Sutherland does not come off much better. His introduction to *Other Canadians* was engagingly humorous. Some of the humour was intentional—he scored some neat hits off A. J. M. Smith, who probably enjoyed the fun as much as anybody—but the funniest parts today are the unintentional humour of remarks like this: "If God still talks to these poets in private, he carries less weight than Karl Marx or Sigmund Freud. The seven-day fireworks of the world's creation matter less than the creation of the socialist state; the cure of earthly ills is to be achieved by economics or psychology rather than by divine intervention. . . . Mr. Smith's oxygen tent with its tap to the spirit will keep a few remnants breathing for a while, but can hardly impede the growth of socialism in Canada, or prevent the radical consequences which must follow for the Canadian writer. The future in this country is already beginning to move".

It is easy to have the wisdom of hindsight; easy to see now how wrong these critics were in thinking that poetry was having any real effect on the war effort or that utopian socialism was soon to be realized in the Dominion of the North. And the poetry was frequently as shallow as the criticism. But at least there was critical excitement, and at least the poet, in the conviction that his words were important, was ready and eager to write. Looking back, we can envy their sense of belonging—envy Anderson's ability to write in full seriousness: "In a people's war the writer can feel at home".

The many poets whom we listed above can be divided into two main groups. There was the group which clustered about Patrick Anderson, and published most frequently in *Preview*. This group included holdovers from the thirties such as F. R. Scott, A. M. Klein and Ralph Gustafson, and new poets such as P. K. Page, Ronald Hambleton, James Wreford and Neufville Shaw. Most of these poets had an English background or were university graduates with intellectual interests and a cosmopolitan outlook. The second group clustered about John Sutherland, published its work mainly in *First Statement,* and included Irving Layton, Miriam Waddington, Louis Dudek, Raymond Souster and Kay Smith. Its members were more Canadian in background and emphasis, more proletarian in origin and affiliation, and emotional rather than intellectual in their approach. (Of course these generalizations are not wholly accurate, but they are broadly true.)

Patrick Anderson (born 1915) severed his connection with Canada soon after World War II, but he deserves a place in this history for the stimulating role he played in Canadian poetry during the forties. He was, if nothing else, a most effective catalyst, an enthusiastic, word-intoxicated man who brought a new sense of excitement into our literary life. Evocative words and images poured from his pen in rich profusion. These opening lines from "Summer's Joe", probably his finest single poem, will give some idea of his fertility of imagery:

> He unlocked an apple first, then lifted the latch
> of the ancestral tree,
> whistled amongst the tall corn gaily
> like a scythe of birds:

on the shore the lion waves lay down on their paws
and above the trodden sand
a storm of gulls made sadness as white
as April does . . . .

Each line is so brilliant, the onward rush is so swift, that we
are dazzled and whirled as if at a carnival. We do not pause
to ask what the poem means: we only know that by the end
we have undergone a tremendously vital experience. But the
meaning is there, if we search for it: if I read the poem
correctly, it is the account of a boy's growth into responsibility, of his dawning recognition that in neither nature nor
love can he escape his social function.

But the meaning somehow seems incommensurate with
the means employed to convey it, and this is a valid criticism
of many of Anderson's poems. The rockets make a brilliant
display, but they trace out a meagre, inconclusive message.
Nowhere is this exhibited more clearly than in the con-
cluding section of his long and intermittently successful
"Poem on Canada". In a splendid burst of rhetoric,
Anderson perorates:

> let the Canadian,
> with glaciers in his hair, straddle the continent,
> in full possession of his earth and north
> dip down his foot and touch the New York lights
> or stir the vegetable matter of the Bahamas
> within the Carib gutter. Let
> the skiers go with slogans of their eyes
> to crowd a country whose near neighbourhood's
> the iron kindness of the Russian coasts—
> through deserts of snow or dreary wastes of city,
> the empty or the emptily crowded North.

We feel our patriotic pulses stirred to action—but what,
precisely, would he have us do?

A similar confusion weakens most of Anderson's pro-
gramme poems. We get not really a programme, but what
Mr. Eliot has called "undisciplined squads of emotion".
Anderson's exuberance is really a form of sentimentality,

and there are other forms of sentimentality in his work, as witness this poem, "The Airmen":

> Then we were drinking, come in from ruin.
> Suddenly our oaths were pitched like tents
> on the dark hill side—under the goatshair
> our whiskey breath moved like lights.
> We were all nomads, and each man mindful
> of tender flock, his milkwhite wishes.

Anderson is at his best when he forgets his desire to "fuse the lyric and didactic elements in modern verse", as he put it in the foreword to *Preview*, and is content merely to sing or to describe a scene. Then, as in the last stanza of "Drinker":

> He tastes with the iron pipe the very roots of water
> spreading under the ground, which in multitudinous dirt
> and infinite threaded dark are purified—
> he drains the long stalk of water up between his lips
> and in his sandy mouth there bursts its melting flower . . . .

or in this stanza of "Camp":

> So all a summer's day
> of a Sunday drowned in green,
> we flourished in that country
> and no one ever came
> but the sun with a hand of brass
> stood in his height of sky
> and poured the map like a cup
> to run upon the place,
> spilling it carelessly . . . .

he is capable of a far more important fusion, the fusion of form and content, of idea and expression.

One of the poets on whom Anderson exerted his fascination was Miss P. K. Page (born 1917). Anderson's influence on her was not, however, wholly salutary. It provoked her into quickened activity, but it led her to essay, like Anderson himself, the role of a propagandist poet. But Miss Page has little talent for propaganda, and most of her programme

poems are even less satisfactory than Anderson's. Her poem
"Generation" reads today like a parody of the early Auden:

> Tragically, Spain was our spade;
> the flares went up in the garden.
> We dug at night;
> the relics within the house
> sagged.
>
> Walking down country lanes
> we committed arson—
> firing our parent-pasts;
> on the wooded lands
> our childhood games grew real:
> the police and robbers
> held unsmiling faces
> against each other.

Miss Page's special gift is for the sympathetic interpretation
of other people rather than for such parlour politics. Nobody
can match her in the capacity for making us feel what it is
like to be a typist in an office or a probationer in a hospital.
Her best work is essentially feminine, the product of intuitive
understanding. Especially well can she convey to us the
world of childhood, as in the lovely final stanzas of "The
Band and the Beautiful Children":

> But the children move
> in the trembling building of sound,
> sure as a choir
> until band breaks and scatters,
> crumbles about them and is made of men
> tired and grumbling
> on the straggling grass.
>
> And the children, lost, lost,
> in an open space,
> remember the certainty of the anchored home
> and cry on the unknown edge of their own city
> their lips stiff from an imaginary trumpet.

The theme of this poem—the quest for beauty, for
innocence or for love—is the dominant theme of Miss Page's

best poetry. We find it in "Personal Landscape", the first poem of her first volume (*As Ten, As Twenty*, 1946), where the search for love is symbolized as a search for solid ground; in "Round Trip", which describes a futile search for home, and in the poignantly tragic "If It Were You".

Miss Page has a very distinctive poetic technique. Her verse is ripe and rich, as sensuous almost as that of Keats. It is packed with alliteration and assonance, and overflowing with images. Images drawn from anatomy and images in which the organic and the inorganic are strangely blended occur frequently and give a peculiar but often very apt effect. Here are a few examples:

> he notes the place where the sienna soil
> makes an incision in the field of mustard . . . .
>> "Round Trip"

> in such sweet rain his ears and armpits grew
> flowers and humming birds were part of him . . . .
>> "Round Trip"

> In countries where the leaves are large as hands
> where flowers protrude their fleshy chins . . . .
>> "Stories of Snow"

All of the qualities we have mentioned—the sympathetic understanding, the symbolic journey, the richness and the peculiar imagery—occur in what is undoubtedly Miss Page's finest single poem, "The Stenographers". Here is the last stanza:

> In the felt of the morning the calico minded,
> sufficiently starched, insert papers, hit keys,
>> efficient and sure as their adding machines;
> yet they weep in the vault, they are taut as net curtains
> stretched upon frames. In their eyes I have seen
> the pin men of madness in marathon trim
> race round the track of the stadium pupil.

Miss Page published a second volume of poetry, *The Metal and the Flower*, in 1954. This confirmed but did not enhance her reputation. In some of the poems the effect is of ingenuity rather than of genuine skill, and the general impression is of a talent that has worked itself out. In "Photos of a Salt Mine", however, she managed to reach the highest level of her earlier work. In recent years Miss Page has turned from poetry to painting and drawing, and in the new medium she is achieving similar effects of the weird intermingling of the organic and inorganic worlds. Her poetic contribution, though limited, was a real and valuable one. No one in Canada has portrayed more movingly the plight of the vulnerable individual trapped in "a world he never made".

James Wreford (born 1915) was, like Patrick Anderson, something of a bird of passage in Canadian poetry. He arrived in this country just prior to World War II, and left soon after it. His poetry, however, did make a strong impact in Canada, appearing in most of the Canadian literary periodicals, in the joint volume *Unit of Five* (1944), in the anthologies of Smith and Gustafson, and in his book *Of Time and the Lover* (1950). His earlier work was social in emphasis, and revealed the influence of the English left-wing school, particularly that of W. H. Auden. Thus in "Early Willows" we find him writing:

> There is no bargain basement no
> last January sale shall get
> a cut rate peace, a short cut to
> relieve the mounting debt.
>
> The corner drugstore noways can
> both diagnose and salve the grief
> that winters in the heart of man
> despite the swiftly pushing leaf. . . .

and in "Kirkland Lake":

> Under the dark industrial sky
> we wonder why we have to die
> who living, were valued at a wage
> that starved our youth and murdered age.

By the time he published *Of Time and the Lover,* however, his interest in social justice had largely given way to an interest in the joys of love and the flight of time. Echoes of Auden persist, but an even stronger influence here is that of Gerard Manley Hopkins. Many of the poems are marred by lapses of taste, carelessness of structure and lack of melodic richness. It is when Mr. Wreford, who was a professor of geography at McMaster University, draws upon his knowledge of the earth sciences as the source of imagery that he achieves a measure of originality. In his work as a whole there is far too much of the pastiche.

As we have said, Wreford's work appeared first in book form in a joint volume entitled *Unit of Five.* This volume, which also included poems by Louis Dudek, P. K. Page, Raymond Souster and Ronald Hambleton, was edited by the last-named. Ronald Hambleton (born 1917) is a poet quite similar to Wreford, being heavily indebted to Auden for the tone and technique of his verse, and writing of the social problems of the war and post-war period in a metaphysical style. His work has facility and wit, but it often loses its direction in a tangle of verbosity. His only independent volume of verse, *Object and Event,* was published in 1953. More recently he has given most of his attention to radio scripts, and to his comic but inconclusive novel of British Columbia life, *Every Man Is an Island* (1959).

The net product of this school of metaphysical and social poets was, then, rather disappointing. Anderson and Wreford left Canada and virtually gave up the craft of poetry soon afterwards; Miss Page and Hambleton persisted for a few more years, but they too abandoned poetry early in the fifties. They did as a group, however, provide a good deal of excitement during the forties, and they furthered the efforts of the Montreal Group to introduce a new type of poetry into Canada and to discredit the old type of conventionally pretty verse. They gave Canadian poetry a new element of intellectual sophistication and they brought it into closer contact with the realities of an industrial society.

The other main school of Canadian poetry during the
war and immediate post-war years was, if less immediately
exciting, of more lasting significance. Louis Dudek, Irving
Layton, Miriam Waddington and Raymond Souster were
more deeply rooted in the Canadian soil than the meta-
physicals whom we have just been considering, and their
poetry was drawn more directly from the stuff of their own
experience. Although they were influenced to some extent
by the English left-wing school and by American proletarian
poets, they were much less derivative than Anderson,
Wreford and Page. They expressed their dissatisfaction with
the existing state of Canadian society in a more distinctly
North American idiom, and their work was marked rather
by honesty and sincerity than by sophistication and metaphysical ingenuity. They spoke a plainer and more emphatic
language, and addressed themselves bluntly and sometimes
coarsely towards the social issues of their time. Whereas the
metaphysical group began brilliantly and soon lapsed into
repetitiveness or into silence, each member of this social
realist school began hesitantly, rather clumsily, but gradually
acquired greater assurance and authority. All of them continued to practise the craft of poetry through the forties,
fifties and into the sixties.

The senior member of this group, and the one who has
gradually established himself as its leader, is Irving Layton
(born 1912). Layton's first book of verse, appropriately
entitled *Here and Now,* was published by John Sutherland's
First Statement Press in 1945. His dissatisfaction with the
Audenish antics of the metaphysical school, and his own convictions about the nature of poetry, are succinctly expressed
in one stanza in this collection:

>Since Auden set the fashion
>Our poets grow tame;
>They are quite without passion,
>They live without blame.

Thus early, Layton had marked out his own path: poetry must be the product of the poet's own experience rather than of poetic fashion; the poet must wage war upon conventional attitudes and standards of behaviour: poetry must be passionate, it must express what in more recent years he has been prone to call the Dionysiac element in life; and the poet must be free in his personal life and convictions, ready to draw down upon his head the wrath of society for his defiance of their cherished values. This is the manifesto for a poetry of revolutionary individualism.

In the decade and a half since 1945, Layton has certainly practised what he then preached. He has been a most prolific poet, producing no less than fourteen volumes in sixteen years, and he has steadily grown in assurance and authority. He has not allowed himself to be discouraged by early neglect, nor to be spoiled by later adulation. It is true that he has sometimes published poems which would have been better discarded as exercises, and that in some of his prefaces he has been guilty of arrogance and attitudinizing. The fact remains that he has shaped his own poetic instrument with patience and unexcelled devotion, that he has been fearless in revealing to the world his own often unconventional and unpopular beliefs and actions, and that his poetry has gradually acquired that resonant assurance which is the mark of the major poet. It seems indisputable that Irving Layton will be remembered as the major Canadian poet of the mid-twentieth century.

Perhaps the most striking feature of Layton's poetry is its versatility. He can be tender and compassionate, coarse and arrogant, witty and ironical, angry and sarcastic, sensual and passionate. One of the best examples of his gift for tenderness is the title poem of *The Bull Calf and Other Poems* (1956), the first stanza of which reads:

> The thing could barely stand. Yet taken
> from his mother and the barn smells
> he still impressed with his pride,

with the promise of sovereignty in the way
his head moved to take us in.
The fierce sunlight tugging the maize from the ground
licked at his shapely flanks.
He was too young for all that pride.
I thought of the deposed Richard II.

Here we can see many of Layton's qualities. There is his realism, which takes account of the barn smells and refuses to prettify or to turn a blind eye to ugliness and pain. There is his sense of the immense, almost terrifying vitality of nature —"the fierce sunlight tugging the maize from the ground". There is his Blakeian conviction that all that lives is holy: here the calf is invested with a quasi-divine majesty, and in other poems Layton has found a similar magnificence in creatures as conventionally mean and petty as sheep, frogs and even mosquitoes. There is his accurate observation of the appearance of things, seen here in his notice of the tottering stance of the young calf and throughout his poetry in his descriptions of people and places: Layton is a poet who does full justice to the visible universe. There is also —and this in itself is a mark of Layton's versatility, since one tends to think of him as a non-intellectual poet—his erudition, marked by the reference to Richard II. Increasingly Layton's poetry has been enriched by references to the figures of myth and legend, of history and politics, of science and literature. He is not only, in other words, a poet who sees clearly the immediate world about him, but one whose mind is richly stored with a knowledge of other times and other places.

But above all in this brief selection we see the "double vision" of Irving Layton: his simultaneous perception of the glory and horror of life on earth. Layton is a poet who must both curse and bless; he sees the triumphant vitality, the sovereign pride of the calf, but he sees also its imminent destruction. Similarly the sun—which over and over again is a central symbol in his poetry, and which provides the title for his finest collection so far, *Red Carpet for the Sun* (1959)

—is ambivalent. It is creative, bringing growth to the corn
and warmth to the calf, but it is also destructive, fierce,
terrifying.

Even in a few short lines meant to illustrate Layton's
tenderness, then, we have found proof of the versatility of
his gifts and the complexity of his apparently simple vision.
Open his books almost at random and you will find poems
that similarly expand upon reflection into increasingly significant statements. Here, for example, is a brief, unpretentious
little poem called "First Walk in Spring":

> I pass out of the door into the garden.
> From my favourite tree one limb's broken.
> An insect, egotist, strums his soliloquy
> At my ear.  I walk out under the open sky.
>
> Theoretical man, my eyes have marked
> Mounds of earth piled high and dark.
> Earth, shovelsful—think of it—
> In which to be born and buried.
>
> Brown pods, brown leaves that lie
> Beside quickening things, a kind of parody
> On them and their increasing passion
> But that's a thought that's out-of-season
>
> When everywhere beyond my hands I see
> Green shoots, conferva near the railway;
> And grasses, young ferns, that sprout into air
> Wispy as a twelve-year-old's pudendal hair.

This has the casual innocence of a poem by Traherne—but
also Traherne's suggestiveness. Again we have the simultaneous sense of hope and fear, of life and death, of birth
and burial.  The dead pods and leaves make life and struggle
seem faintly ridiculous: but it is the growing things, the
shoots struggling upwards to flowering, that the poet permits
to have the last word. The final line, which at first seems merely
to illustrate what some people have described as Layton's
obsession with sex, is actually an organic part of the poem,
since it relates the cycle of life in the non-human world to

the similar cycle in the world of humanity, and contrasts
the retrospective ("my favourite tree") mature man with the
forward-looking young girl on the verge of adolescence and
fertility.

Indeed a special word should be said on Layton's treatment of sex. Of all Canadian poets, he is easily the most
successful in his handling of this difficult theme. He is
obsessed with sex only in the sense that he recognizes its
central importance in life, and sees that in its combination
of beauty and ugliness, pleasure and pain, it is a microcosm
of the total human condition. As in all other respects, Layton
shows great versatility in his use of sex in poetry. Sometimes,
as in "Earth Goddess" or "The Day Aviva came to Paris",
he is content merely to celebrate the joy of sexual desire and
fulfilment; at other times, as in "Dialogue with a Young and
Pretty Wife", he shows his awareness of the transitoriness
of sexual pleasure; and sometimes, as in "Librarian at
Asheville", he sees the morbid obsession into which sex can
deteriorate.

These four lines serve as the epigraph for Layton's most
recent book, *The Swinging Flesh* (1961), which contains
both short stories and poems:

> "Affirm life," I said, "affirm
> The triumphant grass that covers the worm;
> And the flesh, the swinging flesh
> That burns on its stick of bone."

They sum up more concisely and suggestively than I could
ever hope to do the reiterated theme of Irving Layton's
poetry.

Miriam Waddington (born 1917) also had her first book,
*Green World,* published in John Sutherland's First Statement Press series in 1945. She is a much more quiet and
unspectacular poet than Layton, but she has a persuasive
sincerity that is very winning.

*Green World* established quite clearly the general outlines of her work. The book's dominant theme was the beauty and goodness of the natural world, expressed by recurring images of greenness and growth, and the ugliness and evil of contemporary industrial society, evoked by images of angles, coils, tunnels, walls and "tangles of hot streets". Within human society, the one positive liberating force was seen as love, whether love in the sense of charity or "loving-kindness" or love in the sense of sexual attraction and union. Unlike most of her Canadian contemporaries at that time, Mrs. Waddington did not speak in terms of socialist doctrine, nor indeed of any dogma, and although there were occasional references to the hope for a better social order there was no attempt to be specific about the causes of social chaos or the means of social amelioration. These early poems were simple, colourful, melodic and easy; they had spontaneity and verve, a youthful affirmation and exuberance modified only slightly by twinges of pity, anger or disgust.

In *The Second Silence* (1955) the themes remained much the same. Nature and love were still the main positive attractions, and the sufferings of modern industrial man the main sources of discontent. A decade of experience had, however, broadened the scope of her poetry. Love, especially sexual love, was given more complex treatment, revealed as a source of frustration and pain as well as of satisfaction and pleasure. The discussion of social evils was more specific, being related frequently to the plight of individuals whom Mrs. Waddington had encountered in the course of her duties as a social worker; and the experience of maternity provided her with material for poems on childbirth and the child's view of the world. But if there was a gain in breadth there was something of a loss in verve: there was occasionally a note of weariness or of querulousness. The technique had developed in a similarly paradoxical way: the verse forms were more intricate and skilful, there was more technical sophistication, but at the same time there was a faintly artificial air, a hint of contrivance, in some of the poems. The best poems in this second volume, however, retained the directness of her earlier volume and exhibited a richer sensibility.

Mrs. Waddington's third volume, *The Season's Lovers* (1958), did not mark a spectacular change in either her themes or her techniques. Nature played a slightly less prominent part, but meadows and flowers were still her chief symbols of happiness and of the creative freedom which she finds so sadly lacking in the life of our large cities. She still celebrated love in both its sexual and non-sexual forms as the chief value in human life and, indeed, in several of the poems including the title poem, as a truly miraculous force which transforms the world. She continued to pour out her compassion for those victims of our social disorder whom she encounters in her social work. The only new theme was that of art, seen as another of the forces that can at least temporarily liberate man from suffering.

In technique, there was a more conspicuous development. She has obviously become convinced that the simple free verse technique which she used almost exclusively in her first two volumes needed the disciplines of rhyme and rhetoric. Her use of rhyme is often advantageous, but her attempts at a more sophisticated rhetoric, at metaphysical ingenuity of image and syntax and epigram, often seem merely laboured.

In her poem "The City's Life" Mrs. Waddington writes of herself:

> All she has are her own human channels,
> Eyes that observe, a pulse that beats,
> A heart that moves to other troubled hearts.

and in these lines she has clearly expressed both the strengths and limitations of her poetry. The honest self-evaluation of the passage is symptomatic of the directness with which at her best she responds to the world about her. She is an accurate observer of nature and society, and her pictures of persons and places are frequently the most memorable passages of her verse. Her "pulse that beats" may be taken to symbolize her capacity for passionate response to the call of love: some of her best poems, such as "Arabian", "The Season's Lovers", "In the Mountains" and "In the Sun" are primarily love poems. As for the "heart that moves to other troubled hearts", this results in the sympathetic studies of the unfortunate which are found in such poems as "Old Women of Toronto", "Three Prison Portraits" and "My Lessons in Jail". The chief desideratum in her poetry is a set of original or strongly-held ideas: there is something passive about her poetry, a lack of passionate conviction and assurance. For this lack, however, she largely atones by the quickness and sensitivity of her emotional responses.

Louis Dudek (born 1918) has been a very active figure on the Canadian literary scene since he made his first debut in the early forties in the pages of *First Statement* and in *Unit of Five*. He has subsequently published eight volumes of poetry—*East of the City* (1946), *The Searching Image* (1952), *Twenty Four Poems* (1952), *Cerberus* (jointly with Layton and Souster, 1952), *Europe* (1955), *The Transparent Sea* (1956), *En Mexico* (1958) and *Laughing Stalks* (1958)— has edited, with Irving Layton, an anthology of Canadian poetry, has produced since 1957 the literary magazine *Delta*, has acted as editor of the McGill Poetry Series (a series of volumes by young poets), and has written a number of critical essays on the subject of Canadian poetry.

Although he is a highly educated man, holding a doctorate from Columbia and a professorship of English at McGill, Dudek writes his poetry in a simple, straightforward style. There are far fewer mythological, historical and philosophical references in it than in that of Irving Layton or even of Miriam Waddington. What he is trying to do, he has said, is "to give as purely as possible the experience which is pure and isolated in my mind"; the result is that most of his poems consist of brief descriptions of things or places very much in the Imagist manner, or of expressions of his own state of mind. His poems are very unpretentious, almost at times naive and sentimental. They make their appeal by their honesty and directness, by their capacity to evoke a scene or a mood. In spite of the fact that in his criticism Dudek is often controversial and angry, the prevailing note in his poetry is tender wistfulness. He is a foe of the acquisitive, noisy, mechanical civilization of our day, but he prefers to indict it by implication rather than by explicit condemnation. His favourite device for achieving this effect is to find, in the midst of industrial or urban ugliness, the tree, the bird, the flower or the child which by its simple beauty makes the disorder of its surroundings manifest. It is then, certainly, that he is most successful; when he attempts direct social didacticism he usually falls either into the platitudinous or the pompous.

There would be little point in making a chronological survey of Dudek's poetry, for it has undergone few changes. In the early poems of *Unit of Five* and *East of the City* he makes a few Marxist gestures, but even here the predominant quality is the tenderness of which I have spoken. Gradually such vaguely revolutionary lines as "But carry an axe of stone to this murderous civilization" have disappeared from his work; but they were never very frequent nor uttered with much conviction. His most characteristic and successful work is found in such short lyrics as "Bird at the Window" (from *Twenty Four Poems*) in which the social criticism is implicit:

> Your cracked flute, your hurt
> harmonica, nimble nothing
> at my window, may be a tinkle among
> the traffic, a penny in a blind man's
> teacup, but never mind
> make your song, even though it hurts,
> scratch it out on the sky
> and show them the sharp beauty there is
> in a bird.

This lyrical celebration of life is found also in the love songs which are predominant in his 1956 volume, *The Transparent Sea*. In such poems as "Lover to Lover", "Marriage" and "Divine Touches" Dudek reveals his capacity for evoking genuine emotion and for the melodic arrangement of language. In other poems in this volume, such as "A Man Crying", Dudek evokes successfully a mood of wistful longing, a sense of the loneliness and alienation which the sensitive individual must feel in the present order of things.

Another aspect of Dudek's talent is revealed in *Laughing Stalks*: his gift for light literary and social satire. The volume contains, for example, a delightful sequence of parodies on Canadian poets. There are also some neat gibes at Canadian literary critics. This one I believe should be set down in this book as a reminder to its readers—if any is needed!— that critics are far from infallible:

> The beauty of being a critic
> is that one can write as if one were infallible
> and be forever wrong.
> For if one makes a howling error
> of judgment such as casting talent
> aside, or throwing obloquy
> on genius, or praising an ass
> one can forget, later, like one's readers
> and praise what one called a bore
> as infallibly as before.

Dudek's most ambitious poetic efforts so far have been the two long reflective travelogues, *Europe* and *En Mexico*. In both of these books Dudek combines a skeletal narrative of his own travels, incidental descriptions of persons and places, and social and aesthetic commentary. The result in each case is only intermittently successful, since the loose free verse form which Dudek almost invariably adopts betrays him into diffuseness and repetitiveness. *Europe* is the more

uniformly interesting of the two, and may be used to
illustrate his method. It begins rather flatly with a description of the journey down the St. Lawrence River, but reaches
genuine lyricism in some of the passages describing the
Atlantic Ocean:

> The sea loves to move
>     but it is in no hurry,
> flops over languidly like an easy animal
> waiting for storms,
>     never still.

The second section, dealing with England, has little to say
that is original or striking, and often lapses into such platitudes as "Courtesy is pleasing, saves us from barbarism" or
"And what more pleasant than well-bred English people?"
The sections dealing with the Continent proper are given
some substance and continuity by Dudek's reiteration of two
themes: the deterioration in European art and culture which
set in with the Renaissance (an idea he borrowed from Ezra
Pound, whose disciple in some senses he is), and the contrast
between the meanness of Europe's present and the glories
of its cultural past. His descriptions of places such as the
cathedral at Chartres and of some of the persons he meets on
his travels are often exact and suggestive, but he sometimes
is guilty of surprisingly prudish or priggish remarks
such as "the street urinals of Paris [are] simply disgusting to any aesthetic sense". Poem 63 effectively sums up the
theme of the whole sequence of poems:

> A girl with a load of hay on her head,
>     another leading a donkey . . .
> But slowly one comes to realize
> that the Europe we have come to see
> of old art, stored antiquity
>     and the beautiful customary life
>         of towns and villages,
> hardly exists at all.

A subsidiary theme, that of the relation of art and morality, is summed up in poem 77:

> Good art is the record of a good society,
> A society without art has proved itself corrupt
>     by absolute demonstration.
> We must look to our ethics.

This long sequence of poems is sometimes dull, sometimes platitudinous, sometimes perceptive, always honest and sincere: it is a courageous attempt to record exactly what Dudek saw and felt.

We come back, then, to where we began. The strength of Dudek's work lies in his strenuous attempt to give as purely as possible the experience which is pure and isolated in his own mind. The result is seldom brilliant or profound, but it is always genuine.

Raymond Souster (born 1921), the fourth leading member of this school of social realism, is the most simple and straightforward of them all. Perhaps because of this simplicity, and his complete absence of pretension, he has never received the recognition which is his due. He is in my opinion one of the most delightful and memorable poets whom Canada has produced. Since the early nineteen forties Souster has been consistently producing good poems, and although there has been no significant development in them there has been no deterioration either. He has published some twelve books of verse, including *When We Are Young* (1946), *Go to Sleep World* (1947), *City Hall Street* (1951), *Shake Hands with the Hangman* (1953), *Selected Poems* (1956), *Crepe-Hanger's Carnival* (1958) and *Selected Poems 1955-58*. He has edited the mimeographed little magazines *Contact* and *Combustion,* and has been the moving spirit in Contact Press, a co-operative publishing venture which has brought before the public many books of verse which the commercial publishers would not risk. His influence has been quiet but pervasive and uniformly salutary. At a period when so many

Canadian poets have been turning away from the drabness or the ambiguity of their own society towards the more manageable and obviously attractive world of myth, Souster has consistently kept his eyes on the objects around him, and found the substance of poetry in the stuff of his own experience.

The hasty reader of Souster is apt to derive an impression of monotony from the long succession of brief, casual, matter-of-fact poems. A more careful reading, however, reveals the fact that there is a good deal of variety here. It is a variety of tone and attitude rather than a variety of technique. In the earlier books especially the tone is frequently angry, as Souster rails at the cruelty and futility of war, the injustices of a capitalist society, the ugliness of the industrial landscape. "Phoney War" is a good example of his angry poems:

> It seems that rifles fire blanks or they're all
>     cockeyed to hell like the kind in shooting-galleries,
> And shells merely nudge you on the shoulder if
>     over-slept, or jingle your nerves a bit so you
>     get sick-leave for nothing at all,
> And flame-throwers are just pretty little Roman
>     candles that give the most wonderful lighting
>     effects after dark,
> While the bayonet comes in handy if the
>     roast beef is a trifle rare.
>
> And everybody has weekends off and goes to bed
>     with their lovers or their wives.
> And every man is a hero, his name will be long
>     remembered
> When the war is over, and if you should
>     accidentally die
> Your soul will lie at rest on the breasts of a
>     dozen angels.

Anger at the system of things, of course, implies pity for its victims, and the note of pity is sounded by Souster perhaps more frequently than any other. In the early war poems, it is pity for the ordinary soldiers and airmen who must die in a cause they do not understand.  In the poems of city life, it is pity for the lonely and the outcasts—for old beggars, prostitutes, kids who lack proper playgrounds, lovers who have nowhere to go when they wish to make love.  Here, for example, is "The Penny Flute":

> On the side-street as we came along it in the darkness
> An old man, hat beside him on the pavement, was
>     playing a penny flute.
> The sound was small and sweet, almost a whisper
>     against the muffled roar
> Of the machinery in the cloth factory across the street.
>     He was not playing
> For an audience, but almost for himself.  I wondered
>     who he was
> And how long he'd been standing there piping
> That thin string of music.  But we were late for
>     where we were going
> And young and impatient; we didn't have time for
>     old men and lonely tunes.
> Especially tunes played on a penny flute.

That is very real and moving.  Sometimes, however, Souster's pity degenerates into self-pity and becomes mawkish, as in this "Litter of the Last Rose":

> Litter of the last rose
> Rough-handled by the wind
> And laid out onto the grass.
>
> In the short sundial sweep of your life,
> That happy interval between bloom and the
>     beginning of decay,
> I read my own life
> Climbing swiftly now to its zenith.

Another, more affirmative, tone in Souster's poetry is the passionate celebration of love.  He rivals Irving Layton in the honesty and frankness with which he writes of sex. "When We Are Young", for example, catches very well the way in which two young lovers, caught at a boring party,

yearn to be alone together.  The reality of desire is caught
with equal success in the brief "Poem for Her Picture":

> Behind you the lake, the boat, the sand,
> But I cannot see past your body dressed in its covering,
> Cannot see past your upturned hair, your smile.
>
> You need no backgrounds,
> No one would see them anyway.
>
> O my warm goddess,
> Step down from the wall
> And we will span the blackness of two years
> In our eyes' and our lips' first touching together.

This sense of the wonder of love is complemented by his
wonder at the magical world of nature.  A poem such as
"Lagoons: Hanlan's Point" recaptures that childish awe with
which the young boy greets the world, and "The Lilac
Poem" rivals Herrick in its ability to express delight in
little things:

> Before the lilacs are over and they are only
> Shrunken stalks at the ends of drooping branches,
> I want to write a poem about them and their beauty
> Brief and star-shining as a young girl's promise.
>
> Because there is so much made of strength and wealth
>     and power,
> Because the little things are lost in this world,
> I write this poem about lilacs knowing that both
> Are this day's only: tomorrow they will lie forgotten.

There are many other moods and attitudes which Souster
can recreate successfully—boredom, for example, terror and
gay fantasy—but I hope I have indicated by the illustrations
above that Souster's poetry has range and the ring of truth.
Out of very simple materials, in a simple, colloquial language
and in a very direct, unsophisticated style he has written
poems which, in my opinion, will not be allowed to "lie
forgotten".

In addition to the members of these two main schools of Canadian poetry in the forties, there were a few other poets who made their debut in the period and deserve brief mention. They might, indeed, be said to constitute a third school, since they were mainly university professors who wrote more calmly and traditionally than the members of either the Anderson or the Layton schools. This third group included L. A. MacKay, whose chief book of verse, *The Ill-Tempered Lover*, appeared in 1948; Roy Daniells, author of *Deeper into the Forest* (1948); Charles Bruce (*Grey Ship Moving*, 1945, The *Flowing Summer*, 1947, and *The Mulgrave Road*, 1951); George Whalley, who published his *Poems* in 1946 and *No Man an Island* in 1948; Douglas Le Pan, author of *The Wounded Prince* (1948) and *The Net and the Sword* (1953); Alfred G. Bailey, whose poems were written in the nineteen forties although they did not appear in book form (*Border River*) until 1952; and Ralph Gustafson, better known as an anthologist, but a poet whose published work extends from *Epithalamium in Time of War* (1941), *Lyrics Unromantic* (1942) and *Flight into Darkness* (1944) to *Rocky Mountain Poems* (1960) and *Rivers Among Rocks* (1960).

L. A. MacKay (born 1901), who has been a leading critic of Canadian poetry as well as a poet, had published a chapbook of poems, *Viper's Bugloss,* in 1938. His *Ill-Tempered Lover* reprints the fourteen poems which the chapbook contained and poems which had been appearing in the magazines during the intervening fifteen years. The book is divided into four sections: "The Ill-Tempered Lover", a series of twenty short poems tracing the course of a love-affair from its idyllic beginning through growing frustration and bitterness to a final desolating sense of loss; "1936-46", a group of topical poems on the League of Nations, the Spanish Civil War, appeasement and World War II; "Hay on His Horns", a series of satirical poems on Canadian themes; and "Car-

minis Interea Nostri Redeamus in Orbem", a group of lyrics
and descriptive pieces.  In the first section, the early poems
are more successful: the angry poems are too angry to be
credible, and they are nearer to rhetoric than to poetry.
There is, however, one very vivid sonnet on the theme of
suffering in love—"Stript Bare, Strung up on Tiptoe".  The
poems in the second section express a sour disillusionment
with the course of recent history.  The best poems in the
section are those in which MacKay parodies hymns for
satirical effect—"The Battle Hymn of the Spanish Rebellion"
and "Carol for 1938".  But already most of the poems in this
section have badly faded, for they seldom succeed in univer-
salizing their topical themes.  The same is true of many of
the poems in the third section, but occasionally, as in these
lines satirizing materialistic conceptions of Canadian destiny,
MacKay says something of permanent validity:

> First then, we'll ask
> What's our ambition?  Why, we aim to be
> The Empire's, nay, the whole world's granary.
> A lofty mark, i' faith; to find our place
> Just in the belly of the human race.

But it is in the fourth section, quieter in tone and less angry
in mood, that MacKay is at his best.  In poems such as
"Admonition for Spring", "Hylas", and "Song for a Fence-
post", he reveals a gift for impassioned song and for the vivid
description of landscape.  Here is "Admonition for Spring":

> Look away now from the high lonesome hills
> So hard on the hard sky since the swift shower;
> See where among the restless daffodils
> The hyacinth sets his melancholy tower.
>
> Draw in your heart from vain adventurings;
> Float slowly, swimmer, slowly drawing breath.
> See, in the wild green foam of growing things
> The heavy hyacinth remembering death.

Such polished lyrics are comparatively rare in MacKay's book, but they are the staple product of Roy Daniells (born 1902). His *Deeper into the Forest* is the product of an extremely fastidious sensibility which recoils from the vulgarity and violence of the age and seeks escape in the precision of art, the complexity of myth and the peace of nature and love. The virtues of Daniell's poetry—its exact use of words, its subtle rhythmic effects and its projection of a distinctive personal vision—are limited by his tendency to become somewhat arch and precious in manner and to indulge in private allusions. The first group of poems in his book, the "Anthony" sequence, is particularly vulnerable to these accusations; the third section, "Farewell to Winnipeg", is an attempt at a kind of poetry for which he is not suited; but the title section and the "Epithalamion in Time of Peace" have the virtues almost unalloyed. They coexist most perfectly, perhaps, in this sonnet from the "Deeper into the Forest" sequence:

> Sick with the long displeasure of the chase
> The legendary bird of the burning land
> Halted, and thrust his tired head in the sand.
> Behind him breathed the hunt in rapid race
> Yet for a moment his was darkness, peace.
> The gentle suasion of the abraded grains
> Worn from the rock to softness eased his pains
> With the still dream of a green ancient place
> Remote and safe.  Let us regard this bird
> With compassion and with envy; not for you
> Remembrance (of a voice in the garden heard)
> In timeless quiet e'er the huntsmen strike.
> This microcosmic vision, this review
> Are not for you; think what your end will be like.

Charles Bruce (born 1906), is a pleasant if not particularly forceful poet whose chief talents are for the description of natural scenery in a rather austere, stripped style and for a sort of gentle, relaxed introspectiveness. There is a strongly Wordsworthian quality in his work, a quiet contemplative dignity, an unspectacular strength, a steady accumulation of exact and telling small details. His best book is probably *The Mulgrave Road,* which won the Governor-General's Award as the most distinguished book of verse published in Canada in 1951. In this volume he reminisces about the places and persons of his native Nova Scotia, evoking in apt words and images the slow, repetitive processes of life on the farms and the fishing villages. A traditional talent, then, but not a reactionary one: there is in his work none of that conventional prettiness or sentimental gush which is so often found in regional poetry of this sort.

George Whalley (born 1915) is a similarly quiet and unpretentious poet. Even in *Poems 1939-1944,* which is primarily concerned with his experiences as a naval officer in World War II, the predominant note is one of quietness and peace. He can evoke the mood and sensations of a moment in a few sharply etched lines:

> Under the seawall the rivertide
> plucked softly in the darkness.
> The bridge, black against the night,
> breasted the urgent water
> with a low sound. A duck,
> unseen on the foreshore,
> started and woke, quacked
> in anger at loss of balance,
> was still and slept again.

His portraits of people, such as "W. K. E.", "Q. A. M." and "A Girl in Love", are wistful and tender, the expressions of a restrained and disciplined humanism. His work is lacking in strength and brilliance, but it has great reserves of grace and charm.

Douglas Le Pan (born 1914) is a much more sophisticated and brilliant poet than either Bruce or Whalley. His first volume, *The Wounded Prince,* was introduced by C. Day Lewis, who said of his poems, "They do not innovate technically; nor are they offering a new apocalypse or a guide to the atomic age: they seem to me original in the sense that they spring from an imaginative, serious and intelligent mind, an adult personality, to which poetry is the natural recourse. This is a poetry which comes halfway to meet you. It has an air at once friendly and independent: no confidence tricks, no seeking to flatter or impose upon you, and on the other hand no wrapping itself up in cabbalistic robes and terrified jabber". The main theme of the volume is the plight of humanity caught in the maelstrom of war, and seeking comfort in friendship and love: "There is no fireplace but the warmth of human hands". Le Pan seeks to buttress the human will to endure by recalling the heroic or sacrificial acts of the past, as in the colourful portrait of the mythical "Rider on the Sands", the ultimate reference to Christ's martyrdom in "Canterbury" or the celebration of the courage of the "Coureurs de Bois". A similar theme marks *The Net and the Sword,* where the subject is the experiences of the Canadian Army in Italy. The style is often rich to the point of luxuriance, and he has been nicknamed "peacock Le Pan" and berated for his excess of decoration. Certainly there are poems in which the baroque style seems out of keeping with the brutal matter of death and violence; on the other hand the result sometimes is most memorable. Here, for example, is the beginning of "An Effect of Illumination", describing a bombardment at night:

> A peacock train of stars along the water-stairs
> of the castled hill;
> And the mild eye, innocent of its destiny,

Pale swimmer through blue, planetary light
Now lips the lymph and milky dream of heaven,
Plucks meteors idly like thin, golden threads
That rustle through the lapis lazuli,
Through shot-silk over silent, velvet water.
But those low, lion winks awakening the horizon?
O innocent and distant, chime harmless as
The toll of patiently revolving bell-buoys.

Then systole of sky. Stillness become
A lion's den.
Wild meteors falling in our laps.  Flames.
Dragonish flames and cries that call for breath.

In this passage, surely, the elaborate, ornate language and imagery is very effective in building up just that sense of voluptuous luxury which affords the desired contrast for the sudden brutal ferocity of the raid.

If the texture of Le Pan's verse is somewhat too close and rich for the touch of the ordinary reader, it is as nothing to the metaphysical density and subtlety of the last poet in this group, Alfred G. Bailey (born 1905). Bailey is certainly the most difficult and different poet in contemporary Canada, bringing to bear on his work a mind that is stocked with history and mythology, with anthropological and religious lore. His poems inch their way forward in tortuous, crablike rhythms, giving the reader the feeling that he and the poet together are embarked on a journey through a dark, impenetrable and forbidding wood. The persistent reader, however, finds the journey rewarding: there are fascinating glimpses along the way, and a final vision of man as a wanderer seeking friendship, love and ultimately redemption in a world from which these things have been almost irretrievably lost. The lines, because or in spite of their defiance of the ordinary processes of logic, vibrate and re-vibrate in the head, until they create a logic of their own and impose their meaning. "The Winter Mill" may illustrate the curiously haunting effect of these poems:

> The winter mill will not return this
> often
> a granary for months of ill at
> ease.
> Nor will the thaw engage to round and
> soften
> the burden of its coffin; from the
> knee
> to thigh and upwards cold as any fish
> hook
> will it look to sweep a mist from sunken
> eyes,
> nor gather to its heart its cherished
> april.
> Of it with book and pen record these
> cries.
> The winter ambit has us with its
> finger,
> and muscle hardens when it seems to
> break
> like tooth once bitten and forever
> ache.
> And there's no stoic tethers soul to
> eye
> with batting of this scene that only
> waits.

Ralph Gustafson (born 1909) is also a difficult poet, learned and elliptical. His early work—as indeed the early work of Bailey—was traditional in form and content, but from Gerard Manley Hopkins and Dylan Thomas he learned to distort syntax in order to achieve added emotional effect, and to use words in unusual combinations. This gives to much of his verse a mannered quality which scarcely seems appropriate: one feels that basically Gustafson is a romantic poet whose eager response to love and nature might be more fittingly presented in simple form. In some of his poems he is more direct, and in them he reveals a melodic gift of a high order. The constant theme of his poetry, early and late, is the splendour of the natural environment and the delight of human love: he is always seeking the "rivers among rocks", the life-giving forces which exist among the harsh and dangerous circumstances of war and social disorder.

The thirty years from 1920 to 1950, then, saw much activity in Canadian poetry. The emergence of E. J. Pratt and of the Montreal School in the twenties marked the beginning of the modernist movement; in the thirties there was a slackening caused largely by the depression and the difficulty of finding publication; but in the forties Pratt and the Montrealers were joined by a whole host of new poets. Never before had there been so many interesting poets writing in Canada at a time. Birney and Livesay wrote their poems of social protest and humanitarian zeal; Patrick Anderson, P. K. Page and their school united political radicalism with metaphysical wit and passion; Dudek, Layton, Souster and Waddington wrote their moving personal lyrics or their bitter commentaries upon a disordered civilization; the academic poets brought learning and sophisticated craftsmanship. It was a period of great excitement and promise, of the spawning of new periodicals and presses, of impassioned debates about the nature and aims of poetry and in particular about its responsibility to society. And the appearance in 1949 of James Reaney's *The Red Heart* indicated that the excitement and achievement might well continue into the fifties.

# CHAPTER SEVEN

# Modern Canadian Fiction
## 1920 – 1950

As WE have seen, the great bulk of Canadian fiction in the nineteenth and early twentieth centuries took the form of either the historical romance or the regional idyll. The thirty years 1920-1950 did not see a sharp break with those traditions: both forms were extensively cultivated, and in quantity novels and short stories of these two types still predominated. But the scope of Canadian fiction broadened in these three decades, and in this broadening lay the chief hope of the future. The best novels were those which transcended these classifications, especially those of Frederick Philip Grove, who brought a fierce honesty to the regional novel and thus made the term "idyll" singularly inappropriate, of Morley Callaghan, who deliberately set his work in the wider context of American and European fiction, and of Hugh MacLennan, who used a regional base but built on it a national structure.

But Grove, Callaghan and MacLennan were not alone in introducing a new sense of reality into Canadian fiction. Many young novelists turned their critical gaze upon the contemporary scene, and treated it realistically, symbolically or in a manner which combined realism and symbolism. They began to experiment with new techniques and to venture new ideas. The result was that, although no single great novel was produced, and although our fiction still lagged behind our poetry, the average level of craftsmanship perceptibly rose and the gap between the two forms was considerably narrowed.

## I. The Historical Romance

This improvement of quality was true even of the modern Canadian historical romance, for although no writer equalled Kirby's single masterpiece, a number of writers approached it. Laura Goodman Salverson, Frederick Niven, W. G. Hardy, F. E. D. McDowell, Thomas Raddall and Will R. Bird, to name only the most prominent, all wrote novels which combined an interest in vivid scenes and vigorous action with a concern for historical and psychological verisimilitude.

Laura Goodman Salverson (born 1890) specialized in the history of the Icelandic settlers. She began promisingly in 1923 with *The Viking Heart,* which describes the arrival and ultimate assimilation into Canadian life of a group of these settlers. This first novel is unmistakably romantic in emphasis, but it is given substance by an authentic account of the domestic life and early hardships of the pioneers. The hardships are always surmounted, sometimes by rather incredible means, but at least they are not ignored. The whole novel is pleasant in tone and vivid if somewhat flamboyant in style, and at the time of its appearance it was hailed as the initiator of a new era of realism in Canadian fiction. Recent criticism is less enthusiastic, but the novel seems assured of a continuing audience.

In her later novels, Mrs. Salverson has not yet fulfilled the promise of her first. *When Sparrows Fall* (1925) deals less convincingly with second-generation Scandinavian settlers in the northern United States; and *Lord of the Silver Dragon* (1927), *The Dove* (1933) and *Black Lace* (1938) are costume melodramas of the type popular in women's magazines. *The Dark Weaver* (1937) is much better than these, but even it falls short of *The Viking Heart*. Like *The Viking Heart*, *The Dark Weaver* is a chronicle of Scandinavian settlement on the Canadian prairies, and it has authentic touches of observation and description. But the canvas is too crowded, and the total effect is confused; structure, the weakest element in *The Viking Heart*, is also the weakest element in this novel. Her most recent novel, *Immortal Rock*, was published in 1954, and attempts to reconstruct the legendary visit of Norsemen to Minnesota in the fourteenth century. Again an essentially romantic story is given a degree of authenticity by a careful attention to detail and a controlled style.

Probably the most enduring of Mrs. Salverson's books is her autobiography, *Confessions of an Immigrant's Daughter* (1939). This has all the virtues of her two best novels—the power to recreate the details of domestic life, to record the privations and simple joys of the pioneers and to describe the physical environment of western Canada—without their faults of romantic exaggeration and hyperbole.

Frederick Niven (1878-1944) is another historical novelist who dealt with the settlement of the Canadian West. Although Niven had published several novels before coming to Canada in 1920, and continued to write others which have no relation to this country, he can legitimately be considered a Canadian novelist by virtue of his prairie trilogy, *The Flying Years* (1935), *Mine Inheritance* (1940) and *The Transplanted* (1944). *The Flying Years*, as its title suggests, sets out to portray a swift panorama of life in the West from the middle of the nineteenth century to the third decade of the twentieth. Its theme is that of much of Charles Mair's poetry: the decay of the primitive nobility of Indian life as a result of the "progress" of white settlement and civilization. *Mine Inheritance* deals with the earliest period in the history of the West: the Selkirk Settlement of 1812-1821. In this book Niven attempted, somewhat too ambitiously, to represent symbolically the whole history of the West as the primitive life of the Indians and the nomadic activities of the fur traders yielded place to the more stable life of agricultural settlement. *The Transplanted* completes the trilogy by portraying the development of a British Columbia mining town from its raw, lawless beginnings into an orderly community.

As these summaries would suggest, the chief defect of Niven's novels is their tendency to be overweighted with theme and history. His characters are projections of ideas rather than living beings, and no amount of verisimilitude in the account of their dress, speech and customs can make up for this fundamental lifelessness. Another weakness of the novels is the episodic nature of their structure: incident follows incident, but scarcely ever is a scene "arranged", given its full scope and emphasis.

One thing, however, Niven could do extremely well: he could describe the scenery of the West in a prose which was clean, sparse and yet vivid. Exact observation is combined with a fine sense of mood in such passages as this, from *The Flying Years*: "No smoke came from the tepees, but a fire crumbled into ash before them, sending up, as is the way of red-willow well alight, more of odour than of smoke into the air. A mere sift of blue, a haze of blue, ascended from that natural meadow in a long thin wisp, and was caught by the draught of the stream's passage, drawn away trembling above its flow, a pennant of blue turning above the turnings of the creek so that its further course could be traced some distance by that gauzy riband among the tree-tops." Once again, the landscape of Canada elicited from a writer that imaginative sympathy which her people and her history could not elicit.

W. G. Hardy (born 1896), although a resident of the West for many years, has not joined Mrs. Salverson and Niven in writing of that area; rather he has chosen to set his historical novels in the lands bordering the Mediterranean. *Father Abraham* (1935) is a romantic melodrama of the life and loves of the father of Israel; *Turn Back the River* (1938) provides a similar treatment of ancient Rome in the days of Catiline and Clodia; *All the Trumpets Sounded* (1942) seeks to recreate the life, and especially the love-life, of Moses; and *City of Libertines* (1957) , as its title suggests, is a highly-coloured picture of Rome in its period of decadence. These novels certainly possess vigour, and they are based on considerable historical research and antiquarian knowledge, but they are sensational in emphasis, flamboyant in style and too complex in structure. In 1951 Dr. Hardy attempted, with only partial success, a novel of contemporary life in Ontario, *The Unfulfilled*. His best work is found in his short stories, where he is frequently more quiet, modest and truly imaginative.

A conspicuous feature of W. G. Hardy's novels is his attempt to relate the episodes of the past to the issues of the present: in *All the Trumpets Sounded,* for example, a parallel is suggested between the sufferings of the ancient Jews under the Pharaohs and the sufferings of the modern Jews under Hitler. In this he is followed by F. E. D. McDowell (born 1898) who, in *Forges of Freedom* (1943), attempts to establish that the Peasants' Revolt of fourteenth century England forged the freedom of the common man. *Forges of Freedom,* however, is not the novel by which McDowell is apt to be remembered. For his first, and far superior, novel, *The Champlain Road* (1939), he chose a subject more traditional with Canadian writers: the martyrdom of the Jesuit missionaries in old Huronia. Even here McDowell attempts to establish a contemporary relevance, for he sees in the fall of Huronia the key to all North American history. But it is not the thesis which makes this novel one of the finest historical romances yet produced in Canada; it is rather the clever way in which McDowell blends fact and fiction, history and romance. He has followed his documentary sources as closely as Niven followed his, but he has succeeded, as Niven did not, in making the documents live. Where McDowell departs from his sources, however, as he does in his account of the adventures of Godfrey Bethune and Diane Woodville, the novel becomes melodramatic and unconvincing.

A notable development in the modern Canadian historical romance has been the tendency to combine an interest in the past with an interest in a particular region, thus uniting the two main streams of Canadian fiction. This combination, displayed in the work of L. G. Salverson and Frederick Niven in the West, has been equally apparent in the work of two Maritime writers, Will R. Bird and Thomas R. Raddall.

Will R. Bird (born 1891) has been the more prolific of the two. For almost twenty years he worked in obscurity, but he came into national prominence in 1945 when his *Here Stays Good Yorkshire* shared the Ryerson Fiction Award with Philip Child's *Day of Wrath*. He has since published seven novels—*Judgment Glen* (1947), *The Passionate Pilgrim* (1949), *So Much to Record* (1951), *To Love and To Cherish* (1953), *The Shy Yorkshireman* (1955), *Tristram's Salvation* (1957) and *Despite the Distance* (1961)—and a volume of short stories, *Sunrise for Peter* (1946).

Mr. Bird to some extent anticipated the best qualities of his later and better known novels in his early *Maid of the Marshes* (1936), where he selected the region with which he has become identified—the Chignecto Basin of Nova Scotia—and displayed his power to evoke the atmosphere of its marshes and dykes and meadows. But he also revealed his chief weaknesses: his imperfect sense of structure, his tendency towards sentimentality and melodrama and his carelessness of style.

Mr. Bird's most recent novels have a strong family resemblance. They are all set in late eighteenth century Nova Scotia, they are all packed to overflowing with strong-willed, turbulent characters, they are all concerned primarily with the careers of private individuals and only secondarily with the impact of public events upon them, and they are all written with a gusto that carries us irresistibly forward in spite of many misgivings.

*Here Stays Good Yorkshire* is perhaps the best, and may be considered as typical. In the foreword Mr. Bird, following the new fashion in historical fiction, stakes his claim to documentary accuracy: "Every care has been taken to present the arrival and establishment of the Yorkshire families as accurately as possible. The documents dealing with discharged members of the Royal Highland Emigrants are exact copies of originals in the Nova Scotia Archives; only the names are fictitious." Obviously anticipating the charge that his characters are so multitudinous as to be confusing, he then sets out a list of the principal characters which includes the names and basic data of no less than forty-five persons. Characteristically, the novel begins with a fight: Bird is obsessed with physical violence, and fights and brawls of one kind or another occur in almost every chapter. As we follow the course of the story, we are aware that the writer's greatest gift is an abounding vitality. Like a Fielding or a Dickens, if only in this respect, he has an immense narrative fecundity: people and incidents spring to his mind in such rapid succession that he has scarcely time to set them down before they are crowded unceremoniously off the stage by others. There is an obvious lack of artistic discipline, too little regard for selection and arrangement, but the narrative moves so quickly that we have scarcely time to notice those things. Everything is vibrant with activity: a man does not simply take a bath, he takes "a thumping fine bath"; when a girl kisses him, it is a kiss that "sets him back on his heels". And there is plenty of humour too: humour as substantial and as palatable as Yorkshire pudding. The old father enjoys sleeping upstairs alone because he can sleep with his stockings on every night without anyone knowing it; when one of the sons is about to warm the bed for his bride with a warming pan she says, "Jonty, darling, do we need it? I thowt I could warm thee?"

All this is so natural, so vigorous and primitive and heart-warming, that only the carping critic is uneasily aware of a certain slipshod quality in the style and structure.  Bird does not trouble to search for the unusual phrase: the colloquial cliché will serve his turn.  "They had supper in style and Gideon was in his best form."  "She was a worker all right." "It was a grand spring."  He is frequently careless in his sentence structure: "An old person was of no use on a farm, and how could they enjoy life?"  Short, choppy sentences follow one another like chips from the Yorkshiremen's axes: "The settlers answered questions in broken English.  He had been on his land a few years but he did not own cattle. Times were hard."

But such a colloquial, careless style sometimes adds to rather than detracts from the authenticity of the story.  More serious are the structural faults.  The point of view shifts so frequently that we grow bewildered: we are just getting used to the reactions of one individual when we are compelled to see a completely different set of incidents through completely different eyes. As in Niven's novels, we get a series of episodes which are sketched rather than fully rendered.

Will R. Bird is a rough and ready workman, but for his narrative vigour, his ability to bring to life a diverse group of strong characters and his dry folksy humour he has a large popular following.

A much more conscientious craftsman and stylist is his fellow Nova Scotian, Thomas H. Raddall (born 1903) . After serving several years' apprenticeship as a writer of short stories for such magazines as *Blackwood's,* and incidentally attracting the favourable attention of John Buchan, Raddall published his first novel, *His Majesty's Yankees,* in 1942.  He has since published three other historical novels (*Roger Sudden,* 1944; *Pride's Fancy,* 1946; and *The Governor's Lady,* 1960); three novels with a modern setting (*The Nymph and the Lamp,* 1950; *Tidefall,* 1953; and *The Wings of Night,* 1956); three volumes of short stories (*The Pied Piper of Dipper Creek,* 1939; *Tambour,* 1945; and *The Wedding Gift,* 1947) ; and a history of Halifax, *Warden of the North* (1949) .

*His Majesty's Yankees* is a historical novel of Nova Scotia during the American revolution. Like Bird's novels, it is crowded with turbulent characters and with violent events; it differs from Bird's novels in that it is more carefully constructed and written with more distinction of style. The structure is less episodic, and a number of scenes are selected for special emphasis and arranged with telling effect. The attack on Fort Cumberland in particular, the climax of the book, is described with compelling vividness. But, as Stephen Vincent Benét pointed out in a contemporary review, the events which follow this attack are somewhat anticlimactic: "Everything builds up to the attempt upon Fort Cumberland —but the attempt is a failure. After which Mr. Raddall must carry his story on. He does so with skill and interest but the spine of his story has been broken."

*Roger Sudden* is another historical romance based on the rivalry between French and English in Nova Scotia in the eighteenth century. The hero is an outlawed Jacobite who is captured by the Indians, joins the French, but eventually helps in the siege of Louisburg and wins the woman of his heart. As this summary indicates, the material is standard melodrama, but Raddall gives it a certain distinction by his swiftly moving prose and his passion for historical accuracy. His sympathetic account of life among the Indians is especially memorable. But the novel has not the concentrated power of *His Majesty's Yankees* and none of its characters are particularly vivid.

Since *Pride's Fancy,* a swashbuckling tale of colonial privateersmen, represented a further decline from the high standard Raddall had set himself in his first historical romance, it was good to see him turning, in *The Nymph and the Lamp,* to more recent material for fresh inspiration. Already, in some of his short stories, Raddall had revealed a capacity to deal convincingly with the contemporary scene. In this novel he drew upon his own early experiences of life as a wireless operator on lonely outposts off the Nova

Scotia coast.  The chief male character, Matthew Carney, operates a relay station on a barren island, and the novel tells of his first vacation on the mainland, of his marriage and of the difficulties which his wife faces in attempting to adjust to life on the island.  It is in describing the island that Mr. Raddall is most successful: the sea, the fog, the sand, the gulls and other wild life are rendered with convincing realism.  As usual, Raddall also succeeds in keeping the story moving at a rapid pace, and in building up strong suspense.  Carney himself, and the other men of the island, emerge as credible characters, but the woman is, comparatively, a failure, and the last section of the novel is too elaborately contrived.

In *Tidefall* Raddall continued to experiment with more modern material, but disappointingly did not improve on his performance in *The Nymph and the Lamp*.  *Tidefall* is the story of a scoundrel who amasses a fortune in rum-running during the twenties, settles down with his ill-gotten gains in a small Nova Scotia port in 1931, and is thwarted in his hopes of becoming a respectable citizen partly by his own bestiality and partly by the economic depression.  This plot provides opportunities for descriptions of the smuggling activities of the Prohibition Era, of economic conditions in Nova Scotia during the first three decades of this century and of adventures at sea in all kinds of weather and in many types of ships.  All these opportunities, and especially those of describing the sea and ships, Raddall exploits to the full. He is much less successful, however, in dealing with the personal relations of his characters.  The smuggler himself, Saxby Nolan, is too uniformly wicked to be credible or to leave room for suspense about his course of conduct, and the love triangle involving Saxby, his wife and the lonely radio operator fails to convince.

The same strengths and weaknesses marked Raddall's third contemporary novel, *The Wings of Night*.  The setting—a small Nova Scotian town—is rendered accurately and suggestively, but the characters are stereotypes, and the plot becomes increasingly melodramatic as it proceeds.

Perhaps in permanent reaction from the imperfect success of his novels with a contemporary setting, Raddall returned in 1960 to historical romance with *The Governor's Lady,* with which he won a substantial American literary prize and a multitude of readers.

The continuing popular demand for historical romance will no doubt guarantee the survival of this form in Canadian letters, but it is likely to survive merely as a form of popular entertainment rather than as a serious literary enterprise. It is difficult to avoid the conclusion that the long popularity of this form of fiction among Canadian writers arose from a failure of nerve, from a fear of attempting to cope with the complexity and amorphousness of contemporary Canadian society. As that society increasingly takes form, and thus becomes more manageable, it is likely to draw writers away from the past.

## 2. *The Regional Idyll*

The line between the historical romance and the regional idyll, like that between many other literary forms, is by no means sharp and hard. Some historical romances—Salverson's *Viking Heart* and Bird's *Here Stays Good Yorkshire,* for example—are both regional and idyllic, and some regional idylls—such as Mazo de la Roche's *Building of Jalna* and Grace Campbell's *Thorn Apple Tree*—are also historical and romantic. But there are certain differences of tone, emphasis and attitude between the two forms which make the division a convenient one. Whereas the historical romance is concerned to a significant degree with the impact of public events upon its characters, the regional idyll is concerned rather with the private lives of its characters, and if public events occur they are very much in the background. The historical romance tends to be masculine and boisterous in attitude and tone, and is filled with scenes of violent combat and physical passion.  The regional idyll, written predominantly in Canada at least by women, is feminine and domestic in emphasis, and treats of young love, the home and the family.

This form of fiction has not been nearly as prominent in Canada since World War I as it was in the days of L. M. Montgomery, Ralph Connor, Norman Duncan and their lesser contemporaries, but it has had one major exponent and many minor ones.  Of the minor idyllists, perhaps the best known is Grace Campbell (born 1895), who has produced five novels of this type: *Thorn Apple Tree* (1942), *The Higher Hill* (1944), *Fresh Wind Blowing* (1947), *The Tower and the Town* (1950) and *Torbeg* (1953).  The first two of these deal with the lives of the Scottish pioneers in Glengarry in a pleasant, sincere if undistinguished way.  The best element in both books is the vivid re-creation of the daily lives of the settlers, and the love story in each case is merely the sugar on the didactic pill.  The third novel, dealing with the impact of World War II upon a group of young people, has the same wholesome flavour and moral emphasis, but it is marred by a melodramatic final section.  *The Tower and the Town,* like so many novels of this school, is the story of a Protestant minister in a rural Ontario charge.  Mrs. Campbell makes the minister's faith and hardships convincing, but she eventually enmeshes him in a too melodramatic plot.  In *Torbeg* she goes back to the past of the Scottish settlers who constitute the characters of her earlier novels, and deals with the Jacobite rebellion of '45 in a romantic and nostalgic but entertaining fashion.  The work of Grace Campbell typifies very well this school of regional idyllicism: it is honest, wholesome, pleasant and competent, but it lacks depth and scope.

The other minor examples of the regional idyll in this period must be dismissed even more briefly.  They have included Fred Jacob's *Day Before Yesterday* (1925), Patrick Slater's *The Yellow Briar* (1933), Jessie Beattie's *Hill-Top*

(1935), Wilfrid Eggleston's *The High Plains* (1938), Allen
Roy Evans' *All in a Twilight* (1944), Dorothy Dumbrille's
*All This Difference* (1945) and *Deep Doorways* (1947),
Helen Guiton's *A Country Lover* (1948), Roderick Haig-
Brown's *On the Highest Hill* (1949), Jessie McEwen's *Tal-
trees* (1949) and Kathleen Coburn's *The Grandmothers*
(1949). The best of them, probably, are the last four, all of
which are far more distinguished in style and subtle in perception than is usual in this genre.

But by far the most outstanding exponent of this type
of fiction in Canada in the thirty-year period was Mazo
de la Roche (1885-1961). Although she produced a score
of novels, dozens of short stories, several plays, and always
commanded the attention of the leading literary reviews of
the English-speaking world, it is fashionable in Canada to
dismiss her as a mere trifler who persisted in adding novel
after novel to a series in which all but a few die-hards had lost
interest. Her work was declared to be a "triumph of journalistic rather than literary art", and she was accused of falsifying
the Canadian scene, neglecting social history, creating incredible or absurd characters and of being a mere escapist
entertainer. It is my contention that all these accusations
are either false or irrelevant, and that Miss de la Roche was
a far better novelist than most Canadian critics gave her
credit for being.

Professor V. B. Rhodenizer, who accuses her of being a
journalist rather than an artist, supports his contention by
declaring that "Journalistic art seeks the extraordinary, the
unusual, the bizarre, the freakish, the eccentric, and is at
its best when its subject is unique; literary art, especially in
realistic fiction, seeks the typical, the representative, and at
its best attains to universality." Such a statement begs many
questions. If these are the aims of journalistic art, is all
romantic literature, which has substantially these same aims,
to be dismissed as journalism? Is literary art, in the novel,
to be confined to realism? If so, what becomes of such masters

of eccentricity as Sterne, Smollett, and Thomas Love Peacock? Surely the task of the artist is to transmit an imaginative vision of reality. The element of imagination may predominate, as in romantic literature, or the element of reality, as in realistic literature; the test of worth is not in the proportions in which the two are blended (though both must be there) but in the degree of consistency and harmony which is maintained and the power with which the vision is projected.

But the basic fallacy of Professor Rhodenizer's argument is that he condemns Miss de la Roche for not being something which she did not attempt to be. This is true of most of the other charges made against her. Judged as a realistic novelist she was a failure; but judged as a romantic novelist she projected an imaginative vision of reality which was remarkably consistent and, in its admittedly minor way, powerful and compelling. The Canadian scene which she presented is not typical or representative; but Jalna is a landscape of the imagination which has its own reality and is far more vivid than most photographs of actual places. She did not entirely neglect social history—we get many glimpses of the "jazz age" in *Whiteoaks of Jalna,* for example, and of the economic depression in *The Master of Jalna*—but the writing of social history was not an important part of her artistic purpose. Certainly her characters are not average Ontario farmers, but they are very vivid individuals. Miss de la Roche frequently emphasizes in the novels of the Jalna series that the Whiteoaks are not typical, that they are deliberately and defiantly trying to preserve an ancestral British way of life against the growing pressure of American commercial democracy. (Perhaps the most striking example of this is the family's horror when the provincial government proposes to cut down some of the Jalna trees in order to widen a highway.) The greatest character-creation of them all, Grandmother Whiteoak, is consciously and proudly an anachronism; but what Canadian novelist of any period has ever created as memorable a person? She is absurd in her way, yes; but are not Uncle

Toby and Lismahago and Mr. Micawber equally absurd—and equally alive?

Another charge frequently made against Miss de la Roche is that she has needlessly expanded the Jalna series instead of producing novels with other scenes and characters. It is true that some of the items in the series are relatively trivial; it is true that she never quite recaptured the piquant mixture of strength and charm of *Jalna* itself; but it is also true that some of the later novels in the series are stronger than some of the early ones. More important is the fact that none of the novels outside the series are comparable with the best or even the average novels within the series. Mazo de la Roche, in other words, was wiser than her critics in devoting the major part of her writing time to the Jalna books, for it was there that her talents were most suitably employed.

She began in the early twenties with three novels, each of which in some way anticipated the success of *Jalna*. *Explorers of the Dawn* (1922), a very slight book, revealed her gift for whimsical humour and for the fresh treatment of child life; *Possession* (1923) introduced the device of the intruding strange woman and displayed a power of describing the Ontario landscape; *Delight* (1926) re-employed the device of the intruder, gave her the opportunity of deploying eccentric characters, and established the dominant tone of the forthcoming Jalna series—that of high comedy somewhat in the manner of George Meredith.

But none of these novels were comparable in power with *Jalna*, which in 1927 won the *Atlantic Monthly* prize from among twelve thousand entries from all over the world. Canadians, who had virtually ignored her work hitherto, gasped with astonishment. A leading editorial in the recently established journal, *The Canadian Forum*, put it thus: ". . . the award left only one cause for regret. Once again a Canadian novelist has had to await recognition abroad in order to win appreciation at home. . . . It must be discouraging for an author, conscious of her own purposes, to find herself carelessly classed with the novel-smiths, who turn out easy and imitative tales calculated to attract readers of popular fiction and to win a quick return in royalties. That was largely the fate of Miss de la Roche until *Jalna* opened the eyes of the average Canadian to the fact that she possesses distinctive qualities as a writer. Now they are applauding her, not because her earlier books possess subtle merits, but because the Boston *literati* have decided that *Jalna* is worth $10,000."

The Boston *literati* were right. *Jalna* is a very good novel which can still be read with pleasure. In style, in structure, in the arrangement of scenes and the deployment of characters it is far above the Canadian average. Sometimes the style is a trifle too extravagant, but what Canadian novelist can equal Miss de la Roche's gift for similes? "It filled the air with its rich throaty notes, tossing them on to the bright sunshine like ringing coins." "All faces turned toward Renny, as though his red head were a sun and they sun-gazing flowers." "The young trees stood in snowy rows like expectant young girls awaiting their first communion." The characters are strongly individualized, for the most part in the Smollett–Dickens manner of attaching to each a "humour" and a trick of gesture or mannerism, and the setting, above all the old house, "Jalna" itself, is so vividly realized that it too becomes a character, the most important in the book. The house has an atmosphere, a personal emanation, which constantly affects all its inhabitants, and the novel is a continuous succession of strong, fully realized scenes, diverse in nature and yet each related to the whole.

The novel also has a significant theme. The Whiteoak family, and the house in which they live, stand for something which their creator values and makes us appreciate. They stand, interestingly enough, for much the same set of values as Stephen Leacock stood for: for the traditional virtues of a landed and genteel mode of life, and against the shoddy fashions of the new commercial era. This novel, and the

others in the series, are, we might say, an exercise in primitiv-
ism; they exalt the primitive virtues of physical courage,
frank animal passion, simple emotional intensity. It is no
accident that the dominant image—it has almost the status of
a symbol—of the series is an animal image. The characters
are constantly being compared with animals—Renny with the
fox, Pheasant with the bird of the same name, Grandmother
with "some strange beast [that] had a lair beneath the stairs",
Piers with "the wild things of the wood", Finch with a snuffing
spaniel. It is no accident either that the weaklings of the
novels—Alayne Archer, Arthur Leigh, and the rest—are the
products of a sophisticated, urban society. Alayne Archer is
not, as one critic suggested, the "villain" of *Jalna* because she
is an American, but because she represents an alien and
shoddy urban civilization which must either destroy or capitu-
late to the primitive forces of Jalna life.

The subsequent novels of the series—extending from *The
Whiteoaks of Jalna* (1929) to *Morning at Jalna* (1960) —
closely resemble the first novel in style and theme. It is in
structure that most of them are deficient. *The Whiteoaks of
Jalna* retains much of the coherent power of *Jalna* itself, but
a marked decline is obvious in *Finch's Fortune* (1931) and
*The Master of Jalna* (1933). These latter two novels are
loosely episodic in structure: we continually have the feeling
that the author, aware that the narrative is in danger of
collapse, hastily shores it up with one melodramatic incident
after another. Some of the later novels, however, notably
*Whiteoak Harvest* (1936) and *The Building of Jalna* (1944),
approach the level of the first two. They almost all employ
the device of the intruder who in some way disturbs the
pattern of Jalna life; they are all filled with strong characters
whose passions and feelings have an elemental force; they all
have a strong sense of the past and an equally strong sense of
place. Taken as a whole, and considered as frankly romantic
rather than would-be realistic novels, they are impressive.
There is a trace of exaggeration, but more than a trace of

truth, in Allan Nevins' recent pronouncement in the *Saturday Review of Literature* that "the work begins to stand up as one of the best achievements of Canadian literature, in its way almost monumental."

## 3. *Realistic Fiction*

If the regional idyll blends on one side into the historical romance, it blends on the other into realistic fiction. Some of the novels which we have just considered—notably Mrs. Salverson's *The Viking Heart* and the best of the Jalna series —have realistic elements; and many of the novels which we are about to consider are strongly regional in emphasis. The differences, again, are differences of tone and attitude rather than of substance. The novels to be considered now are, generally speaking, more sombre in tone, they probe more deeply into the lives of their characters, they treat more intensively the social environment and they are less given to sentimental and romantic evasions. They seek, with varying degrees of success, to record and interpret the processes of ordinary life.

There were four major exponents of realistic fiction in Canada in the period under review: Frederick Philip Grove, Morley Callaghan, Philip Child and Hugh MacLennan. Before going on to a detailed analysis of their work, however, it seems proper to give a brief chronological résumé of the development of realism in Canada, and to pay tribute to some of its early practitioners.

If we except the very tentative beginnings in the eighteen nineties, realism may be said to have taken root in Canada in the mid twenties of this century. It was in 1925 that Frederick Philip Grove's first novel appeared; in that year also appeared Martha Ostenso's *Wild Geese*; and in the following year Robert Stead's *Grain* was published. Both Miss Ostenso and Mr. Stead have published several other novels, but it is because of these two that they are likely to be remembered.

*Wild Geese* is a sombre study of pioneer life in Manitoba, and its central figure, Caleb Gare, is a cruel taskmaster who sacrifices the members of his family to the cause of material success.   Like *Jalna*, it won an important literary prize in the United States, and it retains much of its interest for the contemporary reader.   It is powerful in characterization, especially in the case of Caleb himself, vivid in description, and unified in structure and tone.   *Grain* is a less sombre book— Stead has a gift for humour which enlivens even the most serious sections of his story—but it is equally successful in capturing the atmosphere of pioneer life.   It too has a compelling central character—Gander Stake—and some vivid passages of description.   Particularly successful, among the latter, are the accurate and detailed accounts of such agricultural operations as harvesting and threshing. But it is Gander Stake who makes the book.   We watch him grow up on a Western farm, we witness his refusal to enlist during World War I because of a combination of shyness and dislike of discipline, and always we feel that he is completely real and credible.   The middle sections of the book, set during World War I, are especially good; the early part is marred by facetiousness and the latter part by an over-complicated and somewhat incredible plot.

At about the same time that Grove, Ostenso and Stead were writing their early novels in the West, two young writers in the East, Morley Callaghan and Raymond Knister, were beginning to contribute realistic short stories to such *avant-garde* magazines as *Transition* and *This Quarter*. Of Callaghan we shall speak at length later. Raymond Knister (1900-1932) published, in his short lifetime, two novels (*White Narcissus*, 1929 and *My Star Predominant*, 1931), several short stories, a number of poems and the first anthology of Canadian short stories.   He had lived for a time in the American mid-west, had come in contact with the work of such writers as Theodore Dreiser, Sherwood Anderson and Sinclair Lewis, and his own work in fiction has similar qualities: sombreness of colouring, an emphasis on pathos and frustration, an interest in morbid mental processes and in their symbolic expression. His stories are set, however, in rural Ontario, and it is in the fresh description of the life and scenery of that part of Canada that the chief virtue of his better novel, *White Narcissus*, is to be found. The style is marred by traces of preciousness and selfconsciousness, but is obviously the work of a writer who is determined to wrestle independently with language, and at its best it is lyrical and fresh.

By far the most impressive achievement of these early Canadian realists, however, was that of Frederick Philip Grove (1871-1948). Grove made it his chief business to record one aspect of Canadian life: the struggle of the western pioneer to subdue the wilderness. "These people, the pioneers," he tells us in his autobiography, *In Search of Myself* (1946), "reaffirmed in me my conception of what often takes the form of a tragic experience: the age-old conflict between human desire and the stubborn resistance of nature: order must arise out of chaos; the wilderness must be tamed. No matter where I looked, I failed to see that the task of recording that struggle of man with nature had ever adequately been done. . . ." All of his best work, with the exceptions of his autobiography and his early autobiographical novel *A Search for America* (1927), is set in the Canadian West and has the life of the pioneer as its subject. This work includes two volumes of essays—*Over Prairie Trails* (1922) and *The Turn of the Year* (1923)—four novels—*Settlers of the Marsh* (1925), *Our Daily Bread* (1928), *The Yoke of Life* (1930) and *Fruits of the Earth* (1933)—and several short stories, of which the starkly powerful "Snow" is probably the finest. His novels on other themes and with other settings are distinctly inferior to the four in the prairie series. *Two Generations* (1939), a story of farm life in Ontario, is a relatively pleasant but superficial book, and is marred by serious improbabilities of plot and character. *The Master of the Mill* (1944), a novel of industrial Ontario, is an interesting technical experiment and contains at least one powerful character-study, but it too frequently diverges into melodrama. *Consider Her Ways* (1947), a parable-like story of an expedition of intelligent ants to North America, is a literary curiosity which, for all its occasional insight, added little to Grove's reputation.

His reputation rests firmly on his studies of pioneer life in the West, for which he was almost ideally equipped by training and experience. The son of wealthy Anglo-Swedish parents, Grove was in Paris in the days of Flaubert and Zola and was able to apply the techniques of French naturalism to his study of prairie life. In Paris, in Rome and in Munich he had studied archaeology, and this training, with its revelation of the cyclical rise and fall of civilizations, enabled him to look at pioneer life in the long perspective of human history. After the death of his parents, he was stranded penniless in Toronto in 1893, and for twenty years lived as an itinerant farm-hand in the West: as a result he knew the area thoroughly and was familiar with its people and their problems.

The picture of pioneer life which emerges from Grove's six books with prairie settings is perhaps an unduly stark but certainly a powerful one. He can be accused of omitting many of the more pleasant and positive aspects of that life—the work of the churches, the barn dances, the baseball and hockey games—but this is simply evidence of that process of selection to which any artist subjects his material. If the task of the artist is, as we have suggested, to give us an imaginative vision of reality, then certainly Grove is successful. All of his prairie books convey a vision which is at once distinctive and authentic.

It is also a deeply tragic vision. Life for Grove is "a series of continual conflicts"—conflicts between man and his environment, between man and himself, between man and his fellow-men. Each of his central characters has a dream of future fulfilment, and for each the result is frustration. Their dreams are frustrated sometimes by a universe which, in Grove's view as in Hardy's, is blindly indifferent to man's aspirations: his finest scenes are scenes of storm, in which wind, hail, drought, flood or dust assail his characters. On other occasions the hopes of his characters are frustrated by conflicts within themselves, especially by the conflicts arising out of the sexual impulse, which is, to Grove, often a curse. The conflict between man and his fellows usually takes the form of conflict between the generations, as in *Our Daily Bread, Fruits of the Earth* and *Two Generations,* but the relationships between people in his novels are always tense and at least potentially violent.

But if the vision is thus a tragic one, it is not entirely bleak and forbidding. Grove supplements his negative account of man's prevailingly tragic lot with the portrayal of positive human values. His characters never submit tamely to the forces which seek their destruction, and they always manage to preserve their moral integrity. His strongest characters— John Elliot Senior in *Our Daily Bread,* Abe Spalding in *Fruits of the Earth,* Niels Lindstedt in *Settlers of the Marsh*— cling to their conception of the right whatever the odds against them may be. Grove gives no supernatural sanction to this integrity, but he does suggest that if enough men cling to it long and steadfastly general progress may ensue. In the long run he is a meliorist, not a pessimist. As he himself has put it, in *A Search for America,* "We come indeed from Hell and climb to Heaven; the Golden Age stands at the never-attainable end of history, not at Man's origins. Every step forward is bound to be a compromise; right and wrong are inescapably mixed; the best we can hope for is to make right prevail more and more, to reduce wrong to a smaller and smaller fraction of the whole till it reaches a vanishing point."

Whatever may be the ultimate validity of Grove's attitude towards life, there can be no doubt that it is consistently maintained in his books, and that it gives them a power, a solidity and a unity of tone which add immeasurably to their value. We can be less confident, unfortunately, about their technique. The two volumes of descriptive sketches, *Over Prairie Trails* and *The Turn of the Year*, are almost perfect of their kind, but even his better novels are marred by flaws of style, structure and characterization. *A Search for America* has the swiftest pace of all his novels, but it suffers from a too-hurried conclusion and from a tendency to dogmatic digression; *Settlers of the Marsh* explores depths of psychology seldom sounded in fiction, but some of the events border on melodrama, the characters do not always behave credibly and the structure is loosely episodic in parts; *Our Daily Bread* is the best sustained work of art among his novels, but it is rather over-populated with indistinct secondary characters; *The Yoke of Life* has some splendid scenes of poetic symbolism and of natural description, but its climax is too violent and its treatment of sex is rather too lurid; *Fruits of the Earth* approaches *Our Daily Bread* in sustained power, but its ending is somewhat inconclusive.

The style of all Grove's work is open to the charge of stiffness. English was not his mother-tongue, and he wrote it always as a foreigner who had mastered its grammar but not its idiom. This defect is less noticeable in the more formal parts of his novels—the passages of discussion and description —but it seriously affected his power to write convincing dialogue. There is a certain stiffness, too, about the structure of his novels: we do not slip as easily and naturally into the stream of action as we should like, and the stream itself often flows rather sluggishly forward, impeded and diverted by masses of didacticism and technical detail. A similar tendency is discernible in Grove's treatment of character: he did not mix easily with other people, and there is an aloof reserve in his attitude towards them in his books. He can succeed perfectly only with characters fundamentally like himself: strong, stern, ambitious men like John Elliot Senior and Abe Spalding. His adolescents, for whom he had only a slightly disguised contempt, are seldom convincing, and his women are either colourless or too highly coloured.

But subtle characterization was scarcely needed in Grove's type of fiction. He was consciously acting as the spokesman not for individuals but for a race: the race of pioneers. It is Man who is the hero of Grove's novels: Man pitting his strength against the powers of the Universe and his desire to survive against the destructive pressure of Time. His novels are most aptly conceived as parables, and his characters as symbolic figures playing out their parts on the stage of the earth.

Certainly Grove, for all his limitations, is the most powerful novelist Canada has yet produced. There are depths of philosophical and psychological insight in his work which make him the only Canadian novelist worthy to share the company of such men as Hardy, Balzac and Tolstoi. He is not their equal but, like Leacock, he might sit at the same table without embarrassment.

The second most impressive Canadian realist of this period, Morley Callaghan (born 1903), although he shares Grove's sincerity and singleness of artistic purpose, is a very different type of novelist. Whereas Grove's work is hard and angular, Callaghan's is soft and fluid; whereas Grove deals with the clash of strong men with nature and with their fellows, Callaghan deals with the lost, the lonely and the weak. Grove's best novels are set on the prairies; Callaghan's are set in the large cities of Central Canada. The contrasts between them could be multiplied almost indefinitely: Grove's weakest feature, his style, is Callaghan's strongest; Grove is at his best in the long novel, Callaghan at his best in the short story; Grove achieves his effects by the accumulation of masses of detail, Callaghan his by sudden flashes of insight.

The two writers share, however, two very fundamental qualities: they both see man as the victim of hostile external forces, and the dominant response of each to this tragic situation is compassion. In Callaghan's work, however, it is not so much the universe itself which is blamed for man's misfortunes as an ignorant and falsely motivated society. The enemy for Callaghan, as for Leacock and de la Roche, is a society in which commercial values take precedence over human values.

Callaghan is the author of nine novels—*Strange Fugitive* (1928), *It's Never Over* (1930), *A Broken Journey* (1932), *Such is My Beloved* (1934), *They Shall Inherit the Earth* (1935), *More Joy in Heaven* (1937), *The Varsity Story* (1948), *The Loved and the Lost* (1951) and *The Many Coloured Coat* (1960)—and of four volumes of short stories— *A Native Argosy* (1929), *No Man's Meat* (1931), *Now That April's Here* (1936) and *Morley Callaghan's Stories* (1959). In the novels and the short stories alike, Callaghan portrays the plight of the man or woman who, by reason of inherited temperament or early environment, cannot conform to the social pattern of his or her time. In *Strange Fugitive*, Harry Trotter, bored with his job and his wife, seeks escape through the outlaw life of a bootlegger; in *It's Never Over,* Isabelle Thompson feels herself an outcast because her brother has murdered a policeman in a speakeasy brawl; in *A Broken Journey,* a much weaker novel, the central figure is Marion Gibbons who feels incapable of a normal love relationship because of the wild life which her mother has led; *Such is My Beloved* is the story of a non-conforming Catholic priest and of two outcast prostitutes; *They Shall Inherit the Earth,* the best of his novels, deals sympathetically with the plight of a young engineer who has put himself beyond the pale by deliberately allowing his sister's suitor to drown; *More Joy in Heaven* has as its theme the futile efforts of a paroled convict to re-establish himself in society; *The Varsity Story,* a very slight book, has as its hero a New Zealander who is attempting to establish a significant relationship with a Canadian university; *The Loved and the Lost* has as its heroine a girl whom society betrays because she will not conform to its pattern of behaviour towards Negroes; and *The Many*

*Coloured Coat* is the story of a man whom society almost destroys because it cannot believe that the public relations man for a brewery can be the innocently generous person that he appears to be. A similar analysis might be made of almost all of Callaghan's short stories.

Callaghan, then, has a consistent and significant theme. He also has a consistent attitude; one of charity, tolerance and compassion. Scarcely ever does he hold a character up to contempt or ridicule: even his villains are understood and forgiven. Everywhere the stress is on tenderness, on the necessity for love as the basis of all social relationships. The outlook is strongly Christian, and priests and the Church play a large part in his work. His Christianity, however, is not of the institutional variety: the organized Church almost always figures, in his books, as a reactionary force; the priests he admires are the young enthusiasts who do not conform to the will of the hierarchy.

This means, in effect, that Callaghan, though himself a Catholic, is a proponent of a liberal and humanitarian Christianity. The defect of that type of Christianity, and of much of Callaghan's work, is that it often loses sight of the reality of evil. One feels the lack, in Callaghan's novels and stories, of any definite standards by which his characters are to be judged. He succeeds admirably in revealing the shoddiness of most of the prevailing standards, but when it is a matter of suggesting alternatives he can offer only vague words like simplicity, tenderness and compassion. The result is that all of Callaghan's work has a certain moral flabbiness. This is much less obvious in the short stories than in the novels, because the short story can be made out of a moment of insight, a compassionate glimpse of suffering humanity. Of the novel, however, we demand a firm philosophy, a clearly articulated sense of values, and instead of that Callaghan invites us merely to a feast of pity.

This is a harsh judgment; and one must in fairness hasten to add that in so frequently and so effectively arousing our sense of pity Callaghan has done far more than the average novelist. The point is that Callaghan is potentially a very great novelist who has never quite fulfilled his early promise because he has never fully and firmly made up his mind about the basic issues of life. This can best be illustrated by an analysis of three representative novels: *Strange Fugitive, They Shall Inherit the Earth* and *The Loved and the Lost.*

*Strange Fugitive*, his first novel, is a serious attempt at a modern realistic novel of Canadian life. It resembles the work of Ernest Hemingway in its deliberate simplicity of style, its reliance on understatement and its stress on physical sensation, but it has not the precision of Hemingway nor the clear moral values which inform that author's best work. Callaghan here seems to be toying with the theories of the naturalistic novel, since he talks a good deal about the heredity and environment of his characters and suggests that there is an inevitability in their careers. But he does not succeed in convincing us of this, perhaps because he does not really believe it himself. Harry Trotter goes to his destruction in a series of leaps which seem anything but inevitable: they are not even well motivated. The decision to steal the liquor comes as a sudden surprise, as do the fight with the workman and the deliberate murder of Cosantino. Callaghan seems to have been feeling his way in this novel, and he put into it practically every element fashionable in the advanced literature of the day. He does not seem to have made up his mind whether Harry is a victim of heredity, of unemployment, of a vicious environment, of Fate, or of plain bad luck. The novel, therefore, for all its brilliantly idiomatic style and its vivid descriptions of the urban scene, is soft, vague and directionless. It is not a tragic novel because Harry Trotter is not a tragic hero. We cannot accept his nobility: he is too much the cause of his own downfall, he is too violently impulsive, and he does not struggle sufficiently against the pressure of circumstances.

*They Shall Inherit the Earth* is a much better novel, and

had Callaghan carried on where he left off in it he might already have become one of the great novelists of the English-speaking world.  The characters here are much more clearly portrayed, the theme is more definite and the style is more assured.  But even here there is ambiguity, and an ambiguity which we feel to be not deliberate but the result of indecision in the author's mind.  The explicit theme of the novel, suggested by the title, is that the meek, the poor in spirit, shall inherit the earth.  Of Anna, Callaghan writes: "If to be poor in spirit meant to be without false pride, to be humble enough to forget oneself, then she was poor in spirit, for she gave herself to everything that touched her, she let herself be, she lost herself in the fullness of the world, and in losing herself she found the world, and she possessed her own soul. People like her could have everything.  They could inherit the earth."  But William Johnson, the communist, has explicitly condemned this notion in an equally persuasive passage.  There is, then, no clear certainty yet in Callaghan's mind: he, like his characters, is groping for a faith.  On one point, however, he does seem to have made up his mind: the tendency of the book is to reject naturalistic determinism in favour of a theory of individual moral responsibility.  Generally, the book marks an advance because the issues, though not resolved, are presented more clearly and forcibly, and the author's bewilderment is more honestly portrayed.

Callaghan's more recent novel, *The Loved and the Lost*, reveals that he is still confused.  The heroine, Peggy Sanderson, is a girl who has become familiar with Negroes as a child and who, as an adult in Montreal, deliberately associates with them.  All her white friends are horrified at her behaviour, and she is finally raped and murdered by an unknown assailant.  Callaghan invites us to pity and admire this girl, and to despise the whites who cannot appreciate her saint-like purity.  There is much in the novel to admire: Callaghan is still the master of a supple, idiomatic style, of the revealing phrase and of the description of the urban scene. But the old vagueness is still there also. It is easy enough to agree with the author that the prejudices of most of the white characters are disgusting, but is the heroine's deliberate seeking out of Negroes and of Negro night clubs a proper alternative? The girl, who is compared at various times to a saint, a nun and to Joan of Arc, and who yet seems willing to submit to the amorous advances of almost anyone, is simply too sweet to be wholesome. What precisely is our attitude towards her supposed to be? By what standards are her actions and those of her associates to be judged? To these questions the author provides no answer; again he merely invites us to a feast of pity.

But if Callaghan's novels are partial failures, they are very interesting failures, and one wishes that the history of the Canadian novel contained many more such. No other living Canadian novelist aims so high, or comes so close to achieving a high aim. Callaghan may leave us without definite directions, but at least he makes us think. If he does not resolve issues, at least the issues he raises are basic. And for his style, for his deft handling of scene, dialogue and description, there can be little but praise.

Philip Child (born 1898) is more definite in thematic direction than Callaghan, but he lacks the latter's adroitness of technique and ease of style. His interests are quite similar to those of Callaghan: he too is concerned primarily with the "little man" who feels lost and bewildered in a society which is alien to him. In his first book, *The Village of Souls* (1933), a historical novel set in New France, the central figure is Lys de Faverolles, a girl who has been exiled from France and who bears the mark of shame upon her breast; in *God's Sparrows* (1937) our attention is divided among a group of characters who must survive in the alien environment and atmosphere of World War I; *Day of Wrath* (1945) concerns the efforts of an ordinary man of good will to preserve his integrity and dignity amid the barbarities of Nazi Germany; and *Mr. Ames Against Time* (1949) concerns the efforts of a very similar man to preserve his dignity in a sordid, criminal Toronto underworld.

There is no doubt where Child stands. He is frankly and explicitly a Christian humanist who believes that every individual is supremely important in the eyes of God, and that man best serves and glorifies God by manifesting the dignity of His creature. Indeed Child is rather too insistent in making his attitude clear: perhaps because of his pedagogical experience (Child is a professor of English) he is inclined to indulge in frequent didactic asides which impede the progress of his narratives. His style, too, though much of the time it is brisk and workmanlike, occasionally becomes slightly pompous and self-conscious. In *Day of Wrath,* for example, he writes of a doctor who "took out his stethoscope and listened to nature's powerhouse with the devoted expression of a soothsayer studying the auspices". The didactic habit and the slightly self-conscious style are both illustrated in this sentence from *Mr. Ames Against Time*: "A clock ticked over the door at one end of the room, doubtless to remind the prisoner that time, unlike eternity, is mortal."

But though each of Child's novels is open to objection on the grounds of excessive didacticism and occasional flaws of style, each has much of value to offer us. *The Village of Souls* is brilliant in its evocation of the lonely harshness and strange beauty of the primitive wilderness, and presents, in its three main characters, portraits which are clear and convincing. The first half of the book especially is swift, continuously exciting, and yet perfectly credible. There are some melodramatic twists in the plot towards the end, but there are also some vivid scenes. The conflict of faiths and values between Lys, the representative of a decadent European civilization, Journay, the representative pioneer of a new land, and Anne, the representative of a pagan Indian culture, is cleverly and movingly presented. The novel is not so much a historical romance as a parable of man's fate in the wilderness of the world, and its theme is stated explicitly on the last page: "Only in the consummation of love can a man share his loneliness with another and make for himself a dust-speck world within the infinite wilderness, forgetting for a little its pressure which never entirely ceases upon a man's spirit."

*God's Sparrows* also has some brilliant scenes. The early chapters, which describe family life in Ontario, have something of the nimble adroitness of Virginia Woolf and of the irony of E. M. Forster. Some of the later chapters, especially those which describe battle scenes in France during World War I, are almost equally effective. There are some memorable characters—notably Pennel, Dan and Quentin—and the whole book is informed with Child's gentle, humanist spirit. But the total effect of the book is a confused one. The author has tried to crowd in too much: too many episodes, too many people, too many conflicting ideas. The result is that the story line wavers and the theme is not very clear.

*Day of Wrath* returns to a simpler and clearer theme. Simon Froben, a young Jewish writer living in the Third Reich, is convinced that at all costs he must not meet the brutality of the Nazis with hatred; when, in a moment of extreme provocation, he murders a storm trooper, he undergoes agonies of remorse and finally atones for his desertion of his own principles by an act of supreme self-sacrifice. Only thus, Child insists, can we win true freedom: "To be indifferent to one's own fate and to be absorbed in another's, to forget the shrinking of the body of flesh and nerves as completely as if that body were already in the grave and as if the ghost that had driven and been driven by it were already free of it—this was to know freedom." But it is especially in this novel that the theme is too prominent, with the result that Simon, Anna, Froehlich and the rest become mere symbolic figures rather than living human beings. And Child does not have Grove's power of making symbolic figures so profoundly significant that we cease to resent their lack of flesh and blood reality.

*Day of Wrath,* however, appearing with its lesson of love, tolerance and Christian humanism in the final year of a bitter war, is an important, sincere and frequently moving book. *Mr. Ames Against Time* is a much weaker effort.    The fundamental theme, that of self-sacrificing love, is the same, but it is overlaid with such a series of melodramatic episodes that it is scarcely recognizable.    As if to placate the public that demands thrills and a complicated plot, Child here produced a novel which is half detective story and half sermon. The passages of "tough" dialogue which such a novel demands are quite unconvincing, and the crooks who populate this Toronto underworld are figures from a melodramatic movie.    The frequently mentioned parallels with *Pilgrim's Progress* only serve to emphasize the essential superficiality of the narrative itself.    There are, however, some good things in the novel: there are some vivid descriptions of people and places, the fight scene is a rapid and accurate piece of reporting, and Mr. Ames himself is an interesting and credible character.

Child's novels are the product of a man of good will, of considerable learning and of a fine sense of common humanity. He has not yet found the subject perfectly adapted to his gifts, but in *The Village of Souls* and *Day of Wrath,* especially, he has given us two novels which are sincere and moving parables of man's fate.

Hugh MacLennan (born 1907) is another novelist who has not yet found the perfect subject.    Like Child also, he is a didactic novelist whose didacticism and self-consciousness occasionally impede the flow of his narrative stream.    Rather than with the fate of man in general, however, MacLennan has concerned himself particularly with the fate of Canadians and of the Canadian nation.    His work is the most direct reflection in fiction of the growing national self-consciousness which has been such a conspicuous feature of recent Canadian history.

MacLennan began in *Barometer Rising* (1941) with a semi-historical novel of Halifax during World War I. The climax of the novel is provided by the explosion which almost destroyed that port in 1917, and the account of the events which led up to that explosion, and of the explosion itself, is probably the finest piece of sustained writing that Mac-Lennan has ever produced. By a series of quick touches of atmospheric description he builds up almost unbearable suspense, and the explosion, when it comes, has for the reader almost the force which it must have had for the unfortunate inhabitants. The plot of the novel, however, is unduly complicated, and most of the characters are stock figures of romance. It is in the descriptive passages, and in the frequently shrewd comments on Canadian life, that the chief value of the book resides. The strongly national emphasis of MacLennan's later novels is prefigured in passages such as this: "The railway line, that tenuous thread which bound Canada to both the great oceans and made her a nation, lay with one end in the darkness of Nova Scotia and the other in the flush of a British Columbia noon. Under the excitement of this idea his throat became constricted and he had a furious desire for expression: this anomalous land, this sprawling waste of timber and rock and water where the only living sounds were the footfalls of animals or the fantastic laughter of a loon, this empty tract of primordial silence and winds and erosions and shifting colours, this beadlike string of crude towns and cities tied by nothing but railway tracks. . . ."

In MacLennan's second novel, *Two Solitudes* (1945), the interest suggested by such a passage became his dominant concern. The theme of the novel is the quest for Canadian unity, and particularly for unity between the two dominant cultural groups in Canada, the French and the English. The first half of the novel, which concerns the struggle between Athanase Tallard, a progressively minded French-Canadian, Father Beaubien, a reactionary and racially conscious priest, and a group of English-speaking financiers in Montreal, is extremely good. MacLennan succeeds in making the French-Canadian village as real as he had made Halifax in *Barometer Rising*, and all of the characters are distinctive and credible human beings. Even more important, the didactic elements are perfectly fused with the narrative action: the theme of Canadian unity seems to grow out of the action rather than to be imposed upon it from above.

But the second half of the novel, where MacLennan attempts to resolve the dilemma in which the first part had ended, is much inferior. Paul Tallard, the second son of Athanase, marries Heather, the granddaughter of the most sympathetic English-Canadian character in the book, Captain Yardley, and their marriage is supposed to symbolize the end of the racial division. But Paul is not nearly as credible a creation as his father, the events of the latter half of the book seem contrived, and we are conscious throughout of the author as puppet-master pulling the strings to demonstrate a thesis. For all this, *Two Solitudes* is a fine novel, and seems likely to establish itself as one of the few classics of Canadian fiction.

MacLennan's third novel, *The Precipice* (1948), is an almost complete failure. It is more unified than *Two Solitudes*, but it has none of the power of the first half of that novel and little of the atmospheric authenticity of *Barometer Rising*. Still concerned with the theme of Canadianism, MacLennan here attempts to arrive at the essence of that concept by contrasting the life of a sleepy Ontario small town with that of an American city. But the novel is too self-consciously sociological and contemporary, and MacLennan has nothing very fresh or original to say about the issues which he raises. He is not very clear on what "the precipice" is or how it may be avoided: Marcia turns to Catholicism, Stephen goes back to a simple manual job in the bush, but neither of these solutions is presented with passionate conviction. Like Callaghan, MacLennan seems here to be as bewildered as his characters. And these characters are none of them as distinctive as Athanase Tallard or Captain Yardley. Lucy, the heroine, is a colourless woman in whom our interest is never strongly aroused; Stephen Lassiter, the chief male character, is a type of the young American executive; Carl and Marcia, other young Americans, seem more like characters out of a magazine story than real people. The only really credible and interesting character in the book is Matt McCunn, a resigned Presbyterian minister, a raffish old fellow who drinks excessively and makes engagingly cynical remarks about his twin hates of materialism and Puritanism. Even the setting is less real here than in the first two novels, though there are some good descriptions of the Ontario scene and of the city of New York at night.

As if he were aware that he had been over-ambitious in *The Precipice,* MacLennan returned, in *Each Man's Son* (1951), to a less pretentious subject, one reminiscent of *Barometer Rising.* This novel is a regional study of a Cape Breton coal-mining town in the years immediately preceding World War I, and within its more restricted limits it is a much more satisfying novel than *The Precipice.*

Here MacLennan is content to chronicle the lives of simple people in an isolated settlement. He has not, however, been able to resist his tendency to seek for an apparently significant theme, and there is much talk of the curse of puritanism and of a deep sense of guilt. The talk is not very convincing, and its relation to the action of the novel is tenuous at best. But the characters in this book are vibrantly alive, and the minor characters especially—people like Angus the Barraman and Red Willie MacIsaac—are the most vivid people MacLennan has ever created. Moreover he is obviously at home in the Cape Breton environment in a way that he was not in Ontario and New York, and the region is brilliantly re-created. In spite of a melodramatic climax, *Each Man's Son,* though not comparable with the first half of *Two Solitudes,* is a most convincing novel.

*The Watch that Ends the Night* (1959) is MacLennan's most ambitious and complex novel and, rather surprisingly, became a best-seller in both Canada and the United States. It is the story of the return to Montreal of Jerome Martell, a radical surgeon of the thirties who is believed to have died at the hands of the Nazis, and of the effect of his return upon his wife and the man who has become her second husband, George Stewart. Stewart acts as the narrator, and takes us back in a series of reminiscences to his own childhood and to that of the other two characters. He brings the story up, through the depression years of the thirties and the war of the forties, to the present. In the course of this recital we are presented with many vivid pictures of Canadian places, especially of the woods of New Brunswick in which Martell spent his boyhood, of the streets of Montreal in which the characters spent their later years, and some interesting accounts of the fierce political debates which were characteristic of the Depression. But in this novel MacLennan is not primarily concerned with Canadian places or Canadian politics, but with the efforts of men everywhere to come to terms with existence, with life and with death. Through his contact with Martell and his dying wife Catherine, Stewart comes to realize that: "Life is a gift", and that "it is of no importance that God appears indifferent to justice as men understand it. He gave life. He gave it." After fifty years of uneasiness and fear, Stewart is redeemed and reconciled, aware that: "to be able to love the mystery surrounding us is the final and only sanction of human existence."

This novel has both the strengths and weaknesses of Mac-Lennan's early books: a significant but too explicit theme, characters who are rather too obviously symbols of this or that idea, a strong sense of both place and time. In it, however, the strengths are more conspicuous; in particular, the theme is so basic and is expressed with such clarity and persuasiveness that we are willing to overlook the weaknesses of characterization and plot.

The prominence of themes in MacLennan's novels would lead us to expect that he would be a successful essayist. He has indeed published three volumes of essays—*Cross Country* (1949), *Thirty and Three* (1954) and *Scotchman's Return* (1960)—and in them he seems perfectly at home. Were it not for the tyranny of the novel's popularity, now in force for almost a century, it is probable that MacLennan would have been content to express his attitudes in the essay form. In his essays his wise, gentle, compassionate personality finds full and satisfying play.

Although Grove, Callaghan, MacLennan and Child were the chief Canadian realists of this generation, there were signs in the late thirties and forties that they were not long to stand alone. The signs, however, were surprisingly few and far between until almost the end of the period with which we are now concerned. The economic depression of the thirties, and the example of American novelists such as Sinclair Lewis, John Dos Passos and John Steinbeck, might have been expected to produce a host of novels dealing angrily or bitterly with the unemployment, work camps and bread lines of that era. This trend was apparent in the Canadian short story of the period, particularly in the stories that appeared in the decade in *The Canadian Forum, New Frontier* and *Masses.* But it was not until 1939, with the appearance of Irene Baird's *Waste Heritage* and Ted Allan's *This Time a Better Earth,* that social protest became a significant element in the Canadian novel. The most successful attempts to catch the spirit of this time of social chaos came much later in Hugh MacLennan's *The Watch that Ends the Night* and Earle Birney's *Down the Long Table* (1955).

World War II, however, did give the impetus to Canadian realistic fiction that the depression had surprisingly failed to provide. From 1941 onwards, almost every year brought one or two novels that sought to do justice to the complexities of the contemporary scene. Many of these were first novels by writers whose most significant work was done in the fifties, and will be dealt with in a later chapter.   A few of them, however, should be mentioned here, in order that this account may accurately reflect the conditions of the period between 1920 and 1950.

One group of these realistic novels was made up of books about the War itself: Ralph Allen's *Home Made Banners* (1946), Edward Meade's *Remember Me* (1946), Lionel Shapiro's *The Sealed Verdict* (1947), A. J. Elliott's *The Aging Nymph* (1948), Hugh Garner's *Storm Below* (1949) and Earle Birney's *Turvey* (1949).   None of these novels, with the possible exception of the last two, warrant detailed critical dissection, since they were primarily topical journalism cast in the form of fiction, but collectively they were of some importance in establishing the principle that the pleasant and the unpleasant can play a part in Canadian fiction—a principle that needed establishing in view of the vogue of historical romances and regional idylls.   They were also of some importance in bringing to Canadian fiction a vein of ribald humour.   The over-powering propriety and decorum of Canadian fiction was in desperate need of some such challenge.

Another group of novels of the forties dealt with life on the farms and in the small towns of the prairies.   It is a strange fact that almost all of Canadian realistic fiction, until very recent years at any rate, has been set on the prairies.   It was in novels of the prairies, such as those of Grove, Stead and Ostenso, that Canadian realism began, and to this day one can be fairly confident in predicting that a novel about Saskatchewan, say, will be more in touch with reality than a novel about Ontario.   One can only speculate about the reasons for this: perhaps it is that the West, having less history behind it, has not had the time to develop the inhibitions which seem to beset writers from the eastern parts of Canada; the influence of American realists, most of whom came from or dealt with the mid-west, may be another factor; perhaps the relative harshness of life on the prairies obtrudes itself so powerfully on the writers of that region that they cannot ignore it.  Whatever the reason, the fact remains. In the forties, novels of this sort included Sinclair Ross's *As For Me and My House* (1941) , Christine van der Mark's *In Due Season* (1947), W. O. Mitchell's *Who Has Seen the Wind* (1947), and E. A. McCourt's *Music at the Close* (1947).

Sinclair Ross (born 1908) was already beginning to attract attention by his honest and moving short stories, published for the most part in *Queen's Quarterly,* when *As For Me and My House* appeared.  This novel is certainly one of the most distinctive ever to come out of Canada.  It is an accurate, if sceptical, account of life in a small Saskatchewan town; it is also a searching psychological study of a minister and his overly possessive wife.  The appearance and manners of the town and its inhabitants are brought vividly to life; the main characters are explored with an almost clinical scrupulousness; and there are some excellent atmospheric descriptions of the prairie landscape.  The style is fresh and clear —Ross is never content with the cliché, but uses words with a sensitive awareness of their historical roots and nuances of meaning—and the tone is a piquant combination of astringent criticism and warm sympathy. But it is the almost unbearable tension between the guilt-ridden husband and wife that is the really distinctive feature of the book: Ross's special gift is for the creation of a psychological atmosphere in which the nerves are almost at breaking-point.

*As For Me and My House* gave every promise of marking the arrival of a new major talent in Canadian ficton.  Unfortunately Sinclair Ross's second novel, *The Well*, did not appear until 1958, and was a disappointment.  It concerns a youth from Montreal who, fleeing that city after accidentally killing a man during a robbery, takes refuge on a prairie farm. On the farm he becomes involved in the affairs of an old, half-mad farmer and his young, sensual wife: the farmer claims him as a son, the wife as a lover.  In the conflicts between these three characters there is something of that unremitting, suffocating tension that made *As For Me and My House* so powerful; but in the last third of the book Ross seems undecided how to resolve the conflicts and he finally resorts to a series of melodramatic episodes with a patently contrived happy ending.

The other members of this group have also been a source of some disappointment. Christine van der Mark's *In Due Season* is a carefully observed, tightly plotted and convincingly characterized novel of Western farm life which held out the promise of a number of distinguished successors; so far, however, it is the only novel to her credit. *Who Has Seen the Wind* was, if anything, an even more exciting and promising first novel, in which W. O. Mitchell recorded with sensitivity, humour and pathos the growth to maturity of a young boy in a prairie small town. The town in which Brian O'Connal lives is made quite real to us, populated as it is with a mixture of bigots, eccentrics and plain people of tolerance and good will, but the major emphasis is on the inner life of the boy, on his imaginative response to the world about him. Perhaps the most outstanding feature of the novel is the style: it is poetic and evocative without ever seeming pretentious or contrived. Only in some of the more farcical scenes is a false note struck: here we frequently suspect a desire to achieve popular success by slapstick exaggeration. In his subsequent work, which has taken the form mainly of radio serials and scripts for television, this element of comic exaggeration has almost crowded out the more sensitive and serious qualities in Mitchell's first novel.

E. A. McCourt is the only writer of the four who has continued to produce a succession of novels, and since the bulk of them appeared in the fifties they will be dealt with in a later chapter. To complete the record of this group, however, it may be said here that his later work has not brought the degree of growth that his first novel might have led us to expect.

There was no correspondingly significant group of novels

dealing realistically with the life of eastern Canada. A few isolated examples may however be cited. In 1946 Selywn Dewdney published *Wind Without Rain,* a novel of an Ontario high school in the tradition of Sinclair Lewis's *Babbitt* and *Elmer Gantry.* J. C. Bilbeau, the central character, is a hypocritical educationist (the cant word fits him exactly) whose god is efficiency and whose goal is absolute personal power. His tyrannical methods drive his chief antagonist, the scholarly Angus Macdonald, to despair and eventual suicide. The satire on modern education in this novel is fierce and convincing, but the happy ending does not really ring true and the novel is structurally weak. It did, however, mark a refreshing change from the sweetness and light of most Ontario fiction.

Another such contrast was provided by Joyce Marshall's *Presently Tomorrow* (1946), a novel in which the relationships between a group of girls in a boarding school and the young clergyman who serves as the school's chaplain are sensitively and honestly explored. Miss Marshall's insights into the minds of the girls are very convincing indeed; her touch is less sure with the clergyman; and the final sequences of the novel, in which the clergyman permits himself to be seduced, occasionally strains one's powers of belief. But although the novel is thus only partially successful, its style and psychological accuracy lift it considerably above the average level of the Canadian fiction of its time. Miss Marshall has also written a number of memorable short stories and a second novel, *Lovers and Strangers* (1957). Like so many second novels, *Lovers and Strangers* is disappointing: the record of a marriage which fails, the whole story is so drab and dispiriting that it fails to hold the interest of the most sympathetic reader. Neither of the central characters have enough energy to win our admiration or even our sympathy, and the incidental snapshots of Toronto life, though accurate enough in their way, are insufficiently vivid to compensate for the pallor of the unhappily married couple.

Something of the same drabness vitiates the effect of Len Peterson's only novel, *Chipmunk* (1949). Peterson is better known as a radio playwright, and in such of his plays as "Burlap Bags" he succeeds at once in creating a weird and haunting effect and in making some wry, satirical comments on Canadian society. In his novel, however, the effect is merely repellent: the baker-hero and his girl-friend Faustina are thoroughly disagreeable persons, and the Toronto through which they move is even more unpleasant than that city is in reality. In the whole novel there is no person or thing to which the reader's sympathies can attach themselves, and the inevitable result is that the interest falters.

The final novel from this period which lingers in the memory is *The Rich Man* (1948) by Henry Kreisel. This is an ironic, compassionate study of an Austrian immigrant who returns to his homeland and is falsely assumed to be rich. It is deft in technique, controlled in style, unified in structure and rich both in exact details and in symbolic suggestion. But here again the promise of a fine first novel has yet to be fulfilled. Although Mr. Kreisel has subsequently published some excellent short stories, notably the richly ironic "Travelling Nude", he has yet to produce a second novel.

The history of Canadian fiction would be greatly enriched if one were certain of being able to claim as belonging to it the work of Malcolm Lowry (1909-1957). Certainly his *Under the Volcano* (1947), a powerful, brooding, brilliant study of a man in the grip of alcoholism, is one of the most memorable novels to appear anywhere in English during the decade of the forties. The tendency of recent criticism is to claim Lowry as a Canadian writer, and to assert that he considered himself as such. Lowry was born in England and educated at Cambridge, but he settled near Vancouver in 1939 and lived there almost uninterruptedly until his return to England in 1954. The fifteen years which he spent in Canada are said to have been his most productive: it was in Canada that he finished the last, published version of *Under the Volcano*, and wrote the short stories which appeared in the recently published collection, *Hear Us Oh Lord from Heaven Thy Dwelling Place* (1961). Among the mass of unpublished manuscripts left behind at his death in 1957 are fragments of two novels which, like *Under the Volcano*, are set in Mexico, the almost completed manuscript of a novel, *October Ferry to Gabriola*, which is set in British Columbia, and many poems and short stories, some of which also have Canadian settings or relate to his Canadian experiences. These manuscripts have now been housed in the library of the University of British Columbia, and are being edited for publication by Lowry's widow, Margerie Bonner Lowry, and Professor Earle Birney.

The prospects are, then, that Lowry, who had published one novel, *Ultramarine* (1933) before his arrival in Canada, will soon rank as a major figure in Canadian literary history. Arguing that he belongs to that history, Professor George Woodcock has recently written: "It is not merely that on Canadian soil he produced the final, magnificent version of what many critics regard as the best novel written in our land; nor is it merely that much of his later work was set in Canada. . . . He is not in fact writing about Canada as a transient outsider. He is writing about it as a man who over fifteen years lived himself into the environment that centred upon his fragile home where the Pacific tides lapped and sucked under the floorboards, and who identified himself with that environment—despite trials of flesh and spirit—as passionately as those other strangers who have rendered so well the essence of their particular corners of Canada, Grove and Haig-Brown."

If Professor Woodcock's argument is sustained—and it is a cogent one—the addition of Lowry to the canon of Canadian fiction would do much to redeem this inter-war and post-war period from dullness. Apart from his work, solid contributions were made by Grove, Callaghan, MacLennan and a few promising beginners, but a rigorous standard of criticism would force one to insist that the period was one of solidity rather than of brilliance in our fiction.   The idealized past and the idyllicized present still dominated, and really forthright attempts to grapple with the realities of the contemporary Canadian scene were exceptions rather than the rule. A good deal had been done to create an image of real life on the prairies, but very little to reflect the realities of experience in either the cities or rural areas of the eastern provinces. Callaghan apart, it was only in the fifties that the cities of Canada began to appear regularly and realistically in our fiction.  Until the fifties, the task of interpreting the modern urban life of Canada had been largely left to the poets.

CHAPTER EIGHT

# The Literature of the Fifties

## 1. Introduction

IT WOULD BE presumptuous to attempt, at this early date, a detailed history and appraisal of Canadian writing in the last decade. All that I shall attempt in this chapter is to indicate some of the main trends.

The first thing that strikes one about the literature of the fifties is that it has shown no falling off in either quantity or quality. After the great upsurge of the forties, we might have expected a slackening of literary activity; if anything, the reverse has been the case. In the novel especially, this decade saw more exciting work produced than in any previous period of Canadian literary history.

The reasons for this continued renaissance are somewhat obscure. In many ways the decade was one of vacillation and disillusionment. During and immediately after World War II, Canadians in general and Canadian writers in particular had a sense of common purpose: they were virtually at one in their desire to defeat Hitler and to ensure a just and stable peace. Shortly after the cessation of hostilities, however, the Cold War between Russia and the West destroyed or at least vitiated this unity: there were many who had serious doubts about American foreign policy, especially as practised by John Foster Dulles, and about Canada's support of it. The outbreak of local wars, especially that in Korea, of racial and tribal tension in many parts of Africa and the Far East, and of such crises as those in Berlin,

Hungary, Suez, Laos and the Congo, made the hopes of a peaceful world seem remote and futile. Above all, the sense of impending doom caused by the possession of the atomic bomb by several of the great powers made everyone uneasy and afraid. Even at home, events failed to substantiate the idealistic hopes of the war years. There was no great depression comparable to that of the thirties, but there were several minor recessions, and as the decade neared its end unemployment was rapidly rising.

Such political and social events, although they inevitably affect the writer as a person, do not necessarily impair his continued productivity. The only way in which one would feel confident in arguing that they had a direct effect on our writers is to suggest that they turned the attention of many of them away from their immediate social environment towards the more permanent world of archetypal forms and myths. The tendency of our recent poets to emphasize, in Northrop Frye's phrase, "the formal elements of poetry", may well be associated with this desire to escape or evade the baffling complexity and frustrating inadequacy of their own time and place.

It is when we turn to the cultural situation in Canada that we become aware of positive influences which have supported the continued literary development of the country. Canadian nationalism, which received its first great impetus after Confederation and its second after World War I, entered a third positive phase after World War II. Whereas in the first two phases this nationalism had largely defined itself in opposition to the Imperial connection with Great Britain, it now defined itself in opposition to the economic and cultural domination of the United States. Anti-Americanism became the fashionable Canadian attitude, with the ironic result that writers such as the incisive historian Frank H. Underhill, who had seemed radical in the twenties and thirties by his criticism of Great Britain, now seemed to most Canadian intellectuals a conservative, if not an outright reactionary, because of his defence of the United States. Much of this anti-Americanism was trivial, but it had a serious core in the determination not to allow Canadian identity to be swallowed up by the giant neighbour to the South. The classical expression of this determination was the *Report of the Royal Commission on National Development in the Arts, Letters and Sciences* (1951), commonly known as the Massey Report.

The Massey Report led, in turn, to the establishment in 1957 of The Canada Council, whose avowed purpose was to foster the growth of a national culture. It is too early to assess fully the results of this Council's activities, but its system of grants to artists, scholars and writers has undoubtedly enabled some books to appear which would either not have been written at all or have been written with far greater difficulty. Perhaps its chief function is a symbolic one: it is the tangible expression of our will to cultural identity.

The same spirit of national pride has led to the publication of an increasing number of books devoted to Canadian history, politics and culture. Historians such as A. R. M. Lower (*Canadians in the Making*, 1958), Donald G. Creighton (*Dominion of the North*, 1944; *John A. Macdonald: The Young Politician*, 1952; and *The Old Chieftain*, 1955), J. M. S. Careless (*Canada: A Story of Challenge*, 1953), Gerald S. Graham (*Canada: A Short History*, 1950), Edgar McInnes (*Canada: A Political and Social History*, 1952), Chester Martin (*Foundations of Canadian Nationhood*, 1955), Bruce Hutchinson (*The Struggle for the Border*, 1956), R. M. Dawson (*William Lyon Mackenzie King*, 1958), William Kilbourn (*The Firebrand*, 1956) and F. H. Underhill (*In Search of Canadian Liberalism*, 1960) have done much to enrich our sense of our own past. Our tradition in literature and the other arts has been explored in such books as the various editions of A. J. M. Smith's *Book of Canadian Poetry* (1943, 1948 and 1957), Carl F. Klinck's and

R. E. Watters' *Canadian Anthology* (1955), Julian Park's *The Culture of Contemporary Canada* (1957), Malcolm Ross's *Our Sense of Identity* (1954) and *The Arts in Canada* (1958), and my own *Creative Writing in Canada* (1952) and *Ten Canadian Poets* (1958). The effect of such publications on the Canadian writer and his reader is inevitably to enhance their interest in this country, to give them a sense of excitement. Even if the writer feels the cultural nationalism to be overdone or misconceived, and is provoked to attack or make fun of it, he is still stimulated by it. Thus Norman Levine's *Canada Made Me* (1958), a mordant exposé of the seamier side of Canadian life, is to my mind just as surely a product of the new Canadian nationalism as are the optimistic, roseate pictures of Bruce Hutchinson. The same is true of the gibes at Canadianism in the pages of Irving Layton, James Reaney, Robertson Davies or Mordecai Richler: they are expressions of a real if reluctant involvement in the Canadian situation. In fact, the development of a satirical attitude toward Canadian society is one of the chief signs that this country is gradually taking shape: it was previously too amorphous to be a good target.

The growth of Canadian national feeling in the fifties had other tangible expressions which affected our literature. New literary magazines were established: *The Tamarack Review* in 1956, *Delta* in 1957, *The Waterloo Review* in 1958, *Canadian Literature* in 1959, *Prism* in 1959 and *Alphabet* in 1960. The Canadian Broadcasting Corporation continued and expanded its policy of broadcasting poems and short stories by Canadian writers; a Canadian book club was established in Toronto; publishers, magazines and sororities offered valuable prizes for novels and other forms of writing; the Governor General's Awards for the best Canadian book each year in various categories were taken under the sponsorship of The Canada Council and provided with substantial grants in cash.

There were some losses in the decade—the demise of

*Contemporary Verse* in 1951 and of *Northern Review* in 1956, for example—but on the whole the literary atmosphere was bullish. In a phrase that was politically popular during the decade, Canadian writers "had never had it so good". No wonder that, in spite of the doubts and anxieties caused by the world situation, this was a productive decade.

The second impression that one receives of this decade is that it was a watershed in our literary history. Most of the writers who had dominated the thirties and forties either ceased to write or became relatively inactive, and with a few exceptions the most striking and interesting work was done by newcomers. In poetry, E. J. Pratt's last book of verse, *Towards the Last Spike,* appeared in 1952, A. J. M. Smith's only book of verse in the decade was *A Sort of Ecstasy* (1954), A. M. Klein published nothing, Earle Birney produced only his *Trial of a City* (1952), P. K. Page stopped writing poetry after the publication of *The Metal and the Flower* in 1954, Patrick Anderson turned from poetry to prose travelogues, Charles Bruce and Ronald Hambleton gave up poetry for fiction, and such academic poets as Roy Daniells, Alfred Bailey, Douglas Le Pan and George Whalley became engrossed in administrative and scholarly pursuits. Of the leading poets of the forties, only the social realist group of Irving Layton, Miriam Waddington, Raymond Souster and Louis Dudek continued to publish with unabated vigour in the fifties. Much the same was true in fiction. Frederick Philip Grove died in 1948; Irene Baird published no fiction in the fifties; Laura Goodman Salverson apparently reached the end of a long career in *Immortal Rock* (1954); Philip Child gave up the craft of fiction early in the decade; even promising newcomers of the forties such as Henry Kreisel, Sinclair Ross, Joyce Marshall and Christine van der Mark published little or nothing. Morley Callaghan and Hugh MacLennan continued to publish, but their work did not usually create the same excitement as that generated by the new young novelists who appeared. In both poetry and fiction, the fifties were dominated by new names—by poets such as James Reaney, Jay Macpherson, Daryl Hine and Leonard Cohen; and by novelists such as Ethel Wilson, Robertson Davies, David Walker, Mordecai Richler and Brian Moore. Nor were these writers merely "promising"; in each case they produced a body of work which constituted a substantial achievement.

## 2. *Poetry*

There has been such a plethora of Canadian poets in the past decade that it is difficult to give a clear account of them without falling into the error of gross over-simplification. The new names are so numerous that a mere listing of them could not fail to lead to confusion. Attempts to group poets into "schools" are notoriously dangerous, and particularly so in this instance when there is a great deal of overlapping between the various groups and when several of the poets have not yet clearly established their own identities. The literary historian must, if he is to be clear, risk these errors.

There seem to me, then, to be three main schools of contemporary Canadian poetry, and a few loose fish. The first and in many ways the most brilliant school is that of the mythopoeic poets, whose work draws much of its inspiration from the creative criticism of Professor Northrop Frye in Toronto and which has as its chief luminaries James Reaney and Jay Macpherson. The second school is a continuation of the social realist group active in Montreal in the nineteen forties which has Irving Layton as its chief prophet and practitioner and includes the later work of Dudek, Souster and Miriam Waddington along with that of younger poets such as Leonard Cohen, Alfred Purdy and others. The third group has received far less national recognition, and is basically a school of regionalist verse which finds its focus in *The Fiddlehead,* a magazine of verse (and latterly also of prose) published at the University of New Brunswick since

1945. Prominent in this school are Fred Cogswell, Elizabeth Brewster and Alden Nowlan. It must be emphasized, however, that these schools are groupings of convenience rather than absolutely self-contained units. The mythological poets do not ignore the realities of the world about them, and some of Reaney's comments upon the Canadian social scene are as direct and telling as those of the social realists of Montreal. Conversely, there is a good deal of myth and legend in the work of Layton and Cohen, and indeed in that of Cogswell and Brewster. The differences are those of emphasis: the mythopoeic school is rather more self-consciously "literary", concerned with the formal aspects of poetry and with archetypes of experience rather than with the raw stuff of everyday life; the Montreal school is more conscious of its own immediate urban environment and of its poets' daily emotional crises, and is more interested in the expression of provocative ideas than in the development of a highly sophisticated technique; the Fredericton group resembles the Montreal school in its determination to make poetry out of immediate experience but substitutes a rural or small-town environment for that of the metropolis and writes in regular metres and traditional forms more frequently than in the free verse which is so often the vehicle of the Montreal poets. Another and briefer way of putting it would be to say that the Toronto school is primarily interested in wit, the Montreal school in passion and the Fredericton school in neatness and clarity.

James Reaney (born 1926), the leading practitioner of the mythopoeic school, made his debut in 1949 with *The Red Heart*. This book at once established him as a fresh and exciting figure. Here was none of the earnest social preachment which had marked Canadian poetry during the war and immediate post-war years: in its place was gaiety, irreverence, that rather morbid type of humour which can best be described in the phrase *comédie noire,* a peculiar combination of innocence and sophistication. The imaginative world which he created in this first book had much in common with that which the American novelist Truman Capote was creating at about the same time in books such as *Other Voices, Other Rooms*: a weird, ghostly world in which the innocence of children is confronted with the realities of death and depravity. There is in these poems an unearthly, trance-like effect, created by the use of surprising but, on second thought, apt similes ("The plums like blue pendulums/That thrum the gold-wired winds of summer"), the juxtaposition of homely images with references to death and disease, the alternation of naive perceptions and a world-weary sense of dissolution. The poems often resemble surrealist paintings in their distortions of the familiar into the terrifying. The style is always in keeping: the short lines, the casual rhymes and off-rhymes, the frequently childish diction, the off-hand tone and the series of deliberately flat assertions—these all combine to enhance the main effect, which is one of a fabulous dream or nightmare recounted on the following day.

In the interval between the publication of *The Red Heart* and his second book, *A Suit of Nettles* (1958), Reaney had become a student of Northrop Frye, and had done extensive research on the poetry of Spenser in particular and of the Elizabethan period in general. As a result, he is much more self-conscious here, he models his book upon Spenser's *Shephearde's Calendar,* and freights his poem with a far greater load of erudition and allusion. Some of the virtues of his first book are lost in the process: the vision is less unmistakably personal and distinctive, the charming simplicity has given way to a somewhat affected cleverness. There are, however, compensating advantages: the monotony of *The Red Heart,* the reiteration of an apprehensive nostalgia, is replaced by a much greater variety of tone and increased complexity of theme. The book varies all the way from broad farce through pointed satire to tragic affirmation; perceptive comments are made about Canadian history and politics, about religion, literary criticism and human destiny; and a similar metrical variety is provided by the experiments with sestinas, poulterer's measure, alliterative verse, blank verse and various lyrical forms. Sometimes these prosodic experiments are brilliantly successful, as in this passage from the February Eclogue describing the awkward flutterings of a bat:

> He hangs from beam in winter upside down
> But in the spring he right side up lets go
> And flutters here and there zigzagly flown
> Till up the chimney of the house quick-slow
> He pendulum-spirals out in light low
> Of sunset swinging out above the lawns. . . .

In spite of the brilliance of the poem, however, I cannot escape the feeling that it is a tour-de-force rather than a genuine work of art. We are too conscious here, as we were not in *The Red Heart,* of the poet's artifices, of his determination to impress us. The effect, in other words, is often laboured. However, Reaney's imaginative reserves are obviously so great, his vision is so disturbingly clear, that one feels confident in predicting a series of brilliant successes from his pen. More recently he has turned his attention to drama, and if anyone can breathe life into the hitherto dry bones of Canadian drama it is likely to be James Reaney.

Jay Macpherson (born 1932) resembles Reaney in wit, allusiveness and intricacy of technique, but is a more elegant and reserved poet. She has published two small booklets of verse—*Nineteen Poems* (1952) and *O Earth Return* (1955)—and one beautifully produced volume, *The Boatman,* which received the Governor General's Award as the best book of poetry of 1957. *The Boatman* consists of five sections, variously labelled "Poor Child", "O Earth Return", "The Plowman in Darkness", "The Sleepers", "The Boatman" and "The Fisherman", which are closely interrelated and

which conduct us on a voyage from the fallen world of
sense experience to the redeemed world of divine grace. The
first section portrays the child who feels deserted and lonely,
yearning for the return to Paradise ("wanting/Not childhood's flowers but absolute return"), hunting through the
maze of the fallen world, spiritually blind, waiting for
healing, seeking the True North, longing for maternal
comfort—in short, it presents us with a group of parables
of loss and quest. Section II deals tragically with the fall of
Eve in her various guises—as Sibylla, Eurynome, Sheba and
Mother Earth, while Section III treats the same theme of
seduction and fall lightly and gaily. Section IV is a kind
of magical interlude in which all the characters of the poem
are asleep or enchanted; in Section V they are saved from
disaster by Noah, the boatman or artist; and in Section VI
they are redeemed by the fisherman, Christ. Thus, as
Professor Frye has put it, "the book moves from a 'poor
child' at the centre of a hostile and mysterious world to an
adult child who has regained the paradisal innocent vision
and is at the circumference of a world of identical forms".

This bare summary of the poem's content does far less
than justice to its richness and complexity. Miss Macpherson
has a very delicate sense of poetic structure, and the
individual poems are shaped with a loving care that recalls
the work of seventeenth century poets such as George
Herbert. Similarly, there are cross-references and echoes
back and forth between the individual poems which give
the whole sequence a shaped and closely interwoven effect.
She also has great skill in the disposition of words within
the line, with the result that most of the lines have both an
epigrammatic finality and a fine sense of rhythm and melody.
Tone is beautifully managed and modulated, ranging all
the way from a frolicsome gaiety to a grave solemnity of
utterance. Though the book may at times bewilder us, it
always fascinates us and commands our admiration by its
virtuosity and brio.

A similarly difficult but fascinating poet is Margaret Avison (born 1918). I first became familiar with Miss Avison's poems some twenty-five years ago when I had the pleasure of publishing her early efforts in *Acta Victoriana*; it is characteristic of her modesty and reserve that her first book of verse, *Winter Sun,* did not appear until 1960. Her poems strike us as essentially efforts at self-communion and self-understanding; we are occasionally permitted to overhear her meditations but she has no wish to impose them upon us. In spite of their "private" nature, and their relative fewness, her poems have been eagerly read in the magazines, and her first volume was awaited with an expectation which was not disappointed.

What concerns Miss Avison is the fate of the individual entrapped in a mean, mechanical world but yearning for freedom. Over and over again she contrasts the little time we know with the vast expanses of time and eternity, the little space we inhabit with the great distances from pole to pole and from star to star. "I call to you", she writes, "down the stone corridors that wall me in". Or she beseeches Pandora to

> lift the lid again
> And let the clamoring mysteries be dumb.
> In this clear twilight contour must contain
> Its source, and distances with contours come
> Opening peacock vistas that no man can entomb.

Again, in the poem "Chronic" she complains that her life has become circumscribed to the events recorded in a week's newspapers, and that she cannot even imagine the coming of spring. The individual soul can only escape the trap by a transcendent effort of will: "Nobody stuffs the world in at your eyes./The optic heart must venture: a jail-break/And re-creation". Confinement is death: "The cyanide jar seals life, as sonnets move/towards final stiffness". But many are afraid to venture out of their prison, are unwilling to risk what T. S. Eliot called "the awful daring of a moment's surrender":

> For everyone
> The swimmer's moment at the whirlpool comes,
> But many at that moment will not say
> "This is the whirlpool, then."
> By their refusal they are saved
> From the black pit, and also from contesting
> The deadly rapids, and emerging in
> The mysterious, and more ample, further waters.

Miss Avison's poetry has not the ease and elegance of Miss Macpherson's, nor its melodic precision, but it is more fully rooted in experience. Almost always her poems begin in the observation of an actual event in the here and now—a horse's head staring over the sides of a truck, like God surveying His creation, or a butterfly battered by a storm—and are gradually expanded into a universal statement. Miss Avison's poems also impress one as being more deeply felt, as being the distilled products of personal experience rather than mere literary exercises. Her dislocations of syntax, her choice of unusual and sometimes ugly words, enhance the effect of an honest groping through darkness towards the light.

A fourth member of this mythopoeic school of poetry is Eli Mandel (born 1922). Mandel made his debut in 1954 in the book *Trio*, which also contains poems by Gael Turnbull and Phyllis Webb. His first independent book of verse was *Fuseli Poems* (1960). Like Miss Avison, Mandel translates the stuff of personal experience into mythological forms. In his contribution to *Trio*, the Minotaur poems, the central myth is that of the maze and the monster; in the *Fuseli Poems* it is that of a castle complete with moat and dungeon in which the poet is now king, now hunchback and now the prisoner in the dungeon. The overall effect is that of horror, of a nightmare world of lust and greed, redeemed only by the poet's compassion for suffering humanity, "those lost and stoned and silent faces". He would wish, he assures us, to sing a happy song, but the horror keeps breaking in:

> I think about my past and try to change
> Into a singing metaphor a silent heart,
> A frail red parrot perched within its cage
> Repeating what it hears and cackling without change
> All that ear hears and tongue speaks. I form in thought
> The singing form that forms the silent heart.
>
> But parrots bring in sleep only the surly shape
> Of images of man turned into beasts
> Carrying their loads of shame upon their backs,
> That forest where the trees are shapes of girls
> And every stone an image of a face, and eyes
> Are in the flowers, and I could weep for all
> Those lost and stoned and silent faces.

Even in the most innocent objects, such as a children's merry-go-round in a city park, he sees emblems of disaster: of man bound to the wheel of time and going around and around in repetitive futility:

> Sick on that circle you begin to grieve.
> You wish the ride would end and you could park.
> Night follows day, these horses never leave.

The concentrated agony in these poems rivals that in A. J. M. Smith's: voracious insects, cruel beasts, pus, knives, blood, wounds, diseases and deformities are the images that occur and recur throughout the volume. We are repelled, and yet moved to reluctant respect by the obvious sincerity of the poet. This is prophetic poetry for a decadent world.

There are occasional echoes in Mandel's poetry—echoes of Wallace Stevens, T. S. Eliot, William Blake and Christopher Smart—but on the whole he gives the impression of having found a distinctive voice of his own. Outside influences are much more apparent in the work of another Edmonton poet, Wilfred Watson (born 1911). Watson's only book, *Friday's*

*Child,* was published in 1955 and was awarded the Governor General's Award for that year. Because it came with the prestige of a great English publishing house—Faber and Faber—it received rather more acclaim in Canada than was probably its due. Many of the poems are so derivative of Hopkins, Eliot, Yeats, Auden, Donne and Dylan Thomas as to resemble parodies. The framework of ideas in the book— the opposition between the realm of nature and the realm of grace—has become almost a platitude in our time. The picture of man as lost and fallen, and finding in religious surrender and self-denying love the only specific for his ruin, is more freshly and movingly drawn in the poems of Jay Macpherson. Despite the overly derivative nature of much of the book, however, there are a few poems of genuine power. One such is "The Windy Bishop", a terrific poem about fear. The windy bishop is presumably the wind of dissolution, the wind which destroys all earthly things and which reminds the poet that his body is dust and urges him to fit his soul for heaven. Here the searing cold and driving blizzards of a Canadian prairie winter provide an ideal objective correlative for the poem's central theme. Similar memorable poems are "In the Cemetery of the Sun" and "Canticle of Darkness". Watson has eloquence at his command and a great capacity for tenderness; if he can discover a more independent form of utterance he should develop into a poet of the first magnitude.

Unfortunately, there is no possibility of further development in the work of Anne Wilkinson (1910-1961): her recent death was a heavy loss to Canadian life and letters. Miss Wilkinson was the author of two books of poems: *Counterpoint to Sleep* (1951) and *The Hangman Ties the Holly* (1955). The poems in her first book were, for the most part, simple personal lyrics; those in her second had a greater complexity of mythological reference and symbol. Both books, however, revealed her special gifts. One was for the revealing parody of nursery rhymes, ballads and popular songs. Another was her great power of empathy, of entering into the minds of children, and even into the beings of non-human things such as plants and fish. A third gift was her lyrical skill: "In June and Gentle Oven", for example, is a lovely, liquid, sensuous evocation of an Ontario summer. Her poems are witty and wise, yet often melancholy and disillusioned: they modulate from a mood of sophisticated assurance into one of naive wistfulness. Most frequently she achieves this modulation by juxtaposing the innocent child-hood vision with the experienced adult comprehension of the world as a place of frustration and bitterness, as in this poem "Carol":

> I was a lover of turkey and holly
> But my true love was the Christmas tree
> We hung our hearts from a green green bough
> And merry swung the mistletoe
>
> We decked the tree with a silver apple
> And a golden pear,
> A partridge and a cockle shell
> And a fair maiden
>
> No rose can tell the fumes of myrrh
> That filled the forest of our day
> Till the fruit and shell and maid fell down
> And the partridge flew away
>
> Now I swing from a brittle twig
> For the green bough of my true love hid
> A laily worm.  Around my neck
> The hangman ties the holly.

The youngest poet of this group of mythopoeic poets is Daryl Hine (born 1936). Mr. Hine, although still under thirty, has published three small books of verse: *Five Poems* (1954), *The Carnal and the Crane* (1957) and *The Devil's Picture Book* (1961). It is too early to attempt an assessment of his verse, however, since his poetic personality has not yet defined itself.  His first two books were marked by exuberance of fancy and by a bewildering flux of images and symbols. In his more recent poems he seems gradually to be disciplining his utterance, to be seeking greater lucidity of meaning and compactness of form. There is no question of his imaginative fertility, nor of the honesty with which he is seeking for a key to the understanding of his world.

Whatever one's feelings about mythopoeic poetry—and my own prejudice leads me to fear that it too often degenerates into artificiality, into being literature about literature rather than literature about life—there can be no doubt that it is the school which has dominated Canadian poetry in the last decade. It is only the work of older poets such as Louis Dudek, Raymond Souster, Miriam Waddington and, above all, Irving Layton that has kept the Montreal school of social and personal realism in the running at all. The new poets of this school have been disappointingly slow in developing into major or even into distinctive utterance.

Alfred Purdy (born 1918), for example, published his first book of verse, *The Enchanted Echo,* as long ago as 1944; but he still, in *The Crafte So Longe to Lerne* (1959), seems to be groping for the appropriate style and subject. Between these two books he had published *Pressed on Sand* (1955) and *Emu, Remember!* (1956). As at least two of these titles suggest, Mr. Purdy seems to lack self-confidence. His first booklet of poems consisted largely of doggerel-like verse and of echoes of the late romantic poetry of Roberts and Carman (Oh, up my lads, 'tis April, and the boughs are all asway/With tidings of the rover who is coming home today . . .) but by the mid fifties he had gone a long way towards mastering a modern idiom and point of view. In particular, he demonstrated a talent for the macabre ballad, such as "After the Rats" or "For the Record", with its arresting first lines:

> In the past three days I've gone to the door
> For milk, and the bottle's been full of blood . . .

for the light social satire of "Indictment" and "Short History
of X County", and for the ironic relation of history to present
circumstances as in "Who Does Not Understand". His forte
seems to be humour, especially satire, and it is probably on
his willingness to explore this medium more fully that his
future reputation will depend.

A somewhat similar lack of assured direction mars the
work of several other young poets of this group. Peter Miller
(born 1921), author of *Meditation at Noon* (1958) and
*Sonata for Frog and Man* (1959), writes poems at his best
which are rich in sensuous observation, apt imagery and
thematic perception; but at his worst he descends into a
monotonous flatness and prosiness. Henry Moscovitch (born
1941), who while still a student at McGill has produced the
two booklets *The Serpent Ink* (1956) and *The Laughing
Storm* (1961), is still too much under the shadow of Irving
Layton. His tendency is to imitate the most dubious features
of Layton's verse: its four-letter words, its shock tactics. His
more personal poems are too frequently slack and casual,
falling short of the final epigrammatic statement which
poems of this imagistic or ironic sort demand. His gift, if he
can develop it, seems to be for the brief cameo of a social
situation, of an observed event which becomes archetypal, as
in this little poem "Recess":

> Boys rushing out from school
> to play awhile,
> play hard when you are free,
> for soon the silver whistle
> held by the crippled teacher
> will silence all your shouts
> and gather your happy games
> into a silent halt.

George Ellenbogan (born 1934) is another poet of this
group who is as yet only promising: his *Winds of Unreason*
(1958) is a curious combination of adolescent petulance and
genuine feeling.

Rather more substantial is the achievement of Phyllis Webb (born 1927), whose *Even Your Right Eye* appeared in 1956. Her poetry is lyrical, and the direct expression of her own emotional states. She is at her best in finding concrete images with which to express such abstractions as prayer, patience and suffering. At times she becomes artificial by a too deliberate cleverness, but she has a sense of verbal melody and of poetic structure, and the personality which emerges from her poems—that of a sensitive, eager but apprehensive being—is an attractive one.

But easily the most promising in this group of young poets is Leonard Cohen (born 1933), author of *Let us Compare Mythologies* (1956) and *The Spice-Box of Earth* (1961). His finest quality is established by the first poem in his first book, "Elegy":

> Do not look for him
> In brittle mountain streams:
> They are too cold for any god;
> And do not examine the angry rivers
> For shreds of his soft body
> Or turn the shore stones for his blood.
>
> But in the warm salt ocean
> He is descending through cliffs
> Of slow green water
> And the hovering coloured fish
> Kiss his snow-bruised body
> And build their secret nests
> In his fluttering winding-sheet.

Tenderness, sensuousness, mellifluousness, adjectival richness, direct simple statement: these are the qualities that mark the best of Cohen's work. He reminds us of the early A. M. Klein, to whom one of the best poems in his second book is addressed, by his richness of texture, his emotional candour and his sense of wonder. But just as Klein wavers between the blessing and the curse, between exultation and lamentation, so does Cohen: many of his poems are sad or

angry, complaints or protests against a world of racial
intolerance and persecution, hypocrisy, lust and greed. Out
of his anger with things as they are he fashions macabre
ballads in which the horror is made bearable by being
parodied. Some of these ballads—"Song", "Ballad", "Warning" for example—were among the most striking and successful in his first book, and one or two more appear in *The
Spice-Box of Earth*. On the whole, however, the note of
exultation, especially in the delights of love, is more
dominant in this second book. Most of the poems in it are
ecstatic psalms of praise for feminine beauty. The most
hopeful feature of his poetry is its straightforwardness: he
does not take refuge in the ambiguity of myths, but expresses
with engaging candour and simplicity his own personal
response to experience.

Such straightforwardness also marks the work of the third
group of poets in contemporary Canada, the regionalist
group associated with *The Fiddlehead*. The three chief
poets in this group are Fred Cogswell, Elizabeth Brewster
and Alden Nowlan, but there are several other young poets
of promise such as Robert Gibbs and Allan Donaldson.

Fred Cogswell (born 1917) is the author of five books of
verse: *The Stunted Strong* (1954), *The Haloed Tree* (1956),
*The Testament of Cresseid* (1957), *Descent from Eden*
(1959) and *Lost Dimension* (1960). *The Stunted Strong*, a
small chapbook containing sixteen sonnets about the life
and people of the Saint John River Valley, is his most
original production. There are, perhaps, echoes of Edwin
Arlington Robinson in these sonnets, but basically they
strike us as the product of close observation of Cogswell's
social environment. Neatly and sharply they etch in a few
lines the basic lineaments of people who are at once stunted
and strong, objects of compassion and of irony. Only
occasionally do the sonnets seem a little forced, a little
laboured: most of them have a fine inevitability, a justness
of word and phrase and rhythm. In *The Haloed Tree* a

similar precision is evident, but the dominant poetic form is now the ballad or the epigram. Unfortunately, the weaknesses of his first book are also evident, especially the tendency to make rhythms too emphatic, to establish a beat so strong that it eventually becomes oppressive. *The Testament of Cresseid,* a translation of Robert Henryson's fifteenth century narrative, tended to confirm this overly accented style. Cogswell's best book by far is *Descent from Eden,* and especially the first three sections of it: Ballads and Fantasies, Sonnets, Epigrams and Satires. Here he reveals himself as an acute observer of social patterns, a perceptive psychologist and an economical, ironic narrator. His mind is stored with a wealth of learning, and he is able to relate the lives of the rural people with whom he mainly deals to the whole cycle of human history. What he needs in order to become a really first-class poet is more fluidity and ease in his rhythms; in addition, he should acquire more confidence in the value of his own perceptions, and resist the temptation to fall into the current fad of mythologizing.

Elizabeth Brewster (born 1922) has the ease and fluidity which Cogswell often lacks, but she has less energy and variety. She too makes her poetry chiefly out of the observation of the people and scenery of New Brunswick, although she is also very skilful at introspective lyrics in which she examines her own feelings or fantasies. She has two main manners: one a tight, elliptical style in which everything is compressed into the smallest possible compass, and another a more diffuse, meditative style in which the effect is of conversational ease and casualness. Her work, contained so far in the three booklets *East Coast* (1951), *Lillooet* (1954) and *Roads* (1957), is marked rather by delicacy than by depth, by restraint rather than by rhetoric. Her chief affiliations are with American women poets such as Emily Dickinson and Elinor Wylie, and, in her poems dealing with village life, with the eighteenth century English poet Crabbe, on whom she is a specialist.

Alden Nowlan (born 1933) is the youngest and in many ways the most promising of this group. Although he has so far published only two small books of verse—*The Rose and the Puritan* (1958) and *Under the Ice* (1961)—his poems and short stories have appeared in literary magazines all over the North American continent, and he seems to have inexhaustible reserves of energy and imagination. His poems bear the strong imprint of Cogswell's influence, and consist mainly of ironic or compassionate sketches of rural people or incidents. He seems, however, to possess the confidence in the validity of his perceptions that Cogswell is inclined to lack, and he writes of the mingled beauty and horror of rural New Brunswick with a straightforward honesty that shocks and grips the reader. There is nothing of the artificiality of conventional pastoral in this regional poetry: it is direct, sometimes brutal, always authentic.

A poet who somewhat resembles the members of the *Fiddlehead* school—in his wit, his interest in social vignettes, his clipped metres and epigrammatic style—but who writes of an urban or suburban rather than of a rural environment is George Johnston (born 1915). Johnston's poems have been appearing in the magazines since the nineteen thirties, but it was only in 1959 that his first book, *The Cruising Auk*, was published. As this delay in publication would suggest, there is nothing aggressive or pretentious about Johnston. He is a quiet, laconic, casual poet, who looks with an amused but compassionate eye on human foibles. In some ways he reminds us of the English poet John Betjeman, but he has none of Betjeman's prejudices. He is a poet, rare enough in these or any days, who can be read for sheer pleasure. At times he moves us to laughter, at other times almost to tears, but he is always gentle, urbane and tolerant.

There have been so many interesting poets functioning in Canada in the fifties that it is impossible to give separate treatment to them all. Norman Levine produced an interesting first book of verse, *The Tight-Rope Walker*, in 1950, and has subsequently published a novel, *The Angled Road* (1953), and the controversial combination of prose autobiography and social commentary, *Canada Made Me*. Two members of the famous Roberts family, Goodridge Macdonald and Dorothy Roberts Leisner, have produced a number of books of clear, sharp, accurate verse; Kay Smith of Saint John published *Footnote to the Lord's Prayer* in 1951 and a number of poems in magazines such as *The Fiddlehead* and *Northern Review* which reveal a genuine talent for meditative and introspective lyricism; R. A. D. Ford, in *A Window on the North* (1956), produced a book which was grave, intelligent and mature, full of clear vignettes of Canadian life and scenery; John Glassco, in *The Deficit Made Flesh* (1958), published a book of mainly regionalist verse about the Eastern Townships which in many ways resembles the verse of the *Fiddlehead* school; older poets such as Ronald Everson (*Lattice for Momos,* 1958) and George Walton (*The Wayward Queen,* 1959), whose work had been appearing in the magazines since the nineteen-twenties, took advantage of the new interest in poetry to publish belated but none the less welcome collections; and young poets such as Marya Fiamengo (*The Quality of Halves,* 1958), Ronald Bates (*The Wandering World,* 1959), Michael Collie (*Poems,* 1959), Heather Spears (*Asylum Poems,* 1958), John Robert Colombo (*This Citadel in Time,* 1959) and Kenneth McRobbie (*Eyes Without a Face,* 1960) made their debuts.

Whatever else may be said of Canadian poetry in the fifties, it could certainly not be said to be in short supply. In the work of Layton, Souster, Reaney, Macpherson and Avison it reached a standard that would not easily be surpassed, and the promise evident in the plethora of young poets suggested that the high level of achievement would be sustained in the sixties.

## 3. Fiction

Canadian fiction has always lagged behind Canadian poetry in quality if not in quantity. Perhaps the most exciting literary development of the fifties was the way in which fiction made substantial strides towards closing the gap. Never before had there been so many Canadian writers of fiction who took their art seriously, who were determined to be more than mere purveyors of commercial entertainment. For the first time, the actual stuff of contemporary Canadian life, rather than glorified Canadian history or an idyllicized present, became the staple material of our fiction. Above all, a new sophistication, a new urbanity and wit, became part of our tradition in fiction.

Developments in our fiction were heartening from many points of view. Even the short story, which in the forties had with a very few exceptions been practised only intermittently or as an exercise in escapism, showed signs of growth. Only three independent books of short stories were published in the decade—Hugh Garner's *The Yellow Sweater and Other Stories* in 1952, Desmond Pacey's *The Picnic and Other Stories* in 1958 and Morley Callaghan's *Stories* in 1959—but four anthologies of Canadian short stories appeared: Desmond Pacey's *A Book of Canadian Stories*, 1950; Robert Weaver's and Helen James' *Canadian Short Stories*, 1952; *Klanak Islands*, 1959; and Robert Weaver's World's Classic edition, *Canadian Short Stories*, 1960; excellent short stories by such writers as Ethel Wilson, Mordecai Richler, Henry Kreisel, Alice Munro, Douglas Spettigue, Ernest Buckler, David Walker, Ralph Gustafson and Brian Moore were published in periodicals at home and abroad, and as the decade closed there were rumours that collections of stories by several of these writers were imminent.

There were even refreshing changes evident in those two old standbys of Canadian fiction, the regional idyll and the historical romance. The former genre still attracted to itself the great bulk of our writers of fiction, probably because the life of the Canadian farm, village or small town remained more simple and thus more manageable than the life of our cities. But the quality of the regional idyll improved in one of two ways. Either it became, as in the work of Edward A. McCourt, Evelyn Richardson, Vera Lysenko, Margaret Hutchison, Luella Creighton and Charles Bruce, a more accurate reflection of the actual conditions of life in its region, or it took on, as in the work of John Cornish, Barbara Villy Cormack, Basil Partridge, Jan Hilliard, Stuart Trueman and Ronald Hambleton, a new element of sophisticated comedy.

Of the more realistic regionalists, McCourt and Lysenko dealt with life on the prairies, Margaret Hutchison with that of the interior of British Columbia, Luella Creighton with that of rural Ontario, and Mrs. Richardson and Bruce with the life of the Maritimes. McCourt was the most consistently productive of the group, publishing *Music at the Close* in 1947, *Home Is the Stranger* in 1950, *The Wooden Sword* in 1957 and *Walk through the Valley* in 1958. In all four of his novels there is a good deal of social documentation, some fine description of the prairie landscape, thoughtful discussion of moral issues, and a style which is always competent and at moments reaches genuine distinction. Three deficiencies prevent the novels from reaching the highest plane in our fiction. The first of these is McCourt's weakness in characterization: his characters, with the single exception of the boy in *Walk through the Valley,* are wooden. The second deficiency is a matter of plot: McCourt seems eventually always to lose faith in the power of the ordinary processes of life to hold our interest and resorts to melodrama. The third deficiency is a matter of style: although McCourt's style is always competent it is not always in keeping; often he puts into the mouth of a fourteen-year-old boy, say, the language appropriate to a forty-year-old professor of English.

Second in achievement to McCourt in this group of more realistic regionalists is Charles Bruce. Into *The Channel Shore* (1954) and *The Township of Time* (1959) he has put much of that patient fidelity to fact and atmosphere which distinguished his poetry in the forties. The slow, quiet round of life on the farms and fishing villages of Nova Scotia is rendered with great honesty and authenticity. The trouble is, however, that it is all a little too slow: both his books could have profited from a good deal of judicious editing.

The four women in the group have written competently and honestly but without any real flair. Evelyn Richardson's more memorable book was a piece of autobiography, *We Keep a Light* (1945); her novels, *Desired Haven* (1952) and *No Small Tempest* (1957), suffer from crudeness of characterization and a tendency towards sentimental didacticism. Luella Creighton's *High Bright Buggy Wheels* (1951) and *Turn East, Turn West* (1954) are more forthright than most of the regional novels to come out of southern Ontario, but they do not really succeed in capturing the elusive quality of that materially rich but artistically barren area. Vera Lysenko's *Yellow Boots* (1954) and *Westerly Wild* (1956) give us interesting glimpses into the lives of immigrants on the prairies, but the instinct for propriety prevents them from cutting deeply below the respectable surface of things.

The group of regional comedies may be dismissed even more briefly. Novels such as John Cornish's *The Provincials* (1951) and *Olga* (1959)—both of which are set in British Columbia—Barbara Villy Cormack's *Local Rag* (1951) and *The House* (1955), Basil Partridge's *The Penningtons* (1952), *Larry Pennington* (1954), and *Chaplet of Grace* (1956), Jan Hilliard's *A View of the Town* (1954), *The Jameson Girls* (1956), and *Dove Cottage* (1959), and Stuart Trueman's *Cousin Elva* (1955) —novels such as these neither are nor pretend to be anything more than light entertainment. They are of interest only as a group, indicating that the Canadian popular taste in fiction is shifting away from the sentimental didacticism of the old regional idylls of Ralph Connor, Marian Keith and others. The fictional record of the life of our villages and small towns is now acceptable only as a light comedy or possibly, although no one has really tried it, in the form of a thoroughgoing naturalism which would call for an approach altogether different from that of the old idylls.

Another interesting shift in popular taste is evident in relation to the historical romance. The historical romance is still far from dead in Canada, but if we look far enough back in our literary history it is possible to trace its gradual decline. In the nineteenth century it was indisputably the chief form of Canadian fiction, as witness the work of John Richardson, William Kirby and Gilbert Parker; in the first four decades of this century it was still practised by writers with serious literary pretensions — by Franklin Davie McDowell, Thomas Raddall, Laura Goodman Salverson, Philip Child and Frederick Niven; but in the last decade it has become the almost exclusive preserve of women who write for the same audience that reads women's magazines. These women writers include Suzanne Butler (*My Pride, My Folly*, 1953; *Vale of Tyranny*, 1954), Mary Weekes (*Acadian Betrayal*, 1955), E. M. Granger Bennett (*Land for Their Inheritance*, 1955; *A Straw in the Wind*, 1958), Constance Beresford-Howe (*My Lady Greensleeves*, 1955), Gaie Taylor (*Anastasia's Daughter*, 1955), Gladys Lewis (*Joshua Doan*, 1956), Gladys Taylor (*Pine Roots*, 1956; *The King Tree*, 1958) and Nan Shipley (*The Scarlet Lily*, 1959).

The place once held by the historical romance seems likely to be taken by the historical novel, which deals more seriously and accurately with recent history. There have been several quite successful novels of this type in the last decade—novels such as Earle Birney's *Turvey* and *Down the Long Table*, which deal respectively with Canadians in World War II and in the depression days of the thirties, Hugh MacLennan's *The Watch that Ends the Night*, Lionel Shapiro's *The Sealed Verdict* (1947), *Torch for a Dark Journey* (1950) and *The Sixth of June* (1955), Herbert Steinhouse's *Ten Years After* (1958) and Colin McDougall's *Execution* (1958). All of these novels are courageous attempts to deal with the complexity of political and social issues arising in the last quarter century, and although they seldom rise above the level of good journalism they are much more salutary as reading diet than the glamour and escapism of the average historical romance. Those by Steinhouse and McDougall especially, since they are first novels and reveal insight not merely into political events but also into human character, are worth reading as indications of what their respective authors may be expected to do in the future.

The future of the Canadian novel, however, may more surely be entrusted to five writers who may already be considered, in Canadian terms, major novelists and to a further five who have given promise of developing into major novelists. The five who have already produced a substantial body of distinguished work are Ethel Wilson, Robertson Davies, David Walker, Brian Moore and Mordecai Richler; the five who have made auspicious beginnings are Ernest Buckler, Adele Wiseman, John Marlyn, Charles Israel and Sheila Watson. I think it is true to say that never before has Canada had ten such deft novelists writing at any one time.

Ethel Wilson (born 1890) is the senior member of the group. Her short stories began to appear immediately prior to World War II, but her first novel, *Hetty Dorval*, was not published until 1947. She has subsequently published three other novels—*The Innocent Traveller* (1949), *Swamp Angel* (1954) and *Love and Salt Water* (1956)—and two novelettes, "Lilly's Story" and "Tuesday and Wednesday", under the joint title *Equations of Love* (1952). In all of these books she writes urbanely and casually of people living in her home province of British Columbia. Her novels, however, are not regional idylls. Although the region is brought vividly to life, it is clear that the region is not her primary concern, but rather human character in its universal manifestations; and although there are idyllic interludes in her stories, there is also a full recognition of the powers of evil in the world. On the other hand, although there are persons and events in her books which in the hands of another writer might have become the material of melodrama, she is so given to muted effects of understatement, and to the persistent search for clarity and honesty, that she avoids the fault of romantic exaggeration. She is not one of those writers who set out to dazzle you with their brilliance, shock you with their brutality or overpower you with their passionate rhetoric. Quietly, simply, matter-of-factly, with dry humour and continuous good sense and taste, she records the events of her story.

She has, in other words, a sense of style. Her words seem to be chosen artlessly, but they are always exact and revealing. Her sentences and paragraphs are short and they flow into one another naturally—but they are so arranged as to achieve the maximum of effect with the minimum of fuss. Her novels are structural wholes, cunningly arranged around a few key episodes and symbols, but there is no evidence of artifice in them.

There is about her work, then, a deceptive simplicity—deceptive because the patient recital of events has undertones and overtones, echoes and reverberations. Simple objects such as a revolver become suggestive symbols; ordinary people reveal extraordinary capacities; what appears to be a simple declarative sentence proves to be ironic and ambiguous. Mrs. Wilson is fond of watching, and describing, creatures such as kittens, birds, dogs, deer—and watching them so closely that she eventually sees in them manifestations of eternal laws. Her apparent naivete is not naivete but innocence: she has the innocent eye which by patiently looking at things eventually sees into and through them.

And innocence, innocence in conflict with experience, is her main theme. The peculiar effectiveness of *Hetty Dorval* arises from the fact that the adventuress of the title is observed throughout by the eyes of an innocent young girl. In *The Innocent Traveller* the theme is explicit in the title: no matter how strange, eerie or exasperating the people and events Aunt Topaz encounters, she travels imperturbably through them, retaining to the end the unspoiled vision of a child. Myrtle and Mortimer, in "Tuesday and Wednesday", are innocents—and so is Lilly, in "Lilly's Story", in spite of her outwardly sordid experiences. The same theme recurs in the two more recent novels: Mrs. Wilson believes in people, in their capacity ultimately to keep themselves unspotted from the world. As she has Mrs. Severance in *Swamp Angel* put it, "I believe in faith. I believe in God . . . and in man, to some extent at least". Note the final phrase, however: Mrs. Wilson's is no easy optimism, but rather a modest affirmation of man's capacity to endure, to suffer and to love. All her novels are really "equations of love": demonstrations of the way in which imperfect human beings, in an imperfect world, may yet live together in love. Her ethic is a deeply Christian one: its core is compassion and charity.

All of Mrs. Wilson's novels are short. She does not work on a large scale, but she is a fine miniaturist, who gets lasting effects by small, delicate strokes. She knows exactly what she can do, and she does it to perfection.

Something of Mrs. Wilson's wit and urbanity is shared by Robertson Davies (born 1914), but in his work these qualities are conjoined with exuberance and expansiveness. There is more gusto in his novels, a greater element of farce and sheer high spirits. Whereas Mrs. Wilson is a gentle ironist, Davies is an irreverent satirist, mocking the pretensions and pretences of middle class Ontario society. Davies is also a much more prolific writer: he has been a very productive man of letters, producing three books of essays (*The Diary of Samuel Marchbanks*, 1947; *The Table-Talk of Samuel Marchbanks,* 1949; and *A Voice from the Attic,* 1961); seven or eight plays, including *Fortune, My Foe* (1948), *Eros at Breakfast* (1949), *At My Heart's Core* (1950) and *A Jig for the Gypsy* (1955) ; and many columns of literary criticism and social comment in the pages of *Saturday Night,* the Kingston *Whig-Standard,* the Peterborough *Examiner* and other periodicals. More particularly, from our present point of view, he has written three novels: *Tempest-Tost* (1951), *Leaven of Malice* (1953) and *A Mixture of Frailties* (1958) .

Davies' three novels are all set in the small Ontario city of Salterton, which, as someone has put it, bears no striking dissimilarity to the cathedral and university city of Kingston. As he spent much of his early life in that city, he begins with the advantage of close knowledge of his setting, and he has caught its quality to perfection. He has been accused of neglecting the recent industrial developments in that area, but this is not quite fair: he does mention the industries, but points out that they have not yet succeeded in dominating the town. The Salterton that interests him is the "society" that revolves around the university, the cathedral, the Little Theatre and the newspaper: people who are provincial, snobbish, figures of fun in many ways, but who have some interest in ideas, in the free play of mind and sensibility. And I think we may sum up the themes of his novels by saying that he is trying to reduce the provincialism by satirizing it, and to increase the area in which the mind and sensibility may have free play. To say that it is his aim to liberate the Canadian imagination is perhaps to put it too portentously, but it is a statement that has a large element of truth.

Davies has shown good judgment in selecting as the setting of his novels a region that he knows well. In the first two novels, especially, he has also chosen forms of social activity with which he is well acquainted. *Tempest-Tost* is the story of the production by the Salterton Little Theatre of

Shakespeare's *The Tempest,* and as Davies has had a great deal of theatrical experience he is able to recount the inside story of such a venture with brilliant authenticity. Similarly, in *Leaven of Malice,* the local newspaper is at the centre of the plot: and what Mr. Davies does not know about the small city newspapers of Ontario is probably not worth knowing. In *A Mixture of Frailties,* however, Davies has to some extent forsworn these advantages: although the novel begins in Salterton, it moves to London, England; and it deals not with drama or with newspapers but with the world of operatic music. Partly for this reason, *A Mixture of Frailties* is a less consistently assured novel than the others: it has dull passages, its transitions are sometimes awkward, it vacillates between light comedy and an almost religious seriousness.

Davies has many virtues as a novelist. His humour is almost always suave, deft and in good taste; he can arrange a comic scene, such as that of the book auction in *Tempest Tost,* with cunning dexterity and telling effect; he creates characters who, like those of Dickens, are easily identified and long remembered; he can make wise and witty comments on a great variety of subjects; he has an intimate knowledge of Canadian social behaviour, ways of speech and mental patterns; he is a lively satirist who can make current fads such as psychoanalysis, the solemn study of American and Canadian literature ("Am-Can"), standardized urban housing and pedagogical "methods" seem as ridiculous as they really are. Above all, perhaps, his novels are all written "con brio", with a lively, forceful verve that keeps us reading from line to line in eager anticipation. It is true that he is rather too ready to stop the flow of his plot while he lectures us on some side-issue that interests him, that his characters are sometimes rather like caricatures, that he is apt occasionally to blur his comic effect by a passage of high seriousness—but these are to a large extent the defects of his qualities. His quick, civilized mind was very much needed to let a little light into the dark corners of the Presbyterian conscience of Ontario.

There is no question about the Canadianism of Robertson Davies: he can pillory our provincialism so cleverly because he has felt its confining pressure himself. There is some question, however, about our right to claim David Walker and Brian Moore as Canadian novelists. Walker was born and grew up in Scotland, Moore in Northern Ireland; but as both have lived in Canada since the end of World War II, and have done all their writing here, it seems proper to include them among our novelists.

David Walker (born 1911) is something of a virtuoso: he writes well in a variety of styles. His first novel, *The Storm and the Silence* (1949), is a tense novel of adventure set in the Scottish Highlands. Here we witness Walker's power to create suspense, to follow physical action with patient watchfulness, to build up an atmosphere of almost unbearable apprehension. It is, if you like, a thriller, but a thriller of a very superior sort, written in a tense nervous style, with great psychological acumen, and with a careful attention to appropriateness of setting. His second novel, *Geordie* (1950), is a charming idyll of Scottish country life, and tells the story of a gamekeeper's son who by dint of constant exercising develops a physique which enables him to win the shot-put event for Britain at the Olympic Games. This is genre writing at its best: the Highland scenery is lovingly described, the characters are all quaint but kind and good, the atmosphere is one of quiet domesticity. There is not a false note in the book; on the other hand, there is little depth or complexity either in episode or characterization. The third novel, *The Pillar,* is very different again: the story of six British soldiers in a German prison camp during the war, it is primarily a psychological study of the effect of prolonged confinement upon the souls of men. His fourth novel, *Digby* (1953), the story of an American businessman's glorious holiday in the Highlands, has something of the thriller element of *The Storm and the Silence,* something of the idyllicism of *Geordie,* and a new element of uproarious comedy.

In his three most recent novels, Walker has continued to experiment. *Harry Black* (1956) and *Where the High Winds Blow* (1960) are his most ambitious novels to date, and bring together all the qualities which he has shown himself to possess: they are novels of adventure involving, respectively, a tiger hunt in India and efforts to establish great mining holdings in the Canadian north; they have some fine descriptive passages which show the same skill at the precise and evocative limning of natural scenery that was displayed in *Geordie*; they attempt to probe deeply into the psychological motivations and responses of their heroes, as did *The Pillar*; and they even have a certain element of humour, as in *Digby.* The remaining novel, *Sandy Was a Soldier's Boy* (1957), is a boy's adventure story, beautifully sustained for two thirds of its length but diverging into unconvincing melodrama in its conclusion.

Walker, then, has been a most productive novelist, and one who has applied himself assiduously to the task of finding his real métier. Having achieved a sort of limited perfection in *Geordie*, he might well have been content to play minor variations on a proven theme. Instead he has proceeded to try even more ambitious subjects, to develop his literary muscles in very much the same way that Geordie developed his physical muscles.

In contrast with the variety of Walker, Brian Moore (born 1921) is a novelist who has so far applied himself to one particular kind of story: the compassionate, ironic study of misfits. Moore's work has none of the healthy, outdoor atmosphere of Walker's and none of his interest in physical courage and endurance. If we summon up a mental image of his novels, we see a lonely man or woman shut up in a small, ill-furnished room, surreptitiously looking in a mirror in a pathetic effort at self-examination. On the face of it, nothing could be less promising material for distinguished fiction than Moore's heroes and heroines: an alcoholic spinster who pathetically yearns for friendship and love (*Judith Hearne*, 1955); a bachelor schoolmaster whose one serious attempt to seduce a girl is a dismal flop which yet brings him to near-disgrace (*The Feast of Lupercal*, 1957); and a luckless Irish immigrant in Montreal who temporarily loses his wife and his self-respect because he cannot find a job commensurate with his romantic aspirations (*The Luck of Ginger Coffey*, 1960). His novels are studies of frustration, of people who have been dwarfed and stunted by a narrow, provincial environment, whose leaves never are allowed to expand in sunlight. Moore is equally adept both in the delineation of their interior lives and of their exterior environment: person and place are equally clear, and wear against each other with grating harshness.

The strange thing is that for all the sordidness, all the drabness of these stories, their total effect is far from dispiriting. This is partly because of Moore's compassion: no matter how mean the characters may be, we always feel Moore's tenderness for them, and this tenderness gives warmth to the novels, is a touch of sunlight amid the prevailing greyness. It is partly also because of Moore's unobtrusive but pervasive irony: other standards, other possible ways of life and judgment are being implied, thus opening windows from these shuttered rooms into a larger, freer world. Perhaps chiefly the inspiriting effect arises from the fact that none of the characters are totally defeated; indeed, in the sense that they have finally come to terms with themselves and with life, they have achieved a real if limited victory. In the beginning of the novel, Judith Hearne was still a romantic dreamer, refusing to accept the reality of her own age or situation; in its climax, she makes a wild gesture of futile revolt; but at the end she is reassembling the fragments of her life, preparing to face reality without illusion. Diarmuid Devine, in *The Feast of Lupercal*, comes closer to the resignation of defeat, but even he will endure, will carry on with his teaching rather than making any melodramatic gesture such as suicide. And in *The Luck of Ginger Coffey* the positive note is struck most clearly of all. Ginger realizes that "Love isn't an act, it's a whole life" and that: "He had tried; he had not won. But oh! what did it matter? He would die in humble circumstances: it did not matter. There would be no victory for Ginger Coffey, no victory big or little, for . . . he had learned the truth. Life was the victory. . . . Going on was the victory. . . ."

But all this gives a rather false picture of the novels because it leaves out an important element in them, and an element which also does much to redeem them from drabness. Moore has a fine sense of comedy. The attempted seduction in *The Feast of Lupercal*, for example, which has such serious results for Diarmuid, is a brilliantly comic scene. Ginger Coffey is almost as much a comic character, reminiscent of Micawber with his perpetual hopefulness, as he is a pathetic one. It is perhaps Moore's point that laughter, more than any other single factor, makes life endurable.

Laughter is also a very important ingredient in the novels of Mordecai Richler (born 1931), but laughter which, generally speaking, is much more bitter than that of Brian Moore. Richler is a far more boisterous and angry writer than Moore, more discursive and more wide-ranging. He has an enormous appetite for sensations, an interest in almost every type of human being and event. His is not the essentially private world of Moore, but the public world of politics, business, entertainment and social activity.

Richler's first novel, *The Acrobats* (1954), established the breadth of his interests and the bitterly comic nature of his vision. His central figure is a young Canadian painter, André Bennett, who feels himself one of a lost generation, without faith or hope. Living in Spain, Bennett is torn between nihilism, the communism of Guillermo, the domesticity of Toni and the humanism of Chaim. In the end he is killed by his rival for Toni's affections, the ex-Nazi, Roger Kraus. The moral seems to be that by trying to remain uncommitted, Bennett is inevitably destroyed. He is a political acrobat who "did tightrope dances on high and windy places"—and who fell to his ruin. This first novel is far from perfect—the echoes of Hemingway, Dos Passos, O'Hara and other American novelists are too insistent, and the theme is often lost amidst a plethora of rather disconnected episodes—but it has the redeeming grace of liveliness. The novel abounds in vivid crowd scenes, in exact physical details of sight, sound and smell, and in striking character studies.

Richler's subsequent novels have revealed him finding his way to a more distinctive manner and to a more coherent structure and theme. In *Son of a Smaller Hero* (1955) and *The Apprenticeship of Duddy Kravitz* (1959) he turned to his native city of Montreal as the setting, and succeeded in bringing that city to life as no writer had been able to do before. In both of these novels we again get the sense of abounding vitality, the inexhaustible appetite for sensory impressions of all kinds, the delight in crowd scenes, the gift for quickly sketching in eccentric characters of all kinds, but here there is a coherence between the parts which was lacking in the first novel. In part this coherence is achieved by more strongly realizing the central character: beside Noah Adler and Duddy Kravitz, André Bennett is amorphous and wraithlike. In part it is achieved by the use of a thematic motif which runs like a thread through the disparate episodes: the locked strong-box in *Son of a Smaller Hero*, the dream of owning land in *The Apprenticeship of Duddy Kravitz*. Finally, coherence is achieved by a more clearly defined theme, even though the theme in each case is largely a negative one. In *Son of a Smaller Hero*, Noah Adler rejects the way of life of the Jewish community of Montreal because it is based, like his father's supposed "heroism", on false pretences: the ark he seeks out of the flood is integrity and freedom, and these, at the novel's end, he sets out to seek in Europe. In *The Apprenticeship of Duddy Kravitz*, it is the life of materialistic acquisitiveness which is being rejected: Duddy is the inevitable product of a society which has no respect for any values other than material ones.

Richler's third novel, sandwiched between the two we have just mentioned, was *A Choice of Enemies* (1957). It resembles *The Acrobats* in that it is set in Europe (in Germany and England), deals with émigrés, and is mainly concerned with the collapse of the political beliefs of the thirties. It is Richler's most bitter novel—there is satire at the expense of Canada in general and Canadian intellectuals in particular, satire against the intelligent left and against London, and satire at the expense of the émigré colony in the United Kingdom—and it is his most confused. There are some excellent individual scenes, but the characters are almost universally repellent and their search for values in a doomed society seems hardly worth taking seriously.

Richler's vitality is such that one feels secure in predicting a long and productive career for him. If he can continue to improve as rapidly as he did between *The Acrobats* and *The Apprenticeship of Duddy Kravitz*, he should become a very important novelist indeed. His angry jibes are as much needed to stir Canadians out of their complacency as is the more light-hearted raillery of Robertson Davies.

As different as they are, the five novelists of this group have one quality in common: a capacity for wit and sophistication. The best Canadian novels hitherto—those of Grove, Callaghan and MacLennan—had been a little too stiff and solemn. Davies, Richler, Moore and the others have just as significant things to say, but they say them more lightly, casually and easily. Their work marks a most refreshing development in our literary atmosphere.

That we are in for refreshment is suggested by the early work of five other novelists. Ernest Buckler (born 1908), in his first and so far only novel, *The Mountain and the*

*Valley* (1952), gave us the story of the life of a sensitive farm boy in Nova Scotia which, in its honesty and forthrightness, was a far cry from the average regional idyll. His atmospheric power, his skill in the unobtrusive manipulation of symbols and his fine sense of the tensions implicit in personal relationships make him a novelist to watch with delighted anticipation. Adele Wiseman (born 1928) in *The Sacrifice* (1956) and John Marlyn (born 1912) in *Under the Ribs of Death* (1957) produced fine first novels about the lives of European immigrants in the midwestern city of Winnipeg. Sheila Watson's *The Double Hook* (1959) is technically the most adventurous of the group: obliquely and allusively, by a technique which resembles that of gathering what goes on in a closed room by listening at the keyhole, she gradually reveals to us a disturbing story of lust and jealousy in a small British Columbian settlement. Charles E. Israel (born 1920), the last member of this group, produced two novels in the fifties—*How Many Angels* (1956), a political novel set in the Sudentenland, and *The Mark* (1958), a psychological study set in California. The latter is the more impressive, and is the chief reason for believing that Israel, now a Canadian citizen, will eventually rank as an important novelist. *The Mark* is a gentle, sensitive novel using material which could easily have been made merely sensational: a man who sexually assaults a nine-year old girl. The novel is something of a case history in abnormal psychology, but it is much more. Israel makes us believe in and sympathize with his twisted central character, and the theme of the book is human vulnerability, the necessity for compassion.

This brief survey of our recent fiction has, I trust, demonstrated that there is as much current activity in this area as in poetry. What the sixties may bring no one can tell, but that some of the ten novelists we have just considered will bring us something valid and exciting is almost certain. And already there are signs of new writers appearing to challenge them. The future should not be dull.

# CHAPTER NINE

# *Conclusion*

IT IS CLEAR from the preceding survey that Canada has produced a goodly number of talented writers; but she has not as yet produced a single writer of the very first rank. Even the best of her writers—Lampman, Carman, Pratt, Klein and Layton in poetry; Kirby, Grove, Callaghan, Moore and Richler in the novel; and Haliburton and Leacock in prose humour—are, at the most charitable estimate, secondary figures on the world literary stage.

Of the various literary forms, poetry is the one in which Canada's contribution has been most outstanding. At every stage of her literary history, with the possible exception of the colonial period, poetry has been the dominant form of literary expression. The poetry has been, as might have been expected in a vast, thinly populated and beautiful country, primarily a poetry of natural description. It has also been predominantly romantic, personal, and lyrical: partly because Canadian poetry has been contemporaneous with the romantic movement in European literature and partly because Canadian society has not been sufficiently developed to attract the passionate attention of her poets. Only in the last thirty-five years has Canadian society begun to attract such attention, and even yet the landscape tends to overshadow the people, as an examination of the best work of even comparatively socially minded poets such as Birney, Livesay, Anderson, Page and Layton will prove.

Next in importance to poetry in Canada has been prose humour. Haliburton and Leacock are certainly superior to any other Canadian writers of creative prose with the possible exception of Grove, and they are simply the two most outstanding figures in a long and almost continuous line. Haliburton's contemporary, Joseph Howe, could be extremely witty on occasions, and the best passages in the documentary books of Susanna Moodie and Catherine Parr Traill are humorous. Later in the nineteenth century came Edward William Thomson, whose best humorous stories, such as "The Privilege of the Limits", are worthy of Leacock at his best. In the early twentieth century, along with Leacock himself, there appeared Peter McArthur (1866-1924), whose humorous sketches of farm life, such as "Why I Stick to the Farm" with its memorable opening "As well ask a woodchuck why he sticks to his hole", can still be read with delight. In the most recent period, the tradition has been carried on by such writers as John D. Robins, Robertson Davies and Paul Hiebert.

The novel proper, however, until very recently, has not flourished in Canada. The average Canadian novel is well below the average Canadian poem or humorous essay. The great majority of our novelists have devoted themselves to two forms which by their very nature are limited in scope: the historical romance and the regional idyll. The result has been a mass of fiction which is, on the one hand, falsely glamorous and factitiously exciting, and, on the other, sentimental and oversweet. The greatest type of novel, which seeks to penetrate deeply into the consciousness of its characters, into the nature of a society or into the constitution of the universe, was not practised at all in Canada prior to the emergence of Frederick Philip Grove in 1925, and even since that time it has appeared only intermittently and imperfectly. With a few honourable exceptions, our novelists seem cursed with timidity: they make few technical experiments, and they restrict their gaze to the more pleasant and superficial aspects of life.

The reasons for this dearth of powerful Canadian novels are obscure, but we may hazard a guess that the nature of Canadian society has had much to do with it. Great novels are usually the product of a society in process of radical readjustment; and Canadian society has, at any rate until the last few years, developed slowly and unspectacularly. There have been no great crises about which the national imagination could cluster. The War of 1812 was a secondary campaign which deeply affected only Ontario; the rebellions of 1837 were abortive minority movements; Confederation itself was a reluctant and hesitant adventure; the two Great Wars were fought far from our shores. Even should the potential novelist be sufficiently sensitive to respond to the drama which lurks beneath the rather drab surface of Canadian society, the task which then confronts him is one of unusual difficulty. Canada is a vast country of marked regional variations and with two major cultural traditions and many minor ones: the result is that Canadian society, for all its immaturity, is a difficult one for the artist to reduce to order. It is no wonder that most Canadian novelists either retreat to the relatively orderly society of ancient New France or escape to some secluded region.

Two other factors have inhibited the development of serious fiction: our distrust of abstract thought and our lingering puritanism. We can hardly expect our novelists to deal with profound ideas when we as a nation have no philosophical tradition worthy of the name, and when our national policies are constantly improvised rather than based on a reasoned philosophy of government. The influence of puritanism has been more direct: until recently, whenever a Canadian novelist dared to deal frankly with sexual and other controversial questions—as Grove did in *Settlers of the Marsh* or Callaghan in *Strange Fugitive*—the Canadian public reacted with shocked disapproval.

The short story has fared rather better than the novel, though it too has been inhibited by the same forces. The short stories of most Canadian writers of fiction since the late nineteenth century have been of a finer artistic quality than their novels, as witness the work in both forms of Marjorie Pickthall, Mazo de la Roche, W. G. Hardy, Morley Callaghan, Raymond Knister and Sinclair Ross. The short story has not, however, flourished here as it has in the United States, partly because there have been few publishing outlets for serious short stories. Whereas there are literally dozens of magazines which encourage the serious young American writer, there are only two or three Canadian magazines which will accept anything but slick formula stories. The recent policy of the Canadian Broadcasting Corporation of broadcasting good short stories has done something to remedy this situation, but radio is a relatively ephemeral medium which can never take the place of the printed word.

The development of radio broadcasting has also done much to encourage another literary form which has been severely handicapped in Canada: drama. No separate sections on Canadian drama have appeared in this book for the simple reason that our output of dramatic writing has been almost negligible. Such dramas as appeared in Canada up to 1920—Heavysege's *Saul* and Mair's *Tecumseh* and Marjorie Pickthall's *Wood-Carver's Wife*—were closet dramas which interest us as poems rather than as plays. In the nineteen twenties, as the Little Theatre Movement took root in Canada, a start was made on the production of Canadian plays, but very little of permanent interest emerged. Merrill Denison (born 1893) was the most promising playwright, and he produced in *Brothers in Arms, Contract* and *The Prize Winner* three excellent light comedies; but after a decade or so he gave up the effort and emigrated to the greener fields of the United States. Mazo de la Roche also participated only briefly in the movement, and of her four plays only the delightful farce *Low Life* is likely to survive. The Little Theatre Movement almost completely collapsed under the impact of the economic depression, but the initiation of the Dominion Drama Festival in 1933 helped to keep it alive and the return of prosperity during and after World War II has produced a strong revival. In the last few years a number of promising plays have been written and produced. Robertson Davies, in farces such as *Eros at Breakfast* and more serious plays such as *Fortune, My Foe* and *At My Heart's Core,* has shown a capacity to combine witty dialogue with the presentation of provocative ideas; John Coulter, in *The House in the Quiet Glen, Family Portrait* and *The Drums Are Out,* has demonstrated a gift for racy Irish dialogue and for vivid character portrayal; and Gwen Pharis has given us a number of fine dramatic portrayals of the Canadian West, of which the most memorable are the one-act *Still Stands the House* and the three-act *Dark Harvest.*

But legitimate drama in Canada, even today, remains a very delicate growth. Canada has no city large enough to serve as the permanent home of a fully professional company, and the distances between her cities are so great as to make the project of a travelling company a very risky one. The establishment of the Shakespearean Festival at Stratford in the fifties, and the grants from The Canada Council which enable the Canadian Players to travel across the country, may eventually stimulate a native drama; so far their main effect has been to raise the level of Canadian acting and of Canadian dramatic taste.

But radio drama suffers from no such disadvantages, and it is in radio drama that Canadian playwrights have recently been most active. In January, 1944, Andrew Allan inaugurated a series of radio plays under the general title of *Stage 44,* and the series has brought many distinguished performances to Canadian listeners. Joseph Schull, Lister Sinclair and Len Peterson have been the most regular and most significant contributors of original plays to the programme.

Schull, in plays such as *The Bridge* and *The Legend of Ghost Lagoon,* has displayed a command of poetic symbolism and a deep emotive power, though he is inclined to be over-rhetorical and melodramatic; Sinclair, author of *We All Hate Toronto, Socrates* and *Encounter by Moonlight,* is an obvious disciple of Bernard Shaw and has a measure of that master's wit and provocative raillery, though he is less successful when he attempts the role of a serious prophet; Peterson, the most original of the trio, has hauntingly suggested the error of our times in plays such as *They Are All Afraid* and *Burlap Bags.* Unfortunately none of these plays, with the exception of some of Sinclair's in a volume entitled *A Play on Words* (1948), is available in printed form.

It remains to discuss the question of "distinctiveness", which was raised in the Introduction. I suggested that there had been rather too much emphasis on this matter, since it tended to encourage in our writers a self-conscious Canadianism. The writer who consciously attempts to be Canadian, who insists on packing his work with references to the maple leaf and the Laurentian Shield, is almost sure to become smugly provincial and his work is likely to be of merely local interest. But Canadian history and especially Canadian geography inevitably do affect the writer and make his work distinctive if he is a true artist and responds with special intensity to his social and physical environment.

Continually through this book I have attempted to show that an understanding of the development of Canadian society is necessary for an understanding of Canadian literature. Only a tentative beginning has been made on this hitherto almost completely neglected investigation, but the main outlines are clear. The Canadian Oliver Goldsmith's work was partly made possible by the work of his Anglo-Irish grand-uncle, but its appearance and attitudes were at least equally affected by the fact that Goldsmith was the inhabitant of a small colonial society which had reached a provisional stage of cultural maturity and self-consciousness. Thomas Chandler Haliburton and Joseph Howe were products of the same society, and the work of both men represented a response to the social conditions of their time. It is as important for an understanding of *Sam Slick* to know that the colony of Nova Scotia was undergoing a crisis in the mid-eighteen thirties as to know that forms of dialect humour were at that time becoming popular in the American press. John Richardson is a less indigenous figure, but his best novels—*Wacousta* and *The Canadian Brothers*—are strongly influenced by the nascent Canadian nationalism which was produced by the War of 1812. The work of Susanna Moodie and Catherine Parr Traill can most fully be appreciated not by relating it to English romanticism but by seeing in it the reaction of two upper class immigrants to a pioneer society. Charles Sangster, strongly influenced as he was by English poets such as Moore and Tennyson, was even more deeply affected by the national aspirations which were being aroused in Upper Canada in the eighteen forties and fifties and which were ultimately to result in Confederation.

With the writers of the Confederation period, the influences of a phase of Canadian social development are even more obvious. The national excitement of that period is at least partly responsible for the sudden increase in literary activity, and for each of the writers more specific social influences can be isolated. Roberts and Carman were the products of a provincial society in New Brunswick which, after years of slow germination and growth, suddenly burst into flower in the sixties, seventies and eighties of the last century. The poetry of Lampman is the product of the impact upon a sensitive mind of the industrial revolution which occurred in Ontario in the late nineteenth century. In the nature poems he seeks refuge from the new industrialism; in the social poems he attacks it directly.

In this respect Lampman is a key figure, for the dominant

pattern of social response in Canadian literature was set by his work. Since his time, Canadian writers have almost constantly attacked in various ways the excesses and the false values of a commercial and industrial society. Even Marjorie Pickthall, though most of her work represents an escape from the new society, sometimes, as in "The Woodsman in the Foundry", expresses her distaste for industrialism directly:

> Where the trolley's rumble
> Jars the bones,
> He hears waves that tumble
> Green-linked along the golden stones.
>
> Where the crane goes clanging
> Chains and bars,
> He sees branches hanging
> Little leaves against the laughing stars. . . .

We have already seen how Leacock's work consists predominantly of a satirical attack upon the values of commercial society, and the same attitude is evident in the work of Mazo de la Roche and in Frederick Philip Grove's *The Master of the Mill*. E. J. Pratt conforms to the same general pattern by exalting the primitive virtues of courage and loyalty and by delighting in the victory of natural power over mechanical ingenuity in *The Titanic*. The novels of Morley Callaghan all have as their heroes people who feel alien in the commercial civilization of our time, and Hugh MacLennan's *The Precipice* and *Each Man's Son* both contain many passages attacking the values of such a society. Echoes of the same theme may be heard in Thomas Raddall's *The Nymph and the Lamp* and in Will R. Bird's *So Much to Record,* and it is predominant in the novels of Mordecai Richler and in Brian Moore's *The Luck of Ginger Coffey.*

We find the same pattern of response in the poetry of the nineteen thirties and forties. The members of the Montreal Group were all in revolt against commercialism; perhaps the clearest expression of their attitude is found in F. R. Scott's "Saturday Sundae":

> The triple-decker and the double-cone
> I side-swipe swiftly, suck the coke-straws dry.
> Ride toadstool seat beside the slab of morgue—
> Sweet corner drug-store, sweet pie in the sky.
>
> My brothers and my sisters, two by two,
> Sit sipping succulence and sighing sex.
> Each tiny adolescent universe
> A world the vested interests annex.
>
> Such bread and circuses these times allow,
> Opium most popular, life so small and slick,
> Perhaps with candy is the new world born
> And cellophane shall wrap the heretic.

But the reference in this final stanza to "the new world" reminds us that there was a difference between the attitude of the Montreal Group and of more recent poets such as Anderson, Page, Dudek and Souster, on the one hand, and that of most of the writers of whom we have been speaking, on the other. Kirby, Leacock and de la Roche yearned for an earlier, pre-industrial day; the more recent writers, recognizing that industrialism is here to stay, have advocated a new social order in which most of its adverse effects would be mitigated.

The gradual displacement of an agricultural and rural way of life by an industrial and urban one is, however, only the most striking of the social developments of the last half century in Canada. Almost all the other developments—the steady rise of national independence and national consciousness, the involvement in world wars in particular and in world affairs in general, the depression and drought of the thirties, the growth of progressive and collectivist political ideas—have been clearly reflected in our literature and have helped to give it a distinctive quality. Poems such as Anne Marriott's *The Wind Our Enemy* or short stories such as

Sinclair Ross's "The Lamp at Noon" are obvious products of peculiarly Canadian circumstances.

But even more important than our social history in giving our literature a distinctive form and flavour has been the Canadian climate and landscape. Canada is a land of great distances, of rugged mountains and of swiftly flowing rivers; it is a land of violent contrasts, of abrupt seasonal changes, of almost incredibly bright colours; it is also a northern country, a land of ice and snow, of dazzling whiteness and of the luminous spectrum of the *aurora borealis*. Such an impressive environment could not fail to affect the country's artists. It is interesting to observe that the English and French critics, when the paintings of the Group of Seven were first exhibited in London and Paris in the nineteen twenties, compared them to the work of Scandinavian and Russian painters, and that English reviewers of the early novels of Mazo de la Roche and Frederick Philip Grove detected in them a quality which they could best describe as Russian. In all cases the comparison was apt, not because there was an appreciable or direct Russian or Scandinavian influence on the Canadian work, but because it was the product of a similar geography.

The artistic response to these geographical conditions is difficult to resolve into a neat formula. Northrop Frye, in a brilliant review of Smith's *Book of Canadian Poetry* (*The Canadian Forum*, December, 1943), chose to describe it as "the evocation of stark terror", but this phrase, suggestive as it is, is not sufficiently inclusive. Terror there is in Canadian literature—terror of the wilderness, of storm and flood, of savages and of the intense extremes of cold and heat. But there is also exultation, the fascination as well as the fear of great strength. Perhaps the most inclusive phrase for the dominant reaction, though even it is not fully satisfying, is the expression of a sense of awe.

Wherever we look in Canadian literature we find variations on this theme. Sometimes it is the awe inspired by the sheer solitariness of the Canadian scene, as in these early, awkward lines by Oliver Goldsmith:

> When, looking round, the lonely settler sees
> His home amid a wilderness of trees:
> How sinks his heart in those deep solitudes,
> Where not a voice upon his ear intrudes;
> Where solemn silence all the waste pervades. . . .

This sense of loneliness we find expressed by almost every Canadian writer—by Susanna Moodie, Charles Sangster, Charles Mair, Bliss Carman, Archibald Lampman and Duncan Campbell Scott in the nineteenth century; and by Pratt, Grove, Birney, Anderson, F. R. Scott, Morley Callaghan, Hugh MacLennan and Philip Child in the twentieth. Perhaps Duncan Campbell Scott, in lines such as these:

> So lone is the land that in this lonely room
> Never before has breathed a human being. . .

Frederick Philip Grove, in his frequent pictures of man dwarfed by the stretching immensities of the Western prairies, and A. J. M. Smith in his "Lonely Land", have expressed this feeling most powerfully.

Sometimes the sense of awe takes the form of fear of the violence which lurks in those lonely stretches of country— the violence of storm, of heat or of cold, or of the savage inhabitants. Violent storms play a large part in the work of Isabella Valancy Crawford, D. C. Scott, Grove and Pratt. The fearful fascination of intense heat we find in Mair's "August" and in Lampman's "Heat", and that of intense cold in stories such as Grove's "Snow" and poems such as Carman's "Northern Vigil". Mair writes of a Canadian summer:

> When every morn is fiery as the noon,
> And every eve is fiery as the morn,
> And every night a prison hot and dark. . .

and Carman of a Canadian winter:

> The windows of my room
> Are dark with bitter frost,
> The stillness aches with doom
> Of something loved and lost.

The fear of the violence of the savage inhabitants of the wilderness is expressed most fully in the massacre scene of Howe's "Acadia", in several poems by D. C. Scott, in Lampman's "At the Long Sault" and in Pratt's *Brébeuf and His Brethren*.

But sometimes the sense of awe holds more of exultation than of fear. Even Charles Heavysege, who was almost immune to the influences of his environment, felt the fascination of a Canadian sky at night, as is shown by these lines from his sonnet "The Winter Galaxy":

> The stars are glittering in the frosty sky,
> Frequent as pebbles on a broad sea-coast;
> And o'er the vault the cloud-like galaxy
> Has marshalled its innumerable host.
> Alive all heaven seems! with wondrous glow
> Tenfold refulgent every star appears,
> As if some wide, celestial gale did blow,
> And thrice illume the ever-kindled spheres.

Patrick Anderson, in his "Poem on Canada", exults in the fact that the land is greater and stronger than the men who have tried to conquer it:

> And, despite the traders, despite the coureurs de bois
> and the voyageurs, and those who slung canals
> and fastened bridges above them or sharpened their dreams
> to the wizened and hungry winter of the rails
> westward, forever—or fenced and festooned the miles,
> this Laurentide land, boosted with water power
> and blown from the North, was greater and grander by far.

A similar exultation in unconquerable natural force is found in D. C. Scott's "The Eagle Speaks", in Pratt's "The

Cachalot" and *The Titanic* and in many passages of Grove's essays and novels.

This response to the overwhelming facts of geography, to the pressure of a frightening but alluring climate and landscape, has had important consequences for the Canadian writer's attitude toward his fellow-men. In the first place, the geography has been so impressive that man has been dwarfed by it: our best poetry has been landscape poetry and the best passages in our novels have been descriptive passages. Secondly, the facts of geography have engendered in our writers a sense of humility. North American literature, as might be expected of the literature of a newly settled continent, has been predominantly optimistic; but Canada's optimism has been much more restrained than that of the United States. Our writers have been much less inclined to boast than such United States authors as Whitman and Sandburg because they have lived in a physical environment which is much more forbidding and more humbling. Grove, with his portrayal of a progress slowly and hardly earned by labouring pioneers, gives us a very different sense of the pioneer process than Whitman, and one which is certainly more in accord with Canadian experience. Canadian literature, in other words, is recognizably North American in its vigour, range and optimism, but it is less spectacular than that of the United States because it has been restrained by the pressure of a stern environment.

It would be idle to blame the shortcomings of Canadian literature upon geography and climate. Perhaps the most blighting of all influences have been the lack of a genuine sense of identity in Canada and the lack of a proper sense of self-respect. It is difficult to sort out cause and effect here. Certainly a powerful literature can do much to give a nation a sense of identity; on the other hand, the writer cannot create entirely out of nothing. It is only when a society has achieved some sort of provisional stability or sense of destiny that a strong literature emerges to modify or solidify that tentative pattern. Only in recent years, and then only to a very limited degree, has this Canadian image begun to appear. A favorite parlour and panel game in Canada is still to argue "what is a Canadian?" or such topics as "the price of being Canadian". Our very preoccupation with such questions betrays our insecurity and uncertainty. We still have no national flag, no agreed national anthem, no real cultural centre. I think the recent appearance of novels such as those of Mordecai Richler about Montreal or Adele Wiseman and John Marlyn about Winnipeg indicate that our cities are beginning to have a pattern that the writer can profitably examine, and that these novels will in turn help to define and clarify this pattern. But the process is still in its initial stages.

But in writing in this depreciatory vein I am probably betraying the fact that I am a victim of another Canadian trait, that of self-depreciation. Recently, on the centenary of the birth of Bliss Carman, there was almost no recognition of the event in Canada; it was left to the Russians in Moscow to hold a memorial banquet in his honour and to read his poems. Because Carman is a minor poet, we are afraid to praise him at all, for fear of being thought to have low standards. Almost invariably we wait for the critics of London or New York or Paris to praise a Canadian writer before we dare to do so ourselves. To show any enthusiasm for Canadian writing is felt to be vulgar, proof of a preference for the second-rate.

The difficulty, of course, is to escape this excessive modesty without falling into the trap of national vaingloriousness. Much of the wry timidity with which we now speak of Canadian literature and culture is a reaction against the blatant boosterism of the twenties, when mediocre books by Canadian writers were declared to be world classics. But surely it is possible to be interested in our literary past and present without falling into either undue self-abasement or unwarranted self-glorification. Our literature is not yet one of the world's great literatures, and may never be; but it is our own, and it has its moderate successes as well as its dismal failures. Even in the failures, even in the Heavyseges and the Sangsters and the Mairs, there may be a legitimate Canadian interest. Our literary history may not be glorious, but it is ours and we should be aware of it—even if only to learn from our own mistakes. It is to help provoke such awareness that this book has been written.

# Suggestions for Further Reading

## A. RECENT ANTHOLOGIES OF CANADIAN LITERATURE

Ethel Hume Bennett, *New Harvesting: Contemporary Canadian Poetry 1918-38*, Toronto, 1938.

Earle Birney, *Twentieth Century Canadian Poetry*, Toronto, 1953.

Bliss Carman, Lorne Pierce and V. B. Rhodenizer, *Canadian Poetry in English*, Toronto, 1954.

Louis Dudek and Irving Layton, *Canadian Poems 1850-1952*, Toronto, 1952.

Ralph Gustafson, *Canadian Poetry (English)*, Harmondsworth, Toronto and New York, 1942.

Ralph Gustafson, *Canadian Accent*, London and New York, 1944.

Ralph Gustafson, *The Penguin Book of Canadian Verse*, Harmondsworth, Toronto and New York, 1958.

C. F. Klinck and R. E. Watters, *Canadian Anthology*, Toronto, 1955.

Raymond Knister, *Canadian Short Stories*, Toronto, 1928.

Desmond Pacey, *A Book of Canadian Stories*, Toronto, 1947, 1950, 1952, 1961.

John D. Robins, *A Pocketful of Canada*, Toronto, 1946.

John D. Robins and Margaret Ray, *A Book of Canadian Humour*, 1951.

Malcolm Ross, *Our Sense of Identity: A Book of Canadian Essays*, Toronto, 1954.

A. J. M. Smith, *The Book of Canadian Poetry*, Toronto, 1943, 1948, 1957.

A. J. M. Smith, *The Oxford Book of Canadian Verse*, Toronto, 1960.

John Sutherland, *Other Canadians*, Montreal, 1947.

Robert Weaver and Helen James, *Canadian Short Stories*, Toronto, 1952.

Robert Weaver, *Canadian Short Stories* (World's Classics edition), Toronto, 1960.

## B. RECENT STUDIES OF THE CANADIAN BACKGROUND

George W. Brown, editor, *Canada*, United Nations Series, Berkeley, 1950.

A. L. Burt, *A Short History of Canada for Americans*, Minneapolis and Toronto, 1942.

J. M. S. Careless, *Canada: A Story of Challenge*, Cambridge, England, 1953.

H. M. Clokie, *Canadian Government and Politics*, Toronto, 1944.

Donald G. Creighton, *Dominion of the North*, Boston, 1944, Toronto, 1946.

Donald G. Creighton, *The Story of Canada*, Toronto, 1959.

R. M. Dawson, *The Government of Canada*, Toronto, 1947.

Bruce Hutchison, *The Unknown Country*, New York and Toronto, 1942.

A. R. M. Lower, *From Colony to Nation,* Toronto and New York, 1946.
A. R. M. Lower, *Canadians in the Making,* Toronto, 1958.
Hugh MacLennan, *Cross-Country,* Toronto, 1949.
Edgar McInnes, *Canada, a Political and Social History,* New York and Toronto, 1947.
Chester Martin, *Foundations of Canadian Nationhood,* Toronto, 1955.
Vincent Massey, *On Being Canadian,* Toronto, 1948.
Julian Park, editor, *The Culture of Contemporary Canada,* Ithaca, New York, 1957.
Lorne Pierce, *A Canadian People,* Toronto, 1945.
Report of the Royal Commission on National Development in the Arts, Letters and Sciences, Ottawa, 1951.
Malcolm Ross, editor, *The Arts in Canada,* Toronto, 1958.
F. R. Scott, *Canada Today,* Toronto, 1938.
André Siegfried, *Canada,* London, 1937.
Mason Wade, *The French Canadians,* London, 1955.
W. S. Wallace, *The Growth of Canadian National Feeling,* Toronto, 1927.
Carl Wittke, *History of Canada,* New York, 1941.
George M. Wrong, *The Canadians: The Story of a People,* 1938.

## C. STUDIES OF CANADIAN LITERATURE

### 1. Books

R. P. Baker, *English-Canadian Literature to the Confederation,* Cambridge and Toronto, 1920.
Arthur S. Bourinot, *Five Canadian Poets,* Ottawa, 1954.
Arthur S. Bourinot, *At the Mermaid Inn,* Ottawa, 1958.
J. G. Bourinot, *Our Intellectual Strength and Weakness: A Short Historical and Critical Review of Literature, Art, and Education in Canada,* Montreal and London, 1893.
E. K. Brown, editor, *Canadian Literature Today,* Toronto, 1938.
E. K. Brown, *On Canadian Poetry,* Toronto, 1943, 1947.
L. J. Burpee, *A Little Book of Canadian Essays,* Toronto, 1909.
W. E. Collin, *The White Savannahs,* Toronto, 1936.
Wilfrid Eggleston, *The Frontier and Canadian Letters,* Toronto, 1958.
J. D. Logan and D. G. French, *Highways of Canadian Literature,* Toronto, 1924.
Archibald MacMechan, *Headwaters of Canadian Literature,* Toronto, 1924.
Archibald MacMurchy, *Handbook of Canadian Literature,* Toronto, 1906.
E. A. McCourt, *The Canadian West in Fiction,* Toronto, 1949.
T. G. Marquis, *History of English-Canadian Literature* (Canada and its Provinces, Volume XII), Toronto, 1914.
Desmond Pacey, *Ten Canadian Poets,* Toronto, 1958.
W. P. Percival, *Leading Canadian Poets,* Toronto, 1948.
Arthur L. Phelps, *Canadian Writers,* Toronto, 1952.
Lorne Pierce, *Outline of Canadian Literature,* Toronto, 1927.
R. E. Rashley, *Poetry in Canada: The First Three Steps,* Toronto, 1958.
V. B. Rhodenizer, *Handbook of Canadian Literature,* Ottawa, 1930.
Lionel Stevenson, *Appraisals of Canadian Literature,* Toronto, 1926.
George Whalley, editor, *Writing in Canada,* Toronto, 1956.

## 2. ARTICLES

Margaret Avison, "Poets in Canada", *Poetry* (Chicago) 94: 182-5 (June, 1959).

A. G. Bailey, "Creative Moments in the Culture of the Maritime Provinces", *Dalhousie Review* 29: 231-244 (October, 1949).

A. G. Bailey, "Literature and Nationalism after Confederation", *University of Toronto Quarterly* 25: 409-24 (July, 1956).

Earle Birney, "To arms with Canadian poetry", *The Canadian Forum* 19: 322-4 (January, 1940).

Earle Birney, "Advice to anthologists; some rude reflections on Canadian verse", *The Canadian Forum* 21: 338-40 (February, 1942).

Earle Birney, "Has Poetry a Future in Canada?" *Manitoba Arts Review,* Volume V, no. 1: 7-15 (Spring, 1946).

Claude Bissell, "Literary Taste in Central Canada during the late Nineteenth Century", *Canadian Historical Review* 31: 237-251 (September, 1950).

Claude Bissell, "A Common Ancestry: Literature in Australia and Canada", *University of Toronto Quarterly* 25: 131-142 (1956).

E. K. Brown, "The Immediate Present in Canadian Literature", *Sewanee Review* 41: 430-442 (October, 1933).

E. K. Brown, "The development of poetry in Canada 1880-1940", *Poetry* (Chicago) 58: 34-37 (April, 1941).

E. K. Brown, "The Wall Against Canadian Poetry", *Saturday Review of Literature* 27: 9-11 (April 29, 1944).

E. K. Brown, "The neglect of Canadian Literature", *Canadians All,* Autumn, 1944.

E. K. Brown, "L'Age d'or de notre poésie", *Gants du Ciel* 4:5-17 (Spring, 1946).

L. J. Burpee, "Recent Canadian Fiction", *Forum* 27: 752-760 (August, 1899).

L. J. Burpee, "Canadian novels and novelists", *Sewanee Review* 11: 385-411 (October, 1903).

Douglas Bush, "Is there a Canadian Literature?" *Commonweal* 11: 12-14 (November 6, 1929).

Morley Callaghan, "The Plight of Canadian Fiction", *University of Toronto Quarterly* 7: 152-161 (April, 1938).

John Ciardi, "Sounds of the Poetic Voice", *Saturday Review* 42: 18-21 (October 24, 1959).

W. E. Collin, "On Canadian Poetry—The Stream and the Masters", *University of Toronto Quarterly* 13: 221-228 (January, 1944).

J. A. Cooper, "Canadian Poetry", *National Review* (May, 1897).

W. A. Deacon, "Canadian Literature", *Literary Review* 4: 634 (March 29, 1924).

W. A. Deacon, "Canadian Literature", *Saturday Review of Literature* 2: 29 (August 8, 1925).

W. A. Deacon, "The Canadian Novel Turns the Corner", *Canadian Magazine* 86: 16ff. (October, 1936).

C. R. Dehler, "Canada's English Poetry Since 1939", *Culture* 14: 247-55 (Summer, 1953).

D. J. Dooley, "The Satiric Novel in Canada Today", *Queen's Quarterly* 64: 576-90 (Winter, 1958).

Louis Dudek, "The State of Canadian Poetry, 1954", *The Canadian Forum* 34: 153-5 (October, 1954).

Louis Dudek, "The Montreal Poets", *Culture* 18: 149-54 (June, 1957).

Louis Dudek, "Patterns of Recent Canadian Poetry", *Culture* 19: 399-415 (Winter, 1958).

Louis Dudek, "The Transition in Canadian Poetry", *Culture* 20: 282-95 (Summer, 1959).

Pelham Edgar, "English-Canadian Literature", *The Cambridge History of English Literature,* Volume XIV, Cambridge, 1916.

Pelham Edgar, "Canadian Poetry", *Bookman* 49: 623-628 (July, 1919).

Wilfrid Eggleston, "Canadians and Canadian Books", *Queen's Quarterly* 52: 208-213 (Summer, 1945).

Northrop Frye, "Canada and its poetry", *The Canadian Forum* 23: 207-210 (December, 1943).

Northrop Frye, "La tradition narrative dans la poésie canadienne-anglaise", *Gants du Ciel* 4: 19-30 (Spring, 1946).

Northrop Frye, "Preface to an Uncollected Anthology", in *Studia Varia,* Toronto, 1957.

Myron Galloway, "Robert Speaight on Canadian Theatre", *Northern Review,* Volume 3, Number 3: 48-51 (February-March, 1950).

J. Murray Gibbon, "Where is Canadian Literature?" *Canadian Magazine* 50: 333-340 (February, 1918).

A. Gordan, "Comments on Canadian Poetry", *Canadian Magazine* 49: 132-139 (June, 1917).

Harley Granville-Barker, "Canadian Theatre", *Queen's Quarterly* 43: 256-268 (Autumn, 1936).

Frederick Philip Grove, "The Plight of Canadian Fiction?  A Reply", *University of Toronto Quarterly* 7: 451-467 (July, 1938).

Ralph Gustafson, "Anthology and Revaluation", *University of Toronto Quarterly* 13: 229-234 (January, 1944).

Ralph Gustafson, "Writing and Canada", *Northern Review,* Volume 3, Number 3: 17-22 (February-March, 1950).

W. B. Harte, "Some Canadian Writers of Today", *New England Magazine* 3: 21-40 (September, 1890).

Granville Hicks, "Novelists of the Fifties", *Saturday Review* 42: 18-21 (October 24, 1959).

Harold Horwood, "Number Ten Reports", *Northern Review,* Volume 4, Number 2: 16-21 (December-January, 1950-51).

Fred Jacob, "Canadian literati", *American Mercury* 8: 216-221 (June, 1926).

Leo Kennedy, "Future of Canadian Literature", *Canadian Mercury* 1: 99-100 (April-May, 1929).

Leo Kennedy, "Direction for Canadian Poets", *New Frontiers,* June, 1936.

Hugh Kenner, "Regional Muses", *Poetry* (Chicago) 86: 111-6 (May, 1955).

J. Kerr, "Some Canadian Poets", *Empire Review,* July, 1937.

Carlyle King, "Canadian Literature in English", *Food for Thought* 10: 1-8 (May, 1950).

Dorothy Livesay, "This Canadian Poetry", *The Canadian Forum* 24: 20-21 (April, 1944).

F. R. Livesay, "Canadian Poetry Today", *Poetry* 27: 36-40 (October, 1925).

Jack Ludwig, "Clothes in Search of an Emperor", *Canadian Literature,* Number 5: 63-6 (Summer, 1960).

Hugh MacLennan, "Culture, Canadian Style", *Saturday Review of Literature,* March 28, 1942.

Hugh MacLennan, "Canada Between Covers", *Saturday Review of Literature,* September 7, 1946.

E. A. McCourt, "Canadian Historical Novel", *Dalhousie Review* 26: 30-36 (April, 1946).

M. S. McCracken, "Tradition of Pre-Confederation English-Canadian Literature", *Revue de l'Université d'Ottawa,* October-December, 1937.

R. I. McKenzie, "Life in a New Land, notes on the immigrant theme in Canadian fiction", *Canadian Literature* Number 7: 24-33 (Winter, 1961).

W. H. Magee, "Trends in the recent English-Canadian Novel", *Culture* 10: 29-42 (March, 1949).

W. H. Magee, "Local Colour in Canadian Fiction", *University of Toronto Quarterly* 28: 176-89 (January, 1959).

Eli Mandel, "Poetry Chronicle: Giants, Beasts and Men in Contemporary Canadian Poetry", *Queen's Quarterly* 67: 285-93 (Summer, 1960).

Norman Newton, "Vegetable Kingdom", *The Canadian Forum* 29: 129-130 (September, 1949).

Desmond Pacey, "At last—a Canadian Literature?" *Cambridge Review,* December, 1938.

Desmond Pacey, "The Novel in Canada", *Queen's Quarterly* 52: 322-331 (Autumn, 1945).

Desmond Pacey, "Literary Criticism in Canada," *University of Toronto Quarterly* 19: 113-119 (January, 1950).

Desmond Pacey, "Two Accents, One Voice", *Saturday Review of Literature* 35: 15-16 (June 7, 1952).

Desmond Pacey, "Areas of Research in Canadian Literature", *University of Toronto Quarterly* 23: 58-63 (October, 1953).

Desmond Pacey, "English-Canadian Poetry, 1944-54", *Culture* 15: 255-65 (Summer, 1954).

Desmond Pacey, "The Canadian Writer and His Public, 1882-1952", in *Studia Varia,* Toronto, 1957.

Arthur L. Phelps, "Canadian Drama", *University of Toronto Quarterly* 9: 82-94 (October, 1939).

Arthur L. Phelps, "Canadian Literature and Canadian Society", *Northern Review,* Volume 3, Number 4: 23-35 (April-May, 1950).

E. J. Pratt, "Canadian Poetry Past and Present", *University of Toronto Quarterly* 8: 1-10 (October, 1938).

E. Rayson and F. A. Hadland, "A Glance at the Literature of Canada", *Living Age* 291: 284-289 (November 4, 1916).

James Reaney, "The Canadian Poet's Predicament", *University of Toronto Quarterly* 26: 284-95 (April, 1957).

James Reaney, "The Canadian Imagination", *Poetry* (Chicago) 94: 186-9 (June, 1959).

G. B. Roberts, "The Canadian Poets", *King's College Record,* December, 1886.

Samuel Roddan, "Writing in Canada", *Canadian Forum* 26: 137 (September, 1946).

Coleman Rosenberger, "On Canadian Poetry", *Poetry* (Chicago) 63: 281-287 (February, 1944).

Harry Roskolenko, "On poetry: post-war poetry in Canada", *Here and Now* 2: 23-31 (June, 1949).

W. W. E. Ross, "On National Poetry", *The Canadian Forum* 24: 88 (July, 1944).

Duncan Campbell Scott, "Poetry and Progress", in *Transactions of the Royal Society of Canada,* 1922 and in *The Circle of Affection,* Toronto, 1947.

F. R. Scott, "The Canadian Writers' Conference", *University of Toronto Quarterly* 25: 96-103 (October, 1955).

R. Shoolman, "Is there a Canadian Literature?" *Story,* Volume 11, Number 56 (March, 1937).

Lister Sinclair, "Canadian Idiom", *Here and Now* 2: 16-18 (June, 1949).

A. J. M. Smith, "Wanted—Canadian Criticism", *The Canadian Forum* 8: 600-601 (April, 1928).

A. J. M. Smith, "Canadian Poetry—A Minority Report", *University of Toronto Quarterly* 8: 125-130 (January, 1939).

A. J. M. Smith, "Canadian Literature", *Times* (London), May 15, 1939.

A. J. M. Smith, "Canadian Anthologies, New and Old", *University of Toronto Quarterly* 11: 457-474 (July, 1942).

A. J. M. Smith, " 'Our Poets'—a Sketch of Canadian Poetry in the Nineteenth Century", *University of Toronto Quarterly* 12: 75-94 (October, 1942).

A. J. M. Smith, "Colonialism and Nationalism in Canadian Poetry before Confederation", *Proceedings of the Canadian Historical Association,* 1944.

A. J. M. Smith, "Le Nationalisme et les poètes canadiens anglais", *Gants du Ciel* 3: 87-99 (June, 1945).

A. J. M. Smith, "Nationalism and Canadian Poetry", *Northern Review,* Volume 1, Number 1: 33-42 (December-January, 1945-46).

A. J. M. Smith, *Founders' Day Address at the University of New Brunswick,* Fredericton, 1946.

A. J. M. Smith, "Canadian Literature Today and Tomorrow", *Proceedings of the Canadian Library Association,* June, 1947.

A. Stanley, "Our Canadian Poets'", *London Mercury* 26: 537-547 (October, 1932).

A. M. Stephen, "Canadian Poets and Critics", *New Frontier,* Volume 1, Number 5: 20-22 (September, 1936).

John Sutherland, "Critics on the Defensive", *Northern Review,* Volume 2, Number 1: 18-23 (October-November, 1947).

John Sutherland, "Old Dog Trait—an extended analysis", *Contemporary Verse,* Number 29: 17-23 (Fall, 1949).

John Sutherland, "The Past Decade in Canadian Poetry", *Northern Review,* Volume 4, Number 2: 42-47 (December-January, 1950-51).

Grace Tomkinson, "The watched pot of Canadian poetry", *Dalhousie Review* 14: 459-470 (1934-35).

C. J. Vincent, "Canadian Literature. I English", *"Encyclopedia of Literature,* edited by Joseph T. Shipley, New York, 1946.

Gordon Waldron, "Canadian Poetry, a Criticism", *Canadian Magazine* 8: 101-108 (December, 1896).

F. W. Watt, "The Growth of Proletarian Literature in Canada, 1872-1920", *Dalhousie Review* 40: 157-73 (Summer, 1960).

R. E. Watters, "Original Relations: a genographic approach to the literature of Canada and Australia", *Canadian Literature* Number 7: 6-17 (Winter, 1961).

Robert L. Weaver, "Notes on Canadian Literature", *Nation* 162: 198-200 (February 16, 1946).

Robert L. Weaver, "On the novel: a sociological approach to Canadian fiction", *Here and Now* 2: 12-15 (June, 1949).

Robert L. Weaver, "The Economics of our Literature", *Queen's Quarterly* 60: 476-485 (1954).

Henry W. Wells, "The Awakening of Canadian Poetry", *New England Quarterly* 18: 3-24 (March, 1945).

Paul West, "Ethos and Epic: Aspects of Contemporary Canadian Poetry", *Canadian Literature* Number 4: 7-17 (Spring, 1960).

George Whalley, "The Great Canadian Novel", *Queen's Quarterly* 55: 318-326 (Autumn, 1948).

W. P. Wilgar, "Poetry and the Divided Mind in Canada", *Dalhousie Review* 24: 266-271 (October, 1944).

Norman Williams, "Prospects for the Canadian Dramatist", *University of Toronto Quarterly* 26: 273-83 (1957).

Milton Wilson, "Recent Canadian Verse", *Queen's Quarterly* 66: 268-274 (Summer, 1959).

George Woodcock, "A View of Canadian Criticism", *Dalhousie Review* 36: 216-223 (1955).

George Woodcock, "Recent Canadian Poetry", *Queen's Quarterly* 62: 111-115 (Spring, 1955).

## D. STUDIES OF INDIVIDUAL AUTHORS

### 1. MORLEY CALLAGHAN

Margaret Avison, "Callaghan Revisited", *The Canadian Forum* 39: 276-7 (March, 1960).

H. J. Davis, "Morley Callaghan", *The Canadian Forum* 15: 398-9 (December, 1935).

E. A. Koch, "Callaghan: Lend-Lease from the Bohemians", *Saturday Night* 60: 16-17 (October 21, 1944).

Hugo McPherson, "The Two Worlds of Morley Callaghan," *Queen's Quarterly* 64: 350-65 (Autumn, 1957).

Barbara Moon, "The Second Coming of Morley Callaghan", *Maclean's Magazine* 73: 19, 62-4 (December 3, 1960).

Arthur L. Phelps, "Morley Callaghan" in *Canadian Writers*, Toronto, 1951.

B. Preston, "Toronto's Callaghan", *Saturday Night* 51: 12 (January 18, 1936).

J. D. Ripley, "A Critical Study of Morley Callaghan", unpublished M.A. thesis, University of New Brunswick, 1959.

H. Steinhauer, "Canadian Writers of Today: Morley Callaghan", *The Canadian Forum* 12: 177-8 (February, 1932).

F. W. Watt, "Morley Callaghan as Thinker", *Dalhousie Review* 33: 88-101 (Summer, 1953).

Robert L. Weaver, "A Talk with Morley Callaghan", *The Tamarack Review* Number 7: 3-29 (Spring, 1958).

Edmund Wilson, "Morley Callaghan of Toronto", *The New Yorker* 36: 224-236 (November 26, 1960).

### 2. BLISS CARMAN

James Cappon, *Bliss Carman*, Toronto, 1930.

H. D. C. Lee, *Bliss Carman: A Study in Canadian Poetry*, Boston, 1912.

Muriel Miller, *Bliss Carman: A Portrait*, Toronto, 1935.

Odell Shepherd, *Bliss Carman*, Boston, 1924.

William Archer, "Bliss Carman", in *Poets of the Younger Generation*, London, 1902, pp. 66-82.

G. Gray, "The Mystery of Bliss Carman's Ashes", *Maclean's Magazine* 64: 40 (August 1, 1951).

C. Lewis Hind, "Bliss Carman", in *More Authors and I*, London, 1922.

L. A. Mackay, "Bliss Carman", *The Canadian Forum* 13: 182-3 (February, 1933).

Desmond Pacey, "Bliss Carman: a Reappraisal", *Northern Review* 3: 2-10 (February-March, 1950).

Desmond Pacey, "Bliss Carman", in *Ten Canadian Poets*, Toronto, 1958, pp. 59-113.

Desmond Pacey, "A Garland for Bliss Carman", *Atlantic Advocate* 51: 17, 19ff. (April, 1961).

Jessie B. Rittenhouse, "Bliss Carman", in *Younger American Poets*, Boston, 1904, pp. 46-74.

C. G. D. Roberts, "Bliss Carman", *Dalhousie Review* 9: 409-417 (January, 1930).

C. G. D. Roberts, "More Reminiscences of Bliss Carman", *Dalhousie Review* 10: 1-9 (April, 1930).

C. G. D. Roberts, "Some Reminiscences of Carman in New York", *Canadian Poetry Magazine* 5: 5-10 (December, 1940).

Malcolm Ross, "Carman by the Sea", *Dalhousie Review* 27: 294-298 October, 1947).

Arthur Stringer, "Wild Poets I've Known: Bliss Carman", *Saturday Night* 56: 29, 36 (March 1, 1941).

### 3. ROBERTSON DAVIES

Hugo McPherson, "The Mask of Satire: character and symbolic pattern in Robertson Davies' fiction", *Canadian Literature* Number 4: 18-30 (Spring, 1960).

Ivan Owen, "The Salterton Novels", *The Tamarack Review* Number 9: 56-63 (Autumn, 1958).

M. W. Steinberg, "Don Quixote and the Puppets: theme and structure in Robertson Davies' drama", *Canadian Literature* Number 7: 45-53 (Winter, 1961).

### 4. FREDERICK PHILIP GROVE

Desmond Pacey, *Frederick Philip Grove*, Toronto, 1945.

Robert Ayre, "Frederick Philip Grove", *The Canadian Forum* 12: 255-257 (April, 1932).

G. H. Clarke, "A Canadian Novelist and His Critic", *Queen's Quarterly* 53: 362-368 (August, 1946).

W. E. Collin, "La Tragique Ironie de Frederick Philip Grove", *Gants du Ciel* 4: 15-40 (Winter, 1946).

W. B. Holliday, "Frederick Philip Grove: an impression", *Canadian Literature* Number 3: 17-22 (Winter, 1960).

E. A. McCourt, "Spokesman of a Race?" in *The Canadian West in Fiction* (Toronto, 1949) pp. 55-70.

Desmond Pacey, "Frederick Philip Grove," *Manitoba Arts Review*, Volume 3, Number 3: 28-41 (Spring, 1943).

Desmond Pacey, "Some Letters of Frederick Philip Grove", forthcoming in *Canadian Literature*, 1961-2.

Kay M. Rowe, "Here He Lies Where He Longed", *Manitoba Arts Review*, Volume 6, Numbers 2 and 3: 62-64 (Spring, 1949).

B. K. Sandwell, "Frederick Philip Grove and the Culture of Canada", *Saturday Night* 61: 18 (November 24, 1945).

Isabel Skelton, "Frederick Philip Grove", *Dalhousie Review* 19: 147-163 (July, 1939).

Carleton Stanley, "Voices in the Wilderness", *Dalhousie Review* 25: 173-181 (July, 1945).

Carleton Stanley, "Frederick Philip Grove", *Dalhousie Review* 25: 433-441 (January, 1946).

"Canadian Dreiser", unsigned editorial, *The Canadian Forum* 28: 121-122 (September, 1948).

## 5. THOMAS CHANDLER HALIBURTON

V. L. O. Chittick, *Thomas Chandler Haliburton,* "Sam Slick", New York, 1924.

F. B. Crofton, *Haliburton, the Man and the Writer,* Windsor, 1889.

J. D. Logan, *Thomas Chandler Haliburton,* Toronto, n.d. (1923?).

A. H. O'Brien, *Haliburton, a sketch and bibliography,* 2nd edition, Montreal, 1909.

M. P. F. Chisholm, "Sam Slick and Catholic disabilities in Nova Scotia," *Catholic World* (January, 1897).

V. L. O. Chittick, "Pervasiveness of Sam Slick", *Dalhousie Review* 33: 88-101 (Summer, 1953).

V. L. O. Chittick, "Haliburton Postscript I: ring-tailed Yankee", *Dalhousie Review* 37: 19-36 (Spring, 1957).

V. L. O. Chittick, "Haliburton on Men and Things", *Dalhousie Review* 38: 55-64 (Spring, 1958).

V. L. O. Chittick, "Books and Music in Haliburton", *Dalhousie Review* 38: 207-21 (Summer, 1958).

V. L. O. Chittick, "Haliburton's 'wise saws' and homely imagery", *Dalhousie Review* 38: 348-63 (Autumn, 1958).

F. B. Crofton, "Thomas Chandler Haliburton", *Atlantic Monthly* 69: 355-363 (March, 1892).

D. C. Harvey, "The Centenary of Sam Slick", *Dalhousie Review* 16: 429-40 (January, 1937).

J. D. Logan, "Why Haliburton has no successor", *Canadian Magazine* 57: 362-8 (September, 1921).

D. Macdonald, "Sam Slick Slept Here", *Maclean's Magazine* 67: 22-3 (July 1, 1954).

J. McCarthy, "Sketch from Memory", *Portraits of the '60's,* New York, 1903.

R. L. McDougall, "Thomas Chandler Haliburton", in *Our Living Tradition,* 2nd Series, Toronto, 1959, pp. 3-30.

A. W. Mahon, "Sam Slick Letters", *Canadian Magazine* 44: 75-9 (November, 1914).

A. H. O'Brien, "Thomas Chandler Haliburton, 1796-1805: a sketch and a bibliography", *Transactions of the Royal Society of Canada,* 3rd Series, Volume 3, Section 2: 43-66 (1909).

Effie May Ross, "Thomas Chandler Haliburton: Sam Slick, The Founder of American Humor", *Century,* New Series, 41: 45-64 (November, 1921).

S. Seeley, "Clifton", *Canadian Geographical Journal* 48: 40-4 (January, 1954).

R. K. Wood, "Creator of the first Yankee of literature", *Bookman* 41: 152-60 (April, 1915).

### 6. A. M. Klein

W. E. Collin, "The Spirit's Palestine", in *The White Savannahs,* Toronto, 1936, pp. 207-231.

Louis Dudek, "A. M. Klein", *The Canadian Forum* 30: 10-12 (April, 1950).

Leon Edel, "Abraham M. Klein", *The Canadian Forum* 12: 300-2 (May, 1932).

Leon Edel, "Poetry and the Jewish Tradition", *Poetry* (Chicago) 58: 51-3 (April, 1941).

Desmond Pacey, "A. M. Klein", in *Ten Canadian Poets,* Toronto, 1958, pp. 254-292.

A. J. M. Smith, "Abraham Moses Klein", *Gants du Ciel* 11: 67-81 (Spring, 1946).

D. C. Spurgeon, "Whither Green-Haired Poet?" *Saturday Night* 65: 12, 46 (May 23, 1950).

M. W. Steinberg, "Twentieth Century Pentateuch", *Canadian Literature* Number 2: 37-46 (Autumn, 1959).

John Sutherland, "The Poetry of A. M. Klein", *Index,* Volume I, Number 6: 8-12 (August, 1946).

John Sutherland, "Canadian Comment", *Northern Review* 2: 30-4 (August-September, 1947).

Milton Wilson, "A Biographical Note", *Canadian Author and Bookman* 34: 13 (Spring, 1958).

Milton Wilson, "Klein's Drowned Poet", *Canadian Literature* Number 6: 5-17 (Autumn, 1960).

### 7. Archibald Lampman

Carl Y. Connor, *Archibald Lampman, Canadian Poet of Nature,* Montreal, 1929.

Norman G. Guthrie, *The Poetry of Archibald Lampman,* Toronto, 1927.

Munro Beattie, "Archibald Lampman", in *Our Living Tradition,* 1st Series, Toronto, 1957, pp. 63-88.

Jean Burton, "Archibald Lampman's Poetry of Release", *Willison's Monthly* 3: 425-7 (April, 1928).

W. L. Colgate, "Archibald Lampman: a dedication and a note", *The Canadian Forum* 36: 279-80 (March, 1957).

W. E. Collin, "Natural Landscape", in *The White Savannahs*, Toronto, 1936, pp. 3-40.

A. W. Crawford, "Archibald Lampman", *Acta Victoriana* 17: 77-81 (December, 1895).

Louis Dudek, "The Significance of Lampman", *Culture* 18: 277-90 (Summer, 1957).

Ralph Gustafson, "Among the Millet", *Northern Review* I: 26-34 (February-March, 1947).

W. D. Howells, "Editor's Study", *Harper's* 78: 821-3 (April, 1889).

Leo Kennedy, "Archibald Lampman", *The Canadian Forum* 13: 301-3 (May, 1933).

Raymond Knister, "The poetry of Archibald Lampman", *Dalhousie Review* 7: 348-61 (October, 1927).

J. D. Logan, "Literary Group of '61", *Canadian Magazine* 37: 555-563 (October, 1911).

E. R. Macdonald, "A Little Talk about Lampman", *Canadian Magazine* 52: 1012-1016 (April, 1919).

John Marshall, "Archibald Lampman", *Queen's Quarterly* 9: 63-79 (July, 1901).

Bernard Muddiman, "Archibald Lampman", *Queen's Quarterly* 22: 233-43 (January, 1915).

Desmond Pacey, "Archibald Lampman", in *Ten Canadian Poets*, pp. 114-140, Toronto, 1958.

Desmond Pacey, "A Reading of Lampman's 'Heat'," *Culture* 14: 292-7 (September, 1953).

Arthur Stringer, "Archibald Lampman", *Canadian Magazine* 2: 545-8 (April, 1894).

Arthur Stringer, "Wild Poets I've Known: Archibald Lampman", *Saturday Night* 56: 29 (May 24, 1941).

John Sutherland, "Edgar Allan Poe in Canada" (chiefly his influence on Lampman), *Northern Review* 4: 22-37 (February-March, 1951).

S. C. Swift, "Lampman and Lecomte de Lisle", *Canadian Bookman* 9: 261-4 (September, 1927).

Louis Untermeyer, "Archibald Lampman and the Sonnet", *Poet Lore* 20: 432-7 (November, 1909).

G. H. Unwin, "The Poetry of Lampman", *University Magazine* 16: 55-73 (February, 1917).

Ernest Voorhis, "The Ancestry of Archibald Lampman", *Transactions of the Royal Society of Canada*, 3rd Series, Volume 15, Section 2: 103-121 (1921).

F. W. Watt, "The Masks of Archibald Lampman", *University of Toronto Quarterly* 27: 169-84 (January, 1958).

W. L. Wendell, "Sketch", *Bookman* 11: 515-526 (August, 1900).

## 8. STEPHEN LEACOCK

C. K. Allen, *Oh, Mr. Leacock*, Toronto, 1925.

R. L. Curry, *Stephen Leacock, Humorist and Humanist*, New York, 1959.

Peter McArthur, *Stephen Leacock*, Toronto, 1923.

Bruce Barton, "Billionaire of humour", *Collier's* 69: 9 (April 15, 1922).

W. Caldwell, "Visit to a Canadian Author", *Canadian Magazine* 59: 55-60 (May, 1922).

Cyril Clemens, "Evening with Stephen Leacock", *Catholic World* 159: 236-241 (June, 1944).

J. P. Collins, "Stephen Leacock, Ph.D.: savant and humorist", *Bookman* (London) 51: 39-44 (November, 1916).

R. L. Curry, "The Unknown Years of Stephen Leacock", *Maclean's Magazine* 72: 20-1, 45-7 (July 4, 1959), 72: 26-7, 34 (July 18, 1959).

Robertson Davies, "Stephen Leacock", in *Our Living Tradition*, 1st Series, ed. C. T. Bissell, Toronto, 1957, pp. 128-149.

Pelham Edgar, "Stephen Leacock", *Queen's Quarterly* 53: 173-184 (Summer, 1946).

T. G. Frayne, "The Erudite Jester of McGill", *Maclean's Magazine* 66: 18-19, 37-9 (January 1, 1953).

K. E. Gilliss, "Stephen Leacock as a Satirist", unpublished M.A. thesis, University of New Brunswick, 1958.

C. Lewis Hind, "Stephen Leacock", in *More Authors and I*, London, 1922.

W. T. Larned, "Professor Leacock and the Other Professors", *New Republic* 9: 299 (January 13, 1917).

A. R. M. Lower, "The Mariposa Belle", *Queen's Quarterly* 58: 220-6 (Summer, 1951).

D. McCord, "Old Magic", *Saturday Review of Literature* 19: 10 (January 14, 1939).

Howard O'Hagan, "Stephie", *Queen's Quarterly* 68: 135-46 (Spring, 1961).

Desmond Pacey, "Stephen Leacock as Satirist", *Queen's Quarterly* 58: 208-19 (Summer, 1951).

B. K. Sandwell, "Stephen Butler Leacock, 1869-1944", *Proceedings and Transactions of the Royal Society of Canada*, 3rd Series, 38: 105-106 (1944).

B. K. Sandwell, "Leacock Recalled", *Saturday Night* 67: 7 (August 23, 1952).

G. G. Sedgewick, "Stephen Leacock as Man of Letters", *University of Toronto Quarterly* 15: 17-26 (October, 1945).

C. Vining, "Mr. Leacock: a profile", *Maclean's Magazine* 68: 33 (October 15, 1955).

F. W. Watt, "Critic or Entertainer?   Stephen Leacock and the Growth of Materialism", *Canadian Literature* Number 5: 33-42 (Summer, 1960).

J. Wheelwright, "Poet as Funny man", *Poetry* (Chicago) 50: 210-5 (July, 1937).

## 9. HUGH MACLENNAN

M. G. Ballantyne, "Theology and the Man on the Street: a Catholic Commentary on *Cross Country*", *Culture* 10: 392-6 (December, 1949).

Dorothy Duncan, "My Author Husband", *Maclean's Magazine* 58: 7, 36, 38, 40 (August 15, 1945).

Hugo McPherson, "The Novels of Hugh MacLennan", *Queen's Quarterly* 60: 186-98 (Summer, 1953).

Arthur L. Phelps, "Hugh MacLennan", in *Canadian Writers,* Toronto, 1951, pp. 77-84.

R. E. Watters, "Hugh MacLennan and the Canadian Character", in *As a Man Thinks. . . .*, edited by E. Morrison and W. Robbins, Toronto, 1953, pp. 228-43.

George Woodcock, "Hugh MacLennan", *Northern Review* 3: 2-10 (April-May, 1950).

## 10. E. J. PRATT

Carl F. Klinck and Henry W. Wells, *Edwin John Pratt: The Man and His Poetry*, Toronto, 1947.

John Sutherland, *The Poetry of E. J. Pratt*, Toronto, 1956.

Earle Birney, "E. J. Pratt and His Critics", in *Our Living Tradition*, 2nd and 3rd Series, Toronto, 1959, pp. 123-147.

E. K. Brown, "Pratt's Collected Work", *University of Toronto Quarterly* 14: 211-213 (January, 1945).

W. E. Collin, "Pleiocene Heroics", in *The White Savannahs*, Toronto, 1936, pp. 119-144.

Pelham Edgar, "E. J. Pratt", *Gants du Ciel* 11: 31-45 (Spring, 1946).

H. N. Frye, "Introduction", in *The Collected Poems of E. J. Pratt*, Second Edition, Toronto, 1958.

H. Horwood, "E. J. Pratt and William Blake: an analysis", *Dalhousie Review* 39: 197-207 (Spring, 1959).

Carlyle King, "The Mind of E. J. Pratt", *The Canadian Forum* 36: 9-10 (April, 1956).

R. S. Knox, "A New Canadian Poet", *The Canadian Forum* 3: 278-9 (June, 1923).

L. A. Mackay, "The Poetry of E. J. Pratt", *The Canadian Forum* 24: 208-9 (December, 1944).

M. H. McGrath, "Bard from Newfoundland", *Atlantic Advocate* 49: 13-15 (November, 1958).

Desmond Pacey, "E. J. Pratt", in *Ten Canadian Poets*, Toronto, 1958, pp. 165-193.

Mary Lowrey Ross, "Dr. E. J. Pratt: a poet's quarter-century", *Saturday Night* 73: 14-15 (February 1, 1958).

W. J. Scott, "Poetry and Event", *Poetry* (Chicago) 66: 329-34 (September, 1945).

John Sutherland, "The Poetry of E. J. Pratt", *First Statement* 2: 27-30 (February-March, 1945).

John Sutherland, "E. J. Pratt: A Major Contemporary Poet", *Northern Review* Volume 5, Numbers 3-4: 36-64 (April-May, 1952).

Henry W. Wells, "Canada's Best Known Poet: E. J. Pratt", *College English* 7: 452-6 (May, 1952).

Various authors, "A Garland for E. J. Pratt on his seventy-fifth birthday", *The Tamarack Review* 6: 65-80 (Winter, 1958).

## 11. MORDECAI RICHLER

Nathan Cohen, "A Conversation with Mordecai Richler", *The Tamarack Review* Number 1: 6-23 (Winter, 1957).

Nathan Cohen, "Heroes of the Richler View", *The Tamarack Review* Number 6: 47-9, 51-60 (Winter, 1958).

Peter D. Scott, "A Choice of Certainties", *The Tamarack Review* Number 8: 73-83 (Summer, 1958).

## 12. SIR CHARLES G. D. ROBERTS

James Cappon, *Roberts and the Influences of His Time*, Toronto, 1905.
James Cappon, *Charles G. D. Roberts*, Toronto, 1925.
Elsie Pomeroy, *Sir Charles G. D. Roberts: A Biography*, Toronto, 1943.
Lloyd Roberts, *The Book of Roberts*, Toronto, 1923.
William Archer, "C. G. D. Roberts", in *Poets of the Younger Generation*, London, 1902, pp. 362-372.
Pelham Edgar, "Sir Charles G. D. Roberts and His Times", *University of Toronto Quarterly* 13: 117-126 (October, 1943).
Pelham Edgar, "Sir Charles G. D. Roberts 1861-1944", *Proceedings and Transactions of the Royal Society of Canada*, 3rd Series, 38: 105-106 (1944).
Archibald Lampman, "Two Canadian Poets", *University of Toronto Quarterly* 13: 406-23 (July, 1944).
D. Livesay, "Open Letter to Sir Charles G. D. Roberts", *Canadian Bookman* 21: 34-5 (April, 1939).
T. G. Marquis, "C. G. D. Roberts", *Canadian Magazine* 1: 572-5 (September, 1893).
B. Muddiman, "Vignette in Canadian Literature", *Canadian Magazine* 40: 451-458 (March, 1913).
Desmond Pacey, "Sir Charles G. D. Roberts", in *Ten Canadian Poets*, Toronto, 1958, pp. 34-58.
Desmond Pacey, "Sir Charles G. D. Roberts", in *Our Living Tradition*, 4th Series, Toronto, 1961.
Jessie B. Rittenhouse, "Evolution in the poetry of Roberts", in *Younger American Poets*, New York, 1904, pp. 132-50.
A. M. Stephen, "Poetry of Charles G. D. Roberts", *Queen's Quarterly* 34: 48-64 (January, 1929).
W. J. Sykes, "Charles G. D. Roberts", *Acta Victoriana* 17: 112-5 (January, 1894).

## 13. DUNCAN CAMPBELL SCOTT

William Archer, "D. C. Scott", in *Poets of the Younger Generation*, London, 1902, pp. 385-95.
E. K. Brown, "Duncan Campbell Scott, an Individual Poet", *Manitoba Arts Review* 2: 51-4 (Spring, 1941).
Martin Burrell, "Canadian Poet", in *Betwixt Heaven and Charing Cross*, Toronto, 1928, pp. 253-61.
G. H. Clarke, "Duncan Campbell Scott, 1862-1948", *Proceedings and Transactions of the Royal Society of Canada*, 3rd Series, 39: 115-120 (1948).
Pelham Edgar, "Duncan Campbell Scott", *Dalhousie Review* 7: 38-46 (April, 1927).
Pelham Edgar, "Travelling with a Poet", in *Across My Path*, edited by Northrop Frye, Toronto, 1952, pp. 58-74.
Raymond Knister, "Duncan Campbell Scott", *Willison's Monthly* 2: 295-6 (January, 1927).
Bernard Muddiman, "Duncan Campbell Scott", *Canadian Magazine* 43: 63-72 (May, 1914).
Desmond Pacey, "Poetry of Duncan Campbell Scott", *The Canadian Forum* 28: 107-9 (August, 1948).

Desmond Pacey, "Duncan Campbell Scott", in *Ten Canadian Poets,* Toronto, 1958, pp. 141-64.

A. J. M. Smith, "The Poetry of D. C. Scott", *Dalhousie Review* 28: 12-21 (April, 1948).

A. J. M. Smith, "Duncan Campbell Scott: a reconsideration", *Canadian Literature* Number 1: 13-25 (Summer, 1959), (this essay is also found in *Our Living Tradition,* 2nd and 3rd Series, Toronto, 1959).

W. J. Sykes, "The Poetry of D. C. Scott", *Queen's Quarterly* 46: 51-64 (Spring, 1939).

Lionel Stevenson, "Who's Who in Canadian Literature: D. C. Scott", *Canadian Bookman* 11: 59-62 (March, 1929).

### 14. VARIOUS AUTHORS

Conrad Aiken, "Malcolm Lowry—A Note", *Canadian Literature* Number 8: 29-30 (Spring, 1961).

John W. Bilsland, "Vision of Clarity: The Poetry of Wilfred Watson", *Canadian Literature* Number 4: 40-51 (Spring, 1960).

Earle Birney, "Glimpses into the Life of Malcolm Lowry", *Tamarack Review* Number 19: 35-41 (Spring, 1961).

E. K. Brown, "The Whiteoaks Saga", *The Canadian Forum* XII: 23 (October, 1931).

E. K. Brown, "A. J. M. Smith and the Poetry of Pride", *Manitoba Arts Review* 4: 30-32 (Spring, 1944).

W. J. Brown, "Robert Barr and Literature in Canada", *Canadian Magazine* 15: 170-176 (June, 1900).

L. J. Burpee, "Last of the Stricklands: Mrs. Catherine Parr Traill", *Sewanee Review* 8: 207-17 (April, 1900).

L. J. Burpee, "Canadian Poet: W. W. Campbell", *Sewanee Review* 8: 425-436 (October, 1900).

L. J. Burpee, "Isabella Valancy Crawford", *Poet Lore* 13, Number 4: 575-586 (October, 1901).

L. J. Burpee, "Charles Heavysege", *Proceedings and Transactions of the Royal Society of Canada,* 3rd Series, Volume 7, Section II: 17-60 (1901).

W. E. Collin, "Leo Kennedy", *The Canadian Forum* 14: 24-27 (October, 1933).

W. E. Collin, "Arthur Smith", *Gants du Ciel* Number 11: 47-60 (Spring, 1946).

R. H. Craig, "Reminiscences of W. H. Drummond", *Dalhousie Review* 5: 161-169 (1925-26).

T. R. Dale, "The Revolt of Charles Heavysege", *University of Toronto Quarterly* 22: 35-43 (October, 1952).

Roy Daniells, "Earle Birney et Robert Finch", *Gants du Ciel* 11: 83-96 (Spring, 1946).

A. C. de Guttenberg, "William Kirby", *Revue de l'Université Laval* 9: 337-45 (December, 1954).

E. H. Dewart, "Charles Sangster", *Canadian Magazine* 7: 28-34 (May, 1896).

Louis Dudek, "F. R. Scott and the Modern Poets", *Northern Review,* Volume 4, Number 2: 4-15 (December-January, 1950-51).

Louis Dudek, "Layton on the Carpet", *Delta* Number 9: 17-19 (October-December, 1959).

Hugh Eayrs, "Bookman Profiles: Mazo de la Roche", *Canadian Bookman* 20: 17-22 (October, 1938).

Max-Pol Fouchet, "No Se Puede. . ." (re Malcolm Lowry), *Canadian Literature* Number 8: 25-28 (Spring, 1961).

Georg Friden, *The Canadian Novels of Sir Gilbert Parker: Historical Elements and Literary Technique,* Uppsala, 1953.

J. Garvin, "Sir Gilbert Parker and Canadian Literature", *Canadian Bookman* 14: 92ff. (September, 1932).

W. L. Grant, *The Tribune of Nova Scotia, a Chronicle of Joseph Howe,* Toronto, 1920.

E. B. Greenshields, "A Forgotten Poet" (Heavysege), *University Magazine* 7: 343-359 (October, 1908).

Katherine Hale, *Isabella Valancy Crawford,* Toronto, 1924.

E. J. Hathaway, "Isabella Valancy Crawford", *Canadian Magazine* 5: 569-72 (October, 1895).

Leo Kennedy, "Raymond Knister", *The Canadian Forum* 12: 459-461 (September, 1932).

Downie Kirk, "More than Music: Glimpses of Malcolm Lowry", *Canadian Literature* Number 8: 31-38 (Spring, 1961).

A. M. Klein, "The Poetry of A. J. M. Smith", *Canadian Forum* 23: 257-258 (February, 1944).

Carl Klinck, *Wilfred Campbell: A Study in Late Provincial Victorianism,* New York and Toronto, 1942.

Carl F. Klinck, "Early Creative Literature of Western Ontario", *Ontario History* 44: 155-63 (Autumn, 1953).

Carl F. Klinck, "Major Richardson's 'Kensington Gardens in 1830' ", *Ontario History* 48: 101-7 (Summer, 1956).

Carl F. Klinck, "John Galt's Canadian Novels", *Ontario History* 49: 187-94 (Autumn, 1957).

Carl F. Klinck, "Adam Kidd", *Queen's Quarterly* 65: 495-506 (Autumn, 1958).

Raymond Knister, "Wilson MacDonald", *Willison's Monthly,* Volume 2, Number 5, 188-191 (October, 1926).

Victor Lauriston, *Arthur Stringer, Son of the North,* Toronto, 1941.

Jack Ludwig, "The Mirror of Moore", *Canadian Literature* Number 7: 18-23 (Winter, 1961).

J. F. Macdonald, *W. H. Drummond,* Toronto, 1924.

L. A. Mackay, "William Wilfred Campbell", *The Canadian Forum* 14: 66-67 (November, 1933).

W. E. MacLennan, "Real Canadian Literature" (re Martha Ostenso), *Dalhousie Review* 6: 18-23 (1926-27).

William McConnell, "Recollections of Malcolm Lowry", *Canadian Literature* Number 6: 24-31 (Autumn, 1960).

E. A. McCourt, "Roughing It with the Moodies", *Queen's Quarterly* 52: 77-89 (Spring, 1945).

William Meredith, "A Good Modern Poet and a Modern Tradition" (P. K. Page), *Poetry* 70: 208-211 (July, 1947).

Jocelyn Moore, "Mazo de la Roche", *The Canadian Forum* 12: 380-1 (July, 1932).

S. G. Mullins, "The Poetry of Peter Miller", *Culture* XXI: 398-408 (December, 1960).

David Munroe, "Joseph Howe as Man of Letters", *Dalhousie Review* 20: 451-457 (January, 1941).

J. F. Nims, "Five Young Canadian Poets" (Dudek, Hambleton, Page, Souster, Wreford), *Poetry* 66: 334-40 (September, 1945).

J. N. North, "Mercurial" (Patrick Anderson), *Poetry* 69: 284-286 (February, 1947).

Desmond Pacey, "The First Canadian Novel" (Mrs. Brooke's *History of Emily Montague*) *Dalhousie Review* 26: 143-150 (July, 1946).

Desmond Pacey, "Service and MacInnes", *Northern Review*, Volume 4, Number 3: 12-17 (February-March, 1951).

Desmond Pacey, "The Innocent Eye: The Art of Ethel Wilson", *Queen's Quarterly* 61: 42-52 (Spring, 1954).

Desmond Pacey, "A Group of Seven" (review article on new books of verse by Phyllis Webb, Anne Wilkinson, Raymond Souster, Leonard Cohen, Wilfred Watson, Fred Cogswell and Irving Layton), *Queen's Quarterly* 63: 436-443 (Autumn, 1956).

Desmond Pacey, "Colonial Romantic" (a two-part study of John Richardson), *Canadian Literature* Number 2: 20-31 (Autumn, 1959); Number 3: 47-56 (Winter, 1960).

Lorne Pierce, *Marjorie Pickthall: A Book of Remembrance*, Toronto, 1925.

Lorne Pierce, *William Kirby: The Portrait of a Tory Loyalist*, Toronto, 1929.

Lorne Pierce, *Three Fredericton Poets* (Carman, Roberts, Sherman), Toronto, 1933.

E. J. Pratt, "Marjorie Pickthall", *The Canadian Forum* 13: 334-335 (June, 1933).

E. J. Pratt, "Dorothy Livesay", *Gants du Ciel* 11: 61-5 (Spring, 1946).

R. E. Rashley, "W. H. Drummond and the Dilemma of Style", *Dalhousie Review* 28: 387-96 (January, 1949).

James Reaney, "Isabella Valancy Crawford", in *Our Living Tradition*, 2nd and 3rd Series, Toronto, 1959, pp. 268-288.

James Reaney, "The Third Eye: Jay Macpherson's *The Boatman*", *Canadian Literature* Number 3: 23-24 (Winter, 1960).

W. A. Riddell, *John Richardson*, Toronto, 1923.

Hilda M. Ridley, *The Story of L. M. Montgomery*, Toronto, 1956.

J. A. Roy, *Joseph Howe: A Study in Achievement and Frustration*, Toronto, 1935.

B. K. Sandwell, "The Work of Mazo de la Roche", *Saturday Night* 68: 7 (November 8, 1952).

A. J. M. Smith, "New Canadian Poetry" (P. K. Page and Patrick Anderson), *The Canadian Forum* 26: 250-252 (February, 1947).

A. J. M. Smith, "Turning New Leaves" (Finch and Dudek), *The Canadian Forum* 27: 42-43 (May, 1947).

A. J. M. Smith, "The Recent Poetry of Irving Layton", *Queens' Quarterly* 62: 587-91 (Winter, 1956).

Ian Sowton, "The Lyric Craft of Miriam Waddington", *Dalhousie Review* 39: 237-42 (1959).

Ruth Stephan, "A Canadian Poet" (Dorothy Livesay), *Poetry* (Chicago) 65: 220-2 (January, 1945).

John Sutherland, "The Writing of Patrick Anderson", *First Statement* Number 19: 3-6 (May 14, 1945).

John Sutherland, "The Poetry of P. K. Page", *Northern Review*, Volume 1, Number 4: 13-23 (December-January, 1946-47).

John Sutherland, "The Poetry of Anderson and Page", *The Canadian Forum* 27: 17 (April, 1947).

John Sutherland, "Canadian Comment" (on James Reaney), *Northern Review*, Volume 3, Number 4: 36-42 (April-May, 1950).

Warren Tallman, "Wolf in the Snow" (a study of themes in novels by Sinclair Ross, W. O. Mitchell, Hugh MacLennan, Ernest Buckler and Mordecai Richler), *Canadian Literature* Number 5: 7-20 (Summer, 1960); Number 6: 41-48 (Autumn, 1960).

Robert Weaver, "The Poetry of Dorothy Livesay", *Contemporary Verse* 26: 18-22 (Fall, 1948).

Milton Wilson, "The Poetry of Margaret Avison", *Canadian Literature* Number 2: 247-58 (Autumn, 1959).

George Woodcock, "On the Day of the Dead" (*re* Malcolm Lowry), *Northern Review* 6: 15-21 (December-January, 1953-54).

George Woodcock, "Under Seymour Mountain" (*re* Malcolm Lowry), *Canadian Literature* Number 8: 3-6 (Spring, 1961).

Eva-Lis Wuorio, "Mazo of Jalna", *Maclean's Magazine* 62: 19, 39-41 (February 1, 1949).

# Index